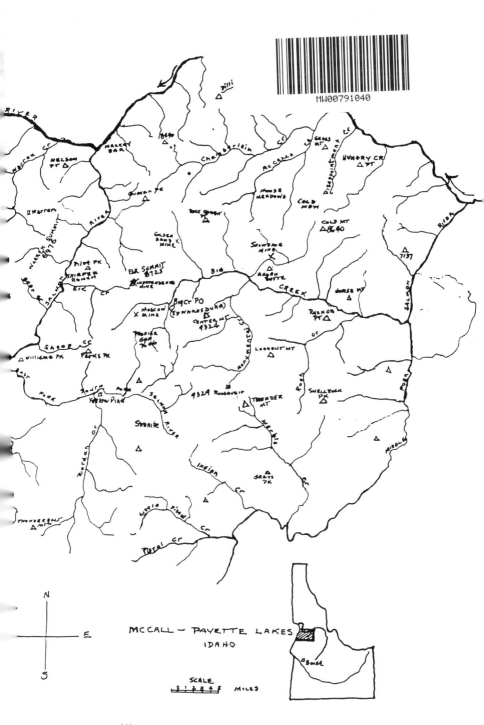

MCCALL ~ PAYETTE LAKES
IDAHO

SCALE
MILES

Historic map by Len B. Jordan, 1960.
Access roads are shown on the modern map on back inside cover.

The # KING'S PINES *of*

IDAHO

A Story of the
Browns of McCall

By Grace Edgington Jordan

J
J

Kirkwood Publishing Company
Fruitvale, Idaho
1998

DEDICATION

To Betty Brown Harwood
and her village McCall
with love.

First Edition, Trade: June, 1998
10 9 8 7 6 5 4 3 2 1

ISBN 1–886609–18–7

About the Cover Photo: "The Brown Tie and Lumber Mill."
©1985 by Earl Brockman reserving all rights. Used with permission.

Book Production by:
Tamarack Books, Inc., PO Box 190313, Boise, ID 83719-0313.
1-800-962-6657   208/387-2656   fax 208/387-2650

Printed and bound in the United States of America.

Published by Kirkwood Publishing Company
2555 Glendale Road
Fruitvale, ID 83620

PROLOGUE

Two of the "King's Pines" were lost with the death of Carl Brown on August 20, 1963, and his wife, Ida, on October 6, 1965. They rest in the family plot at the McCall Cemetery, under a big, beautiful King's Pine. To people who knew and loved trees as the Browns did, the useful life of tall, straight trees does not end when they fall. So might it be with this pioneer couple whom Grace Jordan described in Carl's obituary:

> "The Browns were tireless workers for everything that was good for the community. They gave not just money, they gave themselves."

The New England forests which furnished masts for the Royal Navy 300 years ago are largely gone. But the spirit of the sailing ship lives on in the hearts of those who read colonial history. And the spirit of Carl and Ida Brown lives on for those who read this history of the McCall area. This edition is intended to reaffirm the "Brown spirit" in keeping with Grace Jordan's wording in a 1959 letter to Betty Brown Harwood, the Brown's daughter, when the book was first being considered:

> "I hope to make it a book that makes attractive to readers, not excepting young and impressionable ones, the hard, hard work that goes with ventures in pioneer times, persistence through disaster, faith in a community, the desire to do something for one's state and country, all of it a pronouncement on democracy, for that is what your parents' lives are."

FOREWORD

Idaho is still young and vigorous. Its first permanent settlement, at Franklin, is but a hundred years
old. That means that some of the men and women
credited with its development still live. The story of
one such family, it has seemed to me, should be put
into type. That conviction accounts for this book.

My original aim was to write mostly of Carl and
Ida Brown, of McCall, and to a lesser degree of their
children, Elizabeth, Warren, Dorothy and Margaret.
But as I proceeded I found another image appearing
on my canvas, the town itself. And so my plan had
to be altered, and I shall tell you of the family and
of the village that has known them for more than
50 years.

Built at the south end of the larger of the two
Payette Lakes, McCall would eventually have become
a resort, at least in summer, without any Browns
about. The lake water is a fine sapphire, the air is
high and clean, and the hills are spiked with cool
evergreen timber. But without the payroll of Carl
Brown's lumber mill, operating many years, McCall
would never have become much of a business place.
And without the cooperation, the willing hands and
the brains of the Browns and those the Brown children married, the village would not have attained
such things as its efficient community hospital and
modern high school. Aided and encouraged by the
caring of the Browns, McCall has become a uniquely
satisfactory place to live, self-dependent, spirited, and
beautiful because it is natural and unaffected.

My chronicling has not been easy. The Brown left
hand doesn't even want to know what the right hand
is doing. If you confront a Brown concerning money

or effort that he has given to some good local cause, he may finally admit that Yes, maybe he did do this or that. And then he begins to play down whatever he did. To get any of his goodness or charity on paper requires ingenuity and drudgery.

Paris Martin, editor of the Payette Lakes Star, has permitted me the use of his files, but unfortunately everything before 1940 was destroyed in the fire of that year, and there are great gaps in the remaining years. This may account for happenings that I have missed.

I have dwelt sparingly on the pre-Brown history of the town, which began in 1888 when Thomas McCall first saw the frozen, snow-covered lake and thought it a gigantic meadow. Thanks to the Women's Progressive club, and to Betty Brown Harwood in particular, this history has been preserved in the local library. It is noteworthy, however, that Thomas McCall and the 14 or 15 wagons of settlers who followed him in 1889 had no easy time of it. That first winter was so terrible on stock that though a few of the gaunt, weakened creatures were lured to Meadows, a thousand feet lower, by means of carrots dropped ahead of them on the snow, many head froze standing huddled in the pastures.

Even when one traveled light it took five days to get to McCall from Boise. Neal Boydstun remembers that his grandfather Mark Cole was a member of a party that took 11 days to travel to Roseberry from Weiser with wagons. They forded the brawling Weiser so many times they figured they had forded it lengthwise.

In village affairs I have attempted to include only those moves that Browns were connected with, whether they introduced them or just helped push. However, there have been some exceptions to this plan. For instance, the Browns neither discovered nor named Sharlie, the Payette Lakes serpent. Possibly none of them have seen him, yet many sober McCallites are sure he is real. Because he is good news copy and very strong local medicine, Sharlie is here.

Again, though Betty Brown taught in the district schools and served on the board, and although Warren Brown as a board member fought for seven years for better school buildings, a fight that almost rent the county, the top quality of the youngsters who went through the schools could hardly be laid to the Browns. These youngsters have taken surprisingly many honors in wide fields. They have become not only skiers—a villager skis as soon as he can stand up on slats—but doctors, ministers, designers, soldiers, engineers. Some of these young people are here.

To be serious about one final matter, biography cannot stop with recording. It does not complete its duty without an attempt to adjudge, to evaluate. My summations here are my own, after listening. They may fall short in understanding, but I have sought to be honest.

My chief concern, as it must be with all who write about the living and the doing, has been to do justice, to injure none. My hope has been to make clear that life in a small town can be not only amusing and dear, but to the soul satisfying.

Here are people I have come to love. May you love them too.

Grace Edgington Jordan.

December 1960

ACKNOWLEDGMENTS

In preparing this account I have had the assistance of many. They have probed their memories; they have loaned me clippings, diaries, pictures, promotion booklets; they have shown me heirlooms. I have made use of material from the files of the Boise Statesman, and the Payette Lakes Star of McCall. All this aid has been offered in the spirit of the village itself, warm and free-hearted. Some of my research has taken me to other places within the state of Idaho and even across the continent.

All the Brown family and their relatives by marriage have been helpful. I shall not list each contributing Brown separately except to say that Betty Brown Harwood has secured numerous interviews for me and has used up solid blocks of her time in my behalf. Once she and her mother took me on a two days' trip through the country beyond McCall—to Burgdorf, Warren, Big Creek and Yellow Pine. Of course we had to cross the towering ranges that isolate these places. We spent one night with Grace McRae, less than a mile from the Edwards place, where Carl, Ida and Betty lived for a good many months when Betty was a baby.

To Edna Casler Joll of Boise I owe a debt of gratitude for editorial assistance and encouragement.

For other assistance I should like to express my sincere gratitude to these:

In McCall, John L. Beitia, Les Ulmer, Pat Hayes, Ernest Watkins, Margaret Peck, Grace McRae, Lesta Coonrod, Fay Wallace, Mr. and Mrs. Roy Stover, Ralph McDougal, Helen Luzadder, Helen Markley Miller, Mr. and Mrs. Guy Fairbrother, Paris Martin, William Harp, Elizabeth Harland, Mrs. Irene Vance, Sam Defler, Mark Johannsen, Mr. and Mrs. Melvin (Brownie) Hoff, Mr. and Mrs. L. P. Drew, Mr. and Mrs. Jack Hayes, Mr. and Mrs. Neal Boydstun, Mrs. Joe Kasper, Mrs. Florida Hayes, Mr. and Mrs. Leonard Ackaret, Mr. and Mrs. William Deinhard, and very particularly Mr. and Mrs. Harold (Slim) Vassar.

In Donnelly, Mr. and Mrs. Robert Halferty, Bert Armstrong, and Mrs. Pansy Scheline.

At Cascade, James L. Schoenhut.

At Big Creek, Napier Edwards.

At Warren, Otis Morris.

At Horseshoe Bend, Mr. and Mrs. Theodore Hoff.

In Boise, Mr. and Mrs. Harvey Meldrum, Chester Stephens, Sam D. Hays, Mr. and Mrs. Britt Nedry, Mrs. Don Numbers, Mr. and Mrs. Ralph Paris, Jim Larkin, C. Ben Martin, Mrs. Emmitt Pfost, Mrs. D. L. Crain, Mrs. Mina Buhn, Rev. Meredith Groves, Mrs. Bessie Lambie, and Howard Ahlskog.

At Meadows, Mrs. Ross Krigbaum.

In Cotuit, Massachusetts, Mrs. Julian Rothery.

In Washington, D. C., Mrs. S. L. Broadbent.

In Lincoln, New Hampshire, Mr. and Mrs. Sherman Adams.

In Concord, New Hampshire, the State Historical Society.

PRINCIPAL CHARACTERS OF THIS BOOK

Warren Goodhue Brown, New Hampshire lumberman; his wife Charlotte Elliott; their son Carl Elliott Brown.

Rev. John Sherman Harrington, a minister; his wife Elizabeth Bigham; their daughter Ida Louise.

Elizabeth (Betty), Warren H., Dorothy, and Margaret, children of Carl and Ida Brown.

Stanley W. (Ted) Harwood, husband of Betty.

Jayne Jones, wife of Warren.

Arlen (Tuck) Beyerle, husband of Dorothy.

Homer Davies, husband of Margaret.

Stanley and Ann, children of Betty and Ted Harwood.

Frank and Diane, children of Warren and Jayne Brown.

Karyl and Susan, children of Dorothy and Tuck Beyerle.

Dick, Phil, Don, Sharon, Deborah and Diane, children of Margaret and Homer Davies.

Broadax Bill, Sheepherder Bill, Boston Brown, old-timers from the back country.

Mr. and Mrs. William Edwards, founders of Edwardsville; their son Napier.

Chester Stephens, former Brown employee.

Theodore Hoff, former McCall lumberman; his wife Hannah.

Clem Blackwell, hotel and saloon man; his wife Fanny.

Sam Defler, Supervisor of the Payette Forest.

Lyle Watts and Julian Rothery, former Forest supervisors in McCall.

Helen Wilson Luzadder, McCall school teacher.

Helen Miller, McCall author, teacher.

Beth Rodenbaugh, newspaper woman.

"Aunty Harland," great friend and assistant in the Brown household.

Grace McRae, teacher; her husband Dan, mining man.

Dr. and Mrs. Don Numbers.

Harold (Slim) Vassar, Forest employee; his wife Edith.

Roy Stover, one-time Brown employee; proprietor of The Dog House.

Leslie Ulmer, mill superintendent.

Sharlie, Payette Lakes sea serpent.

CHAPTER ONE

Stuart and Hanover kings demanded of the colonial governments of New England that all white pine trees "fit for masting our Royal Navy" be preserved for that use only. These trees were "hereby granted to his Majesty, his heirs and successors forever."

Baltic countries had previously furnished England with shipbuilding materials, but early in the 17th century America's limitless storehouse of the finest mast and spar material in the world was discovered. Of these woods, the white pine was the commonest and the most easily worked.

Although the ruling was one of but few restrictions laid upon the colonists, and they had only to leave alone all trees marked with the official Broad Arrow, they ignored it when they dared. Sometimes they mobbed the crown's agents when they attempted to punish offenders.

In 1708 all white pines larger than 24 inches in diameter 12 inches from the ground were reserved for the king. In 1732, fines were imposed for cutting trees even 12 inches in diameter at the base.

There were truly noble pine forests in New England in that day. In 1736 a pine cut near the Merrimac river stood "streight and sound, seven feet eight inches in diameter at the butt-end". Trees four or five feet through were rather common. One recorded pine required 55 teams of oxen to draw it to the river. One 38 inches in diameter 60 feet above the butt required 52 ox teams.

Today in New England such trees are hardly more than a memory. But it might be said, fancifully, that this memory is reflected in a certain family in the state of Idaho, whose forbears knew those great pines

1

very well. Leaving New England, moving to the West, these people brought staunchness and honesty, a passion for hard work and a love of timbered hills. In a sense they are King's Pines transplanted.

At the mare's head he stood waiting. Eight years old, slender and lightly built but sturdy, he had blue eyes and fair hair that would darken when he became a man. His hair would be as dark as that of the tall woman standing close by, on the porch.

The boy had brushed and groomed the mare, harnessed and backed her between the shafts of the buggy, properly fastened every hook, buckle and snap. Then he had driven her to the front door of the big house. The house stood at the top of a grassy slope and looked down upon a town and a mill. Beyond this town were hills that appeared soft and rounded only because they were covered with brush and small trees. Through the town rushed a small, excited river.

The woman on the porch was not merely slender; she had dignified beauty, and her white apron was worn for correct appearance at eight o'clock in the morning as much as for utility.

To the boy she said admonishingly: "Remember, Carl, after school you are not to go out to the woods. You are to come home. I do not want you associating with loggers. Their life is rough and dirty. I don't want you working with oxen or hanging around men who drink and smoke and curse. You are meant for better things. Remember what I say."

Perhaps the boy assented without argument—he usually did.

Out of the house strode a square, ruddy man over six feet tall, who gave the woman a brief goodbye and mounted swiftly to the buggy seat. The boy got in too, took up the reins which had been knotted around the whipstock, and spoke to the mare. She set off briskly, wheels flashing in the sun, for the mile run to the mill below. This was the Brown Lumber Mill of Whitefield, northern New Hampshire; and the year was 1886.

Charlotte Brown reentered the two-story house with its attached woodshed and work rooms that were typical of New England, a house "as long as the moral law". Warren Goodhue Brown had built it himself, using the finest pine and hardwood obtainable, for not only did he head his own lumber company, but his father Joseph Brown had lumber mills first on the Pemigewasset above New Hampton Bridge, and later at West Campton. The Browns knew as much about wood as men then could.

When he was only 16, Warren Brown had become a lumberman by working with his father in every phase of the industry. When he was 23, lured by California gold he traveled alone to the Pacific coast, via Panama, crossing the isthmus afoot. Later he found himself in the territory of Washington. Here he made a discovery, the value of Washington white fir as a mast and spar tree. When he returned home he and his brother Alson began shipping this fir by way of Cape Horn to New England, an operation that became so big they built their own ship for the purpose. Their masts were used on vessels built in Maine, Massachusetts and New York, not because New England didn't produce mast timber but because the supply was almost gone.

In 1861 Warren married Ruth Avery, who died a year later of diphtheria. Her infant died with her. In 1865 Warren married Charlotte Elliot, a woman of Scottish descent, and to them were born Josephine, Daisie, Carl Elliott, and Kenneth. Carl was born in 1878, when his father was a vigorous 44 and by no means through his prime, for he was to live to four score, never going near a doctor in his last 57 years.

At eight Carl took full care of his father's driving horses, and drove him each morning to the mill. All his life he would love horses and love working with them. Also he would love the woods. The grandeur of a great tree, the music of the wind in its branches, the sharp smell of fresh sap, this fascination was born in him, never to be lost. But his mother's strictures against woods life were to prove powerful. They would follow him into maturity, into his married life. Of course when he could escape from her vigilance he stole out to watch his father's French Canadians falling trees and drawing them with big draft teams or slow powerful oxen. As they worked, the loggers sang, swinging their axes and saws in rhythm.[1]

Whitefield, named for the great 18th-century evangelist George Whitefield, sits on the St. Johns river, which a few miles to the west pours into the greater Connecticut. Beyond the Connecticut lies Vermont. Whitefield looks northwest to Dalton Mountain, 2100 feet high, due west to Towns Mountain, a hundred feet higher, and east to the White Mountains, which enthrone the Presidential range, with Mt. Washington at 6300 its tallest peak.[2]

New Hampshire landscapes only *look* soft. Hidden in the cover of white pine, tamarack (hackmatack), black spruce, balsam fir, hemlock, white cedar and maple are rocks and fells, cliffs and escarpments. Above a drift of cloud at the craggy edge of Profile Mountain, not far from Whitefield, the Great Stone Face looks into Franconia Notch. And there are other notches, such as Crawford, which is 2000 feet deep and carries the waters of both the Saco and the Ammonoosuc rivers. The word notch seems a typical New England understatement.

In the midst of this rock-ribbed sweep there are sudden lovely little valleys, whose isolation explains the independence, fixed opinions and sparing speech that make the state motto appropriate. That motto is Live Free or Die.

From these woods came the material to feed the mills of Warren Brown and his brother Alson (A. L. and W. G. Brown & Company), a business established in 1864, at one time the largest of its kind in New

Hampshire, possibly in all New England. Besides finished lumber the Browns made doors, mouldings, box-shooks and even butter tubs, as well as exquisite hardwood furniture—the furniture part they would expand as pine and spruce became exhausted.

The boy Carl knew all these useful woods and also the smaller brush that cushioned the abrupt hills. There was basswood, sumac (staghorn), the various cherries, including dwarf, whose insipid dark-red fruit he liked to bite and throw away. He knew service-berry, often pronounced *sar*vice, and also called shad-brush because it bloomed when the shad ascended the rivers.

Part of the boy's passivity came from his adult-dominated life. Even after his sister Josephine, 11 years his senior, married Milford Libby, she lived at home to help care for Daisie, who from birth had never walked. Josephine and Milford had no children to keep them young, and of course Daisie did not marry. There was always a hired girl in the house, and older relatives came for long visits, warmly welcomed by Warren, who liked to be surrounded by people.

Warren had set his house on a foundation of granite. A wood-burning furnace, a sittingroom fireplace that took three-foot logs, and a range in the kitchen tempered the below-zero temperatures and the five-foot snows of Whitefield's winter. On the main floor were formal parlor and comfortable sittingroom separated by a hall, then a large diningroom, the kitchen, the master's bedroom, one for Daisie. Upstairs were other bedrooms. The house had running water and a bath, conveniences not too common in small town New England in 1886. Everything in and about the place was like Charlotte herself, as neat as wax.

In the yard flowers bloomed all summer, and behind the house was a thrifty vegetable garden. The barn was for horses only—the boy Carl had no useful acquaintance with cows.

Whitefield had summer picnics and a booming Fourth of July. In winter young people and children skated on the canal constructed by an underwear manufacturer, a course several miles long. In town the Main street hill was fenced off for coasting. Frequently there were public balls where the French Canadians danced all night, and which could grow riotous. To these last affairs, however, none of the Browns went.

A generation back, Warren Brown's family had been Quaker. He himself was always examining new ideas and this led him and Charlotte into Spiritualism. Among other things Warren came to believe that mines and mining were "favorable" for him, a conviction that would shape his son Carl's life past imagining.

In 1890, when Carl was twelve and still slender because he was too active to put on any fat, he was already a business man. At the mill he put through the circular saw discarded ends of the socket stakes used on lumber cars, cutting them into 16-inch or two-foot lengths for stove wood. After supplying the home woodshed he was free to sell the rest in the village. When this work got too heavy, he hired a couple of friends with handsleds to help him. His father pointed out that ricked wood often settled, and advised Carl to make his cords higher than the standard four feet. He did this, and seventy years later recalled the good Methodist who said he would probably grow up honest because his cords were always over four feet high.

At home Josephine painted and embroidered, Daisie lived in her wheel chair, and Kenneth, seven, who seemed the last child Heaven intended the Browns to have, kept Charlotte busy. Warren's enterprises prospered. At the mill he had a 400-horsepower steam engine; and at an initial cost of $2,200 a "ten lighted machine of the Western Electric Light" enabled the mill to run full time the whole year. In the mills he employed 150 men and in the woods 300 more, who required 200 horses and oxen for their labors.[3]

Carl's mother aimed his life toward the family mercantile business. She encouraged him in his wood sales and urged him to study hard. She called his attention to the great men of New Hampshire, men like Webster and Greeley. She didn't know that once he had driven a team in the woods for a French Canadian logger too drunk to drive.

The boy heard much talk about national issues. His father had cast his first vote for presidential candidate John C. Fremont of the new Republican party. Later Warren decided that the Greenback party more nearly spoke his views; and twice he consented to be its candidate for governor. He also served in the legislature. Often he was away at political meetings, and in 1887 he was sent as a delegate to the convention where the Union Labor party was organized. His own original thinking and his interest in prominent men sent him on long journeys, once into Mexico. Regardless of his strict views on religion and temperance, his courage and honesty made him liked and sought after.

"Always stand by your word when you've given it," he told young Carl. "Be democratic and plain. Be open minded but cautious."

In September 1892, Carl Brown, 14, still rangy, long-boned and light-boned, entered high school. He loved sports only less that he loved horses and threading the deep woods. Baseball was popular and so was the new game of basketball, created only the year before by James Naismith, across in Massachusetts. In fact basketball was sweeping the country. It wasn't rough like football, and Carl's mother didn't object to his playing. And Carl had the necessary quickness and coordination. Indeed, aside from his studies, he liked school.

Without saying much, by going ahead with her own plans, Charlotte was pushing her son toward a life of business. Several summers she sent him to help his aunt who ran a country inn. When he was 17, and his aunt no longer needed him, his mother insisted he start work in the company store.

However, two failures at school had convinced her that he needed a radical change of some sort, so the next year Carl was sent to New Hampton Institute, far enough away that he must live in the dormitory. The president of the school, a Dr. Preston, had a driving horse that Carl at once offered to take care of, much to the owner's satisfaction. And this proved fortunate, for since Carl did not let studies interfere with athletics and good times, some of his instructors distinctly disapproved of the boy with the secretly amused smile. After three years, one in business subjects, he was graduated. This was in 1899, a few months short of his 21st birthday.

Home, willing to try himself at a real job, he went into the store. Here mill employees bought everything: medicines, drygoods, clothing, meat, groceries, tobacco, furniture, hardware—it took 12 clerks to serve them. Times were poor, however, a foreman drawing $3 a day, other workers but $1.50; and family men often fell behind with their store bills. The challenge to keep business moving in spite of the credit lag worried Warren, and after a year he made Carl manager and threw the problem to him. The young fellow leaned into the harness so well and with such results that before long he was offered a position as manager of another store, and at more than the $200 a month his father was paying him. Of course he turned it town.

A friendly alertness accompanied young Brown. Without being told he knew that honey draws more flies than vinegar. Of the clerks he demanded good work, but reserved stern measures until nothing else would do. Natural courtesy made him respect an employee as long as possible. Normally he listened more than he talked; and his appreciation of another's words often made these seem wittier or wiser than they were.

Though the woods and what went on in them pulled him powerfully, he loved his mother and wished to please her. Only on Sundays could he escape from the atmosphere of ledgers and commodities into the green world of the hills. As to Warren Brown, if he had larger plans for his son, he was not ready to speak.

With his position and good salary, young Brown felt his oats a bit, he and the horse that pulled his sparkling rubber-tired buggy. No young man in town was more dapper, and his manner was natural and winning. The feminine hearts of Whitefield must have fluttered when he drove by.

Now to the town's Free Baptist church came Reverend John Sherman Harrington, with a wife and some of their eight children. It was easy to see that the children were a happy lot. Because their father was competent and cheerful and their mother a superb contriver, they did not seem troubled by the fact that ministers' families got along on very little money.

When Carl first saw Ida Louise Harrington, she was past 18. Her hair was brown, soft and fine; her blue eyes sparkled with gold flecks. To Carl, since the Brown women were either tall or big, she seemed very small and delicate. She was indeed small, for she weighed less than a hundred pounds; and until recently she had been in poor health. When she was only 13 a doctor told her parents that she had tuberculosis; and in 1893 the family of the "consumptive" commonly sat down to wait for God in his mercy to call his lamb home. Not so John Harrington. Regardless of what it cost, he took his girl each month to a special doctor in Portland, Maine, and once to North Carolina to try a different climate. Treatment was chiefly rest and diet, and though Ida was so weak at times that she could hardly walk, her father never

9

gave up. At home her brother De Witt took her out for a buggy ride after school each night so she could "get some air".

Her father vigilant, her mother wise and loving, her own spirit determined, Ida Harrington recovered. With a mind sharpened by childish anxiety and suffering, she finished high school quickly, once she was able to attend. Soon after the family moved to Whitefield she began doing millinery. Her eye for style and her nimble fingers made her creations immediately in demand.

The Harringtons were Canadian. John, blue-eyed, bearded and handsome, had decided early in life that nothing would satisfy his soul except to work in God's kingdom. After he married Elizabeth Bigham in 1872 they moved to Hillsdale, Michigan, so he could attend a seminary there. By the time he graduated they had three children. The first two, twin girls, born prematurely, had to be kept in a cardboard box on the oven door, but the tiny creatures survived and grew.[4]

Reverend Harrington had filled several pastorates before Whitefield and one at Littleton afterward. In Whitefield he, like Warren Brown, served in the legislature. He was active in temperance work and on the school board. He raised a big garden, each fall shot one deer for the family larder, took time to enjoy his children and play small jokes on them, and joined the Masons and the Odd Fellows.

In height he was above average, but his wife Elizabeth was small. Small and terribly clean. If her kitchen floor was damp from mopping, not even a cat could cross it. If the cellar steps were damp from mopping, no child could go even half way down for an apple out of the barrel there. She never chilled her offspring with the warning that life dealt as harshly with the just as with the unjust—she was too busy meeting life to quail from it. She dressed the twin girls alike, then dyed and redesigned their outgrown clothes for the younger sisters; and she made

10

many another thrifty turn. Around her, life always arranged to seem sunny.

Young Carl was not a church-goer. He loved to dance, but both the Methodists and the Baptists, who might have drawn him, were violent about dancing. After the arrival of the Harringtons, he sometimes got himself to Baptist services, and probably to the young people's meetings, where sociables were planned. It was some time before he proposed escorting Ida to the John Philip Sousa band concert 30 or 40 miles away at St. Johnsbury, in Vermont. He proposed to drive his buggy horse, called The Pauper because he had been foaled at the county poor farm, and they would have to be away over night, staying with friends. The Harringtons must have felt confidence in their daughter's good sense as well as in young Brown's ability to handle his horse and himself. The trip was made. Probably it jelled something romantic.

Charlotte Brown placed no large obstacles in the way of her son's courtship. She saw that the Harringtons had background and education, and recognized a world of dimensions, yet were devoted to sobriety and goodness. As for Warren, he appreciated Ida's beauty and was pleased with her father's civic spirit. The Harringtons too seemed not displeased. If Carl had competition to overcome, it is not recorded, yet must have existed, for the Harrington family was warm and outgoing and their house always full of young people.

On August 28, 1902, Carl and Ida stood before her father in the parsonage and made their vows. Ida wore a gown described by the local paper as of figured satin foulard, trimmed with panne velvet, white satin and applique that she and her mother had made. The sleeves were long, the collar high-boned, the train short. Ida's thick hair was knotted low at the back.

Following the ceremony, "performed under an archway of ferns and wild flowers", a luncheon was served. Though only close relatives had been invited,

11

they seemed no small number when crowded into the Harrington parlor. Gifts "including cutglass, china and cash" were presented.

The day had special meaning for Ida's parents for it was the 30th anniversary of their own wedding. When they could get away, the bride and groom left for a several days' stay at the Congress hotel in Portland, Maine.

On their return Ida was welcomed warmly in the big house on the hill. Charlotte Brown was wise enough to know that her son and his life now belonged to another woman, a small, pretty, animated person, who would not try to dominate but whose wits could focus sharply, who could speak her piece when necessary.

Warren Brown, however, had not turned over his son's life to anybody.

CHAPTER TWO

Crisp, red-gold autumn. Crystaline winter. Ida in a household not much larger than the one she had known, but financially more secure, spiritually less fluid. Warren Brown, it was clear, liked to show off his daughter-in-law to strangers—she had ease. Charlotte was pleased with her knowledge of good housekeeping and her frugality. And Ida's young husband took on a maturity that surprised even himself. At once he seemed quite settled, quite aware of his relationship to something with perpetuity. And because he loved Ida, with a depth that would steadily increase, he would have to love all women a little. All women but the coarse-fibered. He would love all women and quite a few would love him.

Toward spring, as the northern winter lost its grip, an idea formed in Warren's mind, which turned continually to the West, where forty years before he had discovered a new world. Now Warren proposed a family tour to the Pacific coast—himself and Charlotte, Carl and Ida, and 17-year-old Kenneth. The mill was running smoothly, so was the store and other business adjuncts, and they could get away for a time.

Carl and Kenneth had never been outside of New England, Ida had been only to North Carolina, and Charlotte had made but a few short trips with her husband. Except to much-traveled Warren it would be like setting out for a foreign shore.

They went by Boston and New York, staying a few days in each place. They continued to Washington, D. C., and stayed longer, for to Warren the air of the capital pulsed every moment with political vibration, and one might run into a famous or infamous character on any corner. They traveled south, swung west to New Orleans and found the Mardi Gras in mammoth bloom. On to the Southwest, where the warm winds stirred their New England blood but the brilliant cliffs were sadly bare of timber. They saw a pre-Hollywood Los Angeles, then tolerably innocent, and San Francisco at it was before the quake —a very different city from the one Warren saw in 1857.

They traveled north, sometimes by four-horse stage. Through the redwoods, which Carl and Ida could hardly believe. Through the piney Siskiyous. On into the lush Willamette valley of Oregon. Warren would have crossed the Coast range to the rain forests of the Tillamook, but Portland, named for their own Portland, was beckoning the women. And there was still Washington, now a state, from whose forests Warren and Alson had shipped so many thousand fir masts.

In Seattle they stayed with Amos, Warren's brother, who had come west early enough to homestead where First Avenue now ran. In lumber and real estate Amos had done better than nicely, and the women rested in his superb home while the men went on into British Columbia.

Carl was under a deepening spell. Every business seemed booming, especially any that was touched by the stream of golden trade out of Alaska. And the timber! The wealth of it surpassed even Warren's wondrous tales. From any country road the unbroken stands of blue-black conifers, ridge beyond ridge, reaching back to the misty horizon, filled him with something near ecstasy.

When it was time to turn homeward, Warren took the route through Boise, Idaho, a small, lively and self-conscious capital. Here Ben and Hosea Eastman, who once had lived in Whitefield, and whose sister had been Carl's grade school teacher, entertained them in their houses on Warm Springs avenue. Ida thought she had already seen everything but never before a house heated by natural hot water. Her father had often called her attention to the beneficence of Nature, but fancy Nature heating your house for you.

Their rooms were at the Overland hotel, then referred to as a hostelry, at Eighth and Main, and from its windows they caught glimpses of velvety brown hills rising from a rich valley, hills faintly green now, hills with timber crests.

Carl was more than reluctant when Warren started the party on its way again. They went to Denver to stay two days, and while Warren listened to western political talk he thought constantly in this mile-high setting about mines. For some reason determined by fate, he decided to go next to Topeka and stop.

He looked up a former acquaintance. This man began telling him about an Idaho mine called the Independence back in the mountains somewhere that produced both gold and silver and was a sure-fire thing. Thoughtfully Warren returned to his hotel. If he talked with Charlotte, and if she was unimpressed, the conviction Warren had had for years that mines were "favorable" for him spoke sharply. The next day he gave his acquaintance a check for $20,000.

In late spring the Browns walked into their home on the hill. Daisie was in her wheel chair, Josephine and Milford running the house. Charlotte became busy with her flowers, Carl returned to the store, and with a thoughtful air Warren resumed his desk at the mill office. It wasn't long until he said to Carl: "I can't forget this Idaho mine. I want you to go back out there and look after my interests."

Carl didn't require urging. His first curiosity about the West had developed into a mild obsession. Except that he'd have to be away from Ida . . .

By arrangement he met on the way his father's Topeka friend and other stockholders. They left the Union Pacific at Nampa, turned north, making Council by the Payette and Idaho Northern, then took stage to McCall on Payette lake. Details of the trip north, which was an all-out eye-opener, are now meshed in Carl's mind with details of many another trip, but he remembers getting horses in McCall, a straggling, one-street town on a lovely lake, and pushing into a kind of country he had never dreamed of.

Perpendicular heights, snow-covered even in May; spectral canyons; icy streams gliding over granite beds. They crossed a 6400-foot summit called Secesh (for Secessionists who came in after the Civil war), and stopped over night at Burgdorf, a hot springs place named for the man who ran the primitive inn and tavern. The saddle-weary men who could stand it soaked out some of their stiffness in the hot pool. Carl soaked but briefly—he was afraid of missing something he ought to be seeing.

The next morning they graded around steep hillsides through dense reaches of lodgepole pine. They penetrated cool brakes along quarreling streams, crossed Steamboat and Long Gulch summits at 6600 feet, then dropped to Warren, an almost deserted mining town. In its heyday, about 1880, it had had a

15

population of white and Chinese miners, dance hall girls and Madames, trappers and storekeepers numbering several thousand.

The next day they crossed Warren summit, at nearly 7000 feet, and probably wondered why Nature had to hide her treasures in such remote, lofty crevices. Now they descended through yellow pine, its bark golden to amber, its height often majestic, to the sheltered Shiefer (pronounced Shafer) ranch on the South Fork of the Salmon. And after that they surmounted the highest summit of all, Elk Creek, at 8725 feet. Finally they reached the headwaters of Smith creek, and here at last was the Independence. The thought of arrival was spoiled for some by the realization that all these scoured heights, these knife-thin ridges and vertical drops would have to be negotiated again—they'd have to return the way they came.

Carl was lean-built, eager, adaptable, and the whole thing an unbelievable adventure, every minute to be relished while it lasted. If he ever came back here again, it would be wonderful to bring Ida. These forests were different from those of New Hampshire. The lavas from which they sprang were deeper, they looked down from more soaring heights, but the conifer shape was as thrilling as always. The yellow pine (Ponderosa) seized his imagination. What a rich, clear grain it had. Imagine working with such wood.

The other stockholders may have longed but to be through, to get out of this up-ended country. The only humor of the trip concerned the man who had no mirror and on rising from his blankets was always inserting his artificial eye up-side-down.

If it hadn't been summer they'd never have reached the mine at all, for travel from November to June, they learned, was a snowshoe, dog-sled business. Everything Carl had ever known seemed so far away. This was like frontier, yet not the kind of frontier his great grandparents had known in New Hampshire.

16

He had never conceived of anything like this. Think of the courage, the resourcefulness needed to combat Nature herself here, not to mention fighting other men for her treasures.

Something had got into his blood; he felt excited all the time.

With the other men he returned to Boise, but there he stopped. He stopped and wrote to Ida saying he was staying on and she had better come.

The Harringtons may have questioned the wisdom of Ida's going but not the right of Carl to send for her. John took her to White River junction where she would board her train. It was her wedding anniversary, and her father felt for her, parting on such a day from everybody and everything she knew.

As they waited, a mild-appearing stranger walked down the platform and spoke to Ida. "Would you like to meet the president of the United States?"

Ida hesitated. Her father shook his head slightly.

But before she had to reject the offer, a flustered attendant rushed to them. The man was his charge; they were on their way to an asylum for the insane.

This might have seemed a dubious sign, but Ida brushed such nonsense away—she was going to Carl.

In Boise Carl established his wife in a home at the intersection of Idaho and Warm Springs Avenue while he made trips back to the mine. Ida found it almost easier to make friends here than in Whitefield, and she was often a guest in fashionable homes on Warm Springs avenue or Grove street. Boiseans were not at all provincial. They had wide and varied interests, they often traveled. Nevertheless a woman whispered to Ida at a party, "Would you mind to tell me where you buy your hats?"

Carl bought her a gaited horse, and a man named Max Mayfield taught her some riding points. From the first she refused to ride side-saddle, although she saw some women do it with amazing skill, adapting themselves somehow to the off-center seat. She rode a stock saddle and wore a divided skirt. This was long, as were all skirts, but it enabled her to enjoy many cattle rides with the Mayfields. The girl from the Baptist parsonage missed home, but she wasn't pining.

While he regarded himself as working for his father, Carl Brown began to think about working for himself. That winter while the passes to the Independence lay snow-blocked, he studied assaying. In June he returned to the mountains, this time running a pack-string to carry in supplies. Staying in Burgdorf, he thought about Ida and what her opinion would be of this cross-hatched world. She rode well, she took what came without fussing over small discomforts. Why not find out—he could meet her in McCall.

To Ida the little town on the lovely lake was but one of many stops, and she had no presentiment that it would ever be more to her than a place she had spent a night enlivened until late by considerable roistering along the street.

With Carl she put her horse across roaring creeks where she had to wrap her legs around the saddle-horn to keep dry. At Fisher station John Wannamaker gave them his loft to sleep in. It was the middle of the night when they reached Burgdorf, but the Chinese cook hearing there was a Missy in the party got up and fixed a meal. From then on they slept in odd beds or no beds, ate odd food, rode with odd companions, but Ida greeted everything with animation. If Carl cooked their meal over a fire, she helped him. Finally they arrived at the Independence, and she proceeded to absorb all the mining infor-mation her mind would hold.

They returned by a different route, across Profile Gap[5] through Alpine flowers and wind-twisted spruce, down to a basin of rich yellow pine—and called Yellow Pine—on the East fork of the South fork of the Salmon. Then home, by numerous stops, to Boise.

18

CHAPTER THREE

Carl's Father made one more trip to the West, a move to further affect his son's life although this was imperceptible at the time. Warren Brown even went in to the Independence himself. A man of rugged constitution but past 70 and accustomed to sitting at a desk, if he found the mountains a tough adversary, he didn't complain. Neither did he say much after learning all that he could about the mine. Carl was already convinced that it wasn't going to make anyone wealthy, and he seriously doubted that the spirits that held mining to be "favorable" for his father had been looking at a map of Idaho.

Still silent, Warren stopped over in Nampa to investigate a new kind of prospect, unlike anything he had ever tried, the manufacture of alfalfa meal from hay grown on the wide irrigated flats. To Warren it looked like a bonanza. Enthusiastically he directed Carl to buy quantities of hay, hire four or five men, secure equipment and set up a plant. This done, Warren went home.

Acting for his father, Carl invested the money required, but for some reason the project never got underway, and Carl had on his hands the hay, two wagons and two good teams. So, with the help of one man, he baled the hay to sell. *This project worked.* Carl enjoyed anything that had to do with horses, and he finished up with $2000 that he could consider his own.

He had rented a home in Nampa, neighboring with the Mocks and Steinmeyers, and here, early in 1906, he and Ida became aware that they were to have a child. So much she had never foreseen had come into Ida's life since her marriage, and now this blessing.

19

On October 31, their little dark-haired girl was born. As the child lay against her, Ida Brown dreamed a dream. This little girl would grow up warm and vital, generous by nature, and happy. Possibly she could be a little shy, yet for that very reason comforting to others. Shy but dependable.

As for Carl, he felt grateful that his line continued. They named the baby Ruth Elizabeth.

In the efficient nurse who took care of Ida, fate again stepped into the Browns' lives. She was Mrs. Fred Stewart, graduate of Back Bay Nursing school in Boston. Her husband and Carl were acquainted, and Fred induced Carl to put his hay money into sugar beets on rented land.

Their first crop was a marvel. Their second, through no fault of their own, was a complete failure. Carl and Fred awoke one morning to find themselves $2000 in debt.

Carl had never owed money, but this was 1907, and he was not alone in his troubles. Banks began to close, panic reigned, suddenly there was no employment. Carl had never questioned where money came from. Now he had none, and no way to make any. To Ida with her little Elizabeth in her arms, the whole thing was the horrifying dream that isn't a dream at all.

Even in the short time he had been in Nampa, Carl had impressed people as honest. With Stewart he went to the bank of which their neighbor F. G. Mock was president, and they signed separate notes for $1000 each with interest at 12 percent. Then, out of a clear sky, another Nampan, Hub Frier, offered Carl $2.50 a day to go to work at the Eastern mine on Ramey ridge, hours and hours beyond Burgdorf. The only alternative to accepting this offer was to write his folks for help, something neither Carl nor Ida could bring themselves to do yet.

When the work at the Eastern was done, Frier said,

there would be packing Carl could do. The desperate young pair decided there was only one thing to do.

On his 90-mile treck by snowshoe from McCall, Carl stopped at Big Creek, two summits beyond Warren. Here in a log house, later the Edwardsburg post office, lived William Edwards and his wife. Edwards had come from Georgia three years before to protect the interests of eastern mine investors. Though the Edwardses were obviously used to a wholly different living, and had a small boy named Napier, they had come to stay.

Mr. Edwards was well educated, had been secretary to a southern Senator in Washington D.C., and his wife was a descendant of John Napier who in the 17th Century worked out the first logarithm tables. His *Canonis Descripto*, published in 1614, explained this discovery.[6]

The Edwards house was book-lined, and when Mrs. Edwards set the table for company there was beautiful linen and silver. She was tall and striking, her husband rather small, with pale coloring and a gentleman's manners. He was always addressed as *Mister* Edwards. The pair considered themselves aristocrats, and they looked it.

At the Eastern, life for Carl was no holiday. He snowshoed a mile and a half each blue-edged dawn to his work, drove himself through a long day at toil his muscles were unaccustomed to, and returned to camp in icy twilight. Week after week he did this. Since there was no place to spend money, he sent Ida his check each month and she took payments to the bank. She wrote nothing of their situation to the families at home in Whitefield.

In the spring of 1908 when Frier's work was done, William Edwards made Carl a proposition. If he would bring Ida and the baby in, he would board the three of them free and pay Carl $3 a day for mine assessment work. Edwards wanted another woman for company for his wife.

Carl had given up all hope as to the Independence, and Edwards' offer seemed too good to refuse. In July Ida and Betty set forth from Nampa, traveling by train, stage, then horseback. For a week Betty rode before her mother's saddle on a cushion, over the same summits, through the same streams that Ida had forded before. In spite of uncertainties and alarms, Ida thrilled again to the call of adventure. Even when Betty slept by the hour on her mother's arm, and Ida thought it would break off, she had no desire to turn back.[7]

At the Edwardses they had a room under the slanting, shake roof. And Ida and Mrs. Edwards got along nicely because Ida had resolved they should, but sometimes it took quick thinking. Besides, nearly anything was tolerable so long as she and Betty could be with Carl. She came to love the shut-in peace, and the high peaks that permitted the winter sun only at midday. Especially there was Napier mountain to the east, with its rugged crest and a towering pyramid thrusting from its northern flank.

Ida wasn't worried by stories of wild animals, and once when she was out alone, she all but killed a young bear in a tree. She was carrying a 30:30, which Carl had showed her how to handle. Fortunately a man came along and helped her finish the bear. The bear proved fat as well as young, and not in the least unnerved by her encounter, Ida cooked some of the meat exactly as she would a ham. It came out tender and pleasant.

Ida may have written to the folks in Whitefield about her bear, but not about *the dynamite*. This story got into a Boise paper, was reprinted in an eastern paper and eventually got to Ida's and Carl's folks.

On one of their few holidays they had left Betty and gone on a fishing party. While everybody was sitting around a campfire, somebody tinkered with a fuse that was too short for safety. The dynamite exploded. One man was killed and Sheepherder Bill

Borden had a hole blown in his chest. Many were peppered with gravel, Ida's hair was shaken out of its knot and her knees badly bruised. A dog that was along was deafened.

Bill Borden cried to Ida: "Miz Brown, Miz Brown, I'm a dyin'!"

"No you're not!" Ida told him firmly, taking from her shirt pocket the large clean handkerchief she always carried and pressing it into the hole. This checked the bleeding, but nevertheless a man was dispatched to Thunder Mountain, miles away, for a doctor. The doctor couldn't come, but Ida got her patient to the Edwardses' and nursed him to recovery. Carl wasn't hurt by the blast though for months Ida would be prying gravel from his back with a darning needle dipped in peroxide.

In the fall when Mr. Edwards' work was completed, Carl took a contract with the Independence to dig 110 feet of tunnel at $10 a foot. He would be paid in cash whether or not the tunnel made the Independence produce more for its owners. In order to have his family with him, he arranged to use a two-room cabin at the adjoining Crown mine.

CHAPTER FOUR

Ida Brown's understanding of the people in this strange back country was widening, and now she was to meet more of them, all men. Working on the tunnel with Carl was Broadax Bill. The Browns boarded him and he slept on the kitchen floor. The other room had bunk beds, and it was Ida's private domain. Before daylight the men would start off each morning. They carried lunches, and it would be dark when they got back too exhausted from a day of boring into the earth's iron crust and too sapped by the cold walk to do anything but eat and fall into bed.

Fortunately for Ida, a carrier brought weekly mail, and when all the letters and newspapers had been read the second time the mail order catalogs sustained the mind. Also the Browns had brought an Edison phonograph with a morning glory horn and cylinder records. This was a help, but life was still a far remove from a parsonage and seven brothers and sisters. Such silence, such emptiness. But she had Carl, though he was usually too drugged with fatigue to talk to her; and she had Betty. Betty had no yard to play in because it was eight or 10 feet deep in snow. If they went out merely to see the sky, Ida put on webs and carried the child. Once a lost prospector, stumbling through the great white hummocks, fell literally into the cabin door.

Suddenly Christmas was just around the corner and to the Browns it would be no day at all unless they could share it with others. Of course Carl and Broadax Bill would call off work for the day.

On adjacent ridges two other miners worked, and Carl got word to them to come to dinner. Ida told the mailman to bring two chickens from the Shiefer ranch—keeping the birds cold until cooking time would be no problem.

They had shopped for Betty and each other by way of the catalogs, not forgetting Broadax, and Christmas morning was blissful. With all the culinary resources at hand Ida put her dinner together. As the chickens browned in the little oven, she found herself singing. Now one of the miners arrived. After a long wait for the other man, with the chickens losing their crisp edge, they decided to eat. The day flew, winter afternoon became dusk. Still the other miner hadn't come.

But at mid-morning the next day the belated guest arrived in high spirits, unaware that Christmas had already come and gone.

Suddenly Carl's tunnel was done, and there was no more work. It meant they would have to leave this station in the sky. For several days Carl put Ida on her webs and practiced her in the walking she would have to do. The mail carrier was still using a dogsled and was expecting them to go out with him.

"You'd better stay another week," Broadax Bill told Ida. But she had packed their few clothes and possessions, not including the phonograph, and felt she had had all the isolation she could stand. She was overwhelmed by an obsession to go somewhere, to see another woman. An extra week of waiting, she thought, would simply be the end of her. Some inner voice urged, "Go now!"

For the trip through cold and snow on snowshoes, no riding except possibly for Betty, Broadax Bill loaned her a pair of his trousers. The mail carrier came, Ida was ready in her cut-off pants, Betty muffled to her little nose, Carl anxious to be going. They said good-bye to the cabin. Where were they headed? They didn't know. They'd figure it out when they got to Nampa.

They were on their way, and it would be two weeks before they learned that after their departure a snow-slide swept down the mountain and sliced most of the cabin off into the canyon. It took everything above the second log from the floor, including the top of a trunk. For some reason it spared the phonograph.

Even with the mail carrier's help it was an arduous trip. Eventually they reached the Shiefer ranch, snug and warm in the bottom of the South Fork canyon. Here spring had arrived. The fresh-plowed earth gave off aroma; fruit trees swelled with promise. This place had been a homestead, but after Jack Shiefer drowned, his widow remarried and now the place was for sale.

Carl Brown was convinced that mining was not his future. And he was resolved not to go back to New Hampshire and the store. He pondered this ranch, where they were spending the night, not alone for what it produced, but as a base. He was sure he could get the mail contract from Warren to Edwardsburg, and it could be run from here. The government paid $75 a month for one weekly round trip, in the summer $150 for two such trips. He could also pack freight for miners at three cents a pound. It would mean dogsleds in winter, the rest of the year packhorses. The 80-mile round trip took four days now, three in summer. The summits went up to 9000 feet; the snows got 22 feet deep. But he already knew these heights and depths.

Beyond Warren the ranch was the only stop for travelers, who gladly paid 50 cents for a bed and 50 cents for meals. There was sale for all the eggs and butter and chickens the ranch could spare. Whatever necessities it didn't produce one would have to buy in Warren, at the Kelly and Patterson store.[8]

After supper Carl gave the place a further inspection. Of the 160 tilted acres, some were in hay land, some in steep pasture; there was a good garden and orchard. He saw a few pieces of hard-used farm machinery, three cows, two calves, chickens—all to go with the ranch. It looked as if a little bedding for the house was all one would have to buy.

In their bed in the loft, he and Ida talked, and he didn't fail to mention the strawberry patch. Strawberries, after a winter of dried fruit or none. The thought of strawberries almost upset Ida's mind.

"You've learned to handle sourdough," Carl reminded her. "And light bread—yours is the best! You'll be needing a lot of it."

"Lightbread made with potato water and yeast starter!" Ida added, coming out of her dream.

Carl had $500 saved. In the morning they closed the deal.

The house had three rooms down stairs, one big room above, and a porch wide enough for bedrolls. It had a fireplace and in the kitchen a real treasure, a big fry-top range that the U. S. Forest had once packed into the mountains and declined to pack out again. The home-made furniture and cupboards were adequate, and Ida would soon cover the yellowed newspapers pasted to the walls with color pages from old Ladies' Home Journals.

When they bought the horses and equipment Carl would need, they were in business, Carl as postman and freighter, Ida as innkeeper, gardener and cook. To be ready for emergencies in the house or out, Ida shortened her dresses and braided her hair down her back. Wayfaring strangers would assume that she was somebody's young daughter, unless they saw Betty, who now ran about as free as the dogs and kittens, not in dresses but in rompers.

One of Betty's new companions was George Smeed, a part-Indian boy of 16, who came to the ranch to "help out". From Warren Carl brought a .22 rifle and told George to bring in all the grouse he could. George took the gun when he went for the cows, and usually returned with something for the pot. When George milked, Betty tried to be there to get a squirt of warm milk right in her mouth.

While most of Ida's stoppers proved to be hunters or prospectors, surprises turned up. One night a Professor Holden from Iowa State College arrived. The next day, observing Carl's alfalfa stand and the soil, he advised him to plow the next crop under, for nitrogen. (Carl did this, with good results).

Another evening, and into the yard rode a retinue, no less, of people and packed horses, piloted by Wise Mike Mahan. It was the Medill McCormicks of Chicago. With them came Margaret Cobb, later owner of the Boise Statesman. They had invited Alice Roosevelt too, but she'd had to decline the trip.

At bed time, tactful Mrs. McCormick, fearing that Ida was worried over how to sleep the party, assured her that Mr. McCormick loved to slumber on porches.

True or not, that was where he slept, the ladies snug in the loft room and the rest, all men, taking to the barn.

The men of the party had come to hunt, but the women stayed at the house. Ida found Mrs. McCormick trying to wash a blouse with scented toilet soap—she'd never washed one before, she confessed. So Ida helped her a bit.[9] Whenever the men were in, they preferred to sit on the woodbox in the kitchen while they cleaned their guns. That way they could talk to Ida.

Former Nampa friends, the Tom Cottinghams, wrote from Seattle saying their doctor wanted Tom to get out of his office for a while. And they were both over-weight. Could the Browns make room for them at the ranch?

As soon as winter had broken, Carl met them in McCall with horses. How they stood the ride to the ranch is not recorded, only that they made it. Tom went to work in the garden, toiling heroically. He helped anywhere he could and so did Mrs. Cottingham. In the fall they went back to Seattle well, happy, full of stories to tell, and thinner.

One payoff for the isolated ranch family—isolated but on a good trail—is the rather rare guest who appreciates isolation. If he didn't, he wouldn't have come. He brings in a fresh breath of the outer world and gives her who washes the dishes something different to think about, not necessarily with envy. These visitors differ from the vague and defeated who also come, asking for work but hoping to find very little —just enough to make themselves retainers. Every rancher and his wife come to know both kinds of strangers.

The Browns stayed well. Ida's hard sense forbade needless accidents and preventable illness. For one thing, neither she nor Carl had time to be sick—who'd take their places? Betty, always clean and well-fed, was ever on the go. She had none of the coddling that city children had, and didn't know the difference.

Ida's health reasoning was simply, Obey the laws of Nature. Of course if someone's insides got out of order, yet he had no stomach ache nor abdominal tenderness, she gave liberal physic. For pain or congestion, she applied cold compresses or poultices— poultices of bread, milk and a little soap. For colds, she applied turpentine and lard, externally. For cuts and bruises, Husk's dressing. This was a pinkish salve in a round tin box, and it affected the mind almost as favorably as it did damaged tissue.[10]

Taking thought and obeying Nature's laws was, however, not the whole story. There was discipline too. It was an afternoon when George Smeed and four-year-old Betty walked single file along a steep hillside above the ranch. They were approaching a big pine when George said abruptly, "Betty, don't say anything and don't look around. Keep right on walking."

Usually Betty minded. Once her weary father paddled her for refusing to bring his slippers. This time she did exactly as George told her. That evening George related to Ida and Carl that on a big limb of the pine, just over Betty's head a cougar had lain watching them.

Sometimes when there was illness in the area Ida was sent for, but on account of Betty, she hesitated to go. On a dark night with supper over and the household thinking longingly of bed, a hurried knock sounded. At the door Ida found Pinky Knox, who lived up the river on a poor sidehill ranch.

"Miz Brown," Pinky cried, "my wife's awful sick. I think maybe she's goin to have a baby!"

He *thought*, did he. "Well, don't you *know*?" Ida demanded.

"Well, she thinks so. And she wants you to come right away."

Ida protested that she hadn't had any experience with this kind of thing.

"But she wants you to come anyhow. Right away!"

Finally Ida gave in, but while she was gathering a few things Knox loped off into the dark, leaving her on her own.

Carl was away, but Billy Mitchell, a square-built bachelor neighbor, was at the place. He offered to go with her. Betty was asleep; Billy would come right back to be with her.

Outside it was as dark as Egypt, but Ida got the palouser[11] and lighted it. Thus they made their way along two miles of river trail where rattlesnakes were known to play, to the Knox door. Inside they could hear the woman moaning, and when Ida entered she cried, "I think the baby's about to come!"

It wasn't, not yet, and Ida set Pinky to heating water, lots of it, although all she could think of to sterilize was some string. Fortunately the birth went faster and simpler than Ida expected, and when she tied the cord, she tied it in *three* places, to make good and sure.

Ida stayed into the morning. Mother and child seemed okay and Pinky in possession of his wits, so she went home. In good time Mrs. Knox was on her feet, and the baby lived and throve.

The Browns came to value highly a big-muscled blacksmith from Vale, Oregon, Cash Macey. Drink had downed and defeated him, but at the ranch he got hold of himself, and the place became his heart and home. Betty loved him unreservedly and several times a day she said to her mother, "I must go down now and see what Cash is doing."[12]

If Ida Brown's life was full of hard work, she could take it. The high cold of the Crown cabin had actually brought her to a peak of health that stayed with her now when she went from dawn to dark with little time to rest. However, Carl's life was more than hard. It

30

was grinding, with no respite at all. Except in mid-summer his day began in the dark and ended that way. He always had to hurry with the mail, especially on the Big Creek end, and he strove to make the forks of Elk creek by two in the afternoon so as to feed his dogs, cook a camp meal, and be in bed by six or seven. If he did this and got an early start the next morning for Edwardsburg, he could deliver his mail on time and Mrs. Edwards would not be sharp. As postmistress she insisted on to-the-minute deliveries.

The first winter brought the problem of snowshoes for horses. A horse had to be taught to wear them, and since the horse must not interfere and must also set his feet wide apart, it was better to start the training on a young, gentle animal. At first Carl used wood shoes, later a malleable cast-iron shoe introduced from Minnesota. The wood shoe was made of two ¾ inch slabs bolted together with the grain opposed. A clamp around the horse's pastern held the shoe on, and if he was sharp-shod, his calks sat in holes bored in the wood and gave further leverage. Horses not only learned to walk fast in their snowshoes, they learned to trot.

When the snow piled too deep for horses, Carl turned to dogs. His first were a Dane and a mastiff, but most of the time he drove four. A dog needed to weigh between 100 and 140 pounds. The harness was simple, a collar with traces that attached to a single-tree. As the snow pack increased, Carl went ahead of the team, breaking the trail. They didn't need to be led, they followed. Only when the 10-foot steel-shod sled was empty did Carl ride. Standing at the back he could reach a step-on brake that kept the sled off the dogs if they struck a steep down-pitch. He used no whip, guided by Gee, Haw and Whoa. At night he shut the dogs in or tied them, to discourage secret excursions abroad. On hard-packed snow his dogs pulled from 300 to 400 pounds and kept this up for miles. Deep soft snow cut the payload in half, and twenty miles a day was a good pull.[13]

One thing people along the mail route soon saw was that if horses couldn't make it through, and if dogs wore their hearts or their feet out, still the mail went on. It went on Carl's back. Second class mail he might have to tie high in a tree until he could pick it up again, but all he could load on himself went.

The letter was from the bank in Nampa, and he was suddenly afraid of it. He laid the letter where Ida would see it after he had departed in the chill dawn. It was merely chill here on the South Fork, but before he saw his wife again he would spend a good many hours in below-zero cold, the cold that is treacherous because it is so quiet. It is a time when things seem to hang suspended in the crystaline air, waiting, waiting for the tiny shock, the muted vibration that triggers the roar. He might breast howling summits. Certainly all day he would be subject to the myriad mischances a man faces when he travels alone through empty reaches of ice and snow, where Nature's cynicism can wipe out a man quite casually.

He wore his usual wool outfit, coat, mittens, cap and outerclothing. His underclothes were wool and his socks. His high boots were rubber and canvas. He wore nothing bulky for he must be able to move instantly, unhampered, and to keep warm by keeping active.

He carried no gun on this day or any other, for he never shot deer and didn't count on having to defend himself from men. He carried matches and a pocket knife, little else. On this trip he didn't anticipate any gold bricks in the registered mail. One brick was more than a man cared to drop on his foot, three or four of them making a hefty lift. As usual the first class mail sacks were locked, only the postal people having keys. All his sacks were of waterproof canvas, yet they would sink if he toppled his load into a stream.

He couldn't get the bank letter out of his mind. He was sure Ida hadn't failed in any payments on the note, and at the bank they had never seemed worried. And when the loan was reduced to $500, the bank had offered them a new note with interest lowered to 10 percent. That part he remembered clearly.

Even reduced half, the note still hung over them like a cloud, for until the beet disaster neither of them had known what it was to owe money. Carl thought now of the trifling pleasures they had denied themselves, and of how hard Ida worked. A girl like her coming to this. For himself he didn't mind, but she was so small, so uncomplaining. He was thankful that neither her folks nor his suspected. Besides, his father was having his own worries. Poor investments; bad guesses like the Independence thing.

It was toward evening when he approached the ranch in a state of weariness and depression about the letter. Out of the house Ida came. In her eyes he could see no alarm, no special worry, only happiness that he was home again. When there was a chance he asked, "What about the letter from the bank?"

Ida laughed. "Oh, it was just Fred Mock congratulating us on sending in our last payment. He sent back the second note. Carl, we're all through with it!"

Carl drew a long breath. Then he went in to supper.

CHAPTER FIVE

Actually the canceling of their debt made no great change. The pace they had set for themselves they would not alter. Carl was yet a long way from the point where he could choose work that he liked best, work he felt he was basically equipped to do. But things *looked* brighter.

Their relief was only temporary, for another cloud, small at first but growing from within, began to spread across their sky. For some time Carl had been aware of a pain in his right leg. He kept on the trail doggedly, but now the pain increased to the point where it was nearly impossible for him to walk, and agony even to ride. Ida tried every home remedy she had ever heard of. Nothing helped much or helped long.

There came a night when Carl limped into the house and said, "I can't go on any longer, Ida."

She tried to keep calm, to think. "Maybe we could get Frank Hanthorne to take over the route for a while —just till you feel better."

Carl said nothing, so Ida called Frank at Warren, over the Forest phone line. Yes, Frank said, maybe he could, now the snow was crusting.

For a few days Carl lay on his bed, not moving, but still the torment continued. Some evil force was slowly bending his leg back at the knee. The leg was now two inches shorter than the other one, and he could bear no weight on it at all. He realized that he must get to a doctor at once—besides Ida kept telling him so.

Their savings were so little compared to what it would cost. Doctor bills, probably a stay in a hospital, no pay coming in. Worst of all, he might be permanently crippled. Once more it was the evil dream that proved to be no dream whatever.

Lying desperate, Carl had a sudden idea, and he called his wife to come.

"Fred Stewart owes us for a year's board in Nampa. (Fred was their partner in the sugarbeet deal and had stayed with them when his wife was away working.) If you wrote him about this, maybe he could help— we've never dunned him."

They had Stewart's address, Ontario, Oregon. Tremulously Ida wrote. While they waited for an answer she prayed.

Perhaps Fred was as hard up as they were. Perhaps he'd forgotten he owed them the money or would feel that time had canceled the obligation. Ida thought she remembered that he and his wife had separated— maybe that would make a difference *not* in the Browns' favor. Well, Ida had done all she could; there was nothing to do but wait.

The answer came quickly. If Carl could get himself to Ontario, where there was a hospital, Stewart would pay medical and hospital bills. Carl should come as soon as possible.

But how could Ida even get him to a railroad! She didn't realize yet that in the high back country an honest, hard-driving man can hardly fail to make friends, especially a hearty one who attends to his own business, and more especially one with a wife who also attends. Carl and Ida had far more friends than they knew, and when Carl's plight was learned, they came. Men constructed a litter, swung it tandem between two steady horses, and put Carl on it. They started for Warren, extra men going along just in case they were needed. Winding around the shoulders of straight-off ridges, the little caravan made its way. By the first night they were in Warren. Fresh horses here. The next day the same slow progress, but in Burgdorf beds and again fresh horses. Down through the Secesh meadows. To the head of the lake.

Here they lifted Carl from the litter to a waiting boat. He had suffered agony on the jolting trail. The men had tried to keep him cheered, but though he never said so, he had about lost hope. He just lay in silence. He thought about Ida, left alone with the ranch on her shoulders, and for how long. Maybe he would never be going back.

A woman was waiting also to ride down in the boat. Carl had seen her before, on the street in McCall. The Spanish woman, they called her, her occupation well known, and women did not speak to her. But for stricken Carl her sympathy was instant and overflowing. Down the lake if there was anything she could do to make him more comfortable, she was eager to do it. Gay. Cheerful. It made him feel actually a little better. Imagine so many people really concerned about him. He looked at the Spanish woman more closely . . .

Ida. What was Ida doing at this minute. Probably she was putting all her available help to work in the garden and fields, keeping things up; and *she* was putting out a great big washing. She said when she did a big washing it took her mind.

To his exhausted patient the doctor minced no words. "The casing of the sciatic nerve is fusing with the leg muscle. All I can do for you," he finished, "is to stretch your leg until it's straight, then keep it that way. It's going to be tough. Do you think you can stand it?"

Carl Brown said: "Go ahead."

For two weeks, with no anesthetic, they stretched his leg. Every day they stretched it. Carl thought he'd just as soon die, hell couldn't be any worse. But he never said Stop. The same ordeal every day for two weeks, and the only medication seemed to be a red powder to swallow.

But gradually he felt a little difference, a little less pain. His leg was straightening, it was getting a little longer. When he was sure, he wrote Ida that he was better. Some day, he didn't know when, he'd start home.

The journey back was so different it was almost pleasant. Of course there was still pain and he was very weak, but now he dared to hope.

At Evergreen, which was now the end of the railroad, a woman again waited, to take the stage to McCall. Again it was the Spanish woman, and again she was cheerful and overflowing with sympathy. He couldn't say he was bothered or bored by the trip to McCall. And it would be something to tell Ida the night he got home. To be at home again. Lying at last in his own bed. He'd tell Ida about the Spanish woman and watch her face in the lamplight.

Definitely he was mending.

And what did Ida tell him, that first night at home. Not much about her weeks of worry and hard work, but a great deal about those who had been so good to her while he was away, especially Billy Mitchell.

For yet a while Carl allowed himself the luxury of rest. When he was strong enough to take over the mail route again, summer was coming around the corner.[14]

CHAPTER SIX

When the mail contract expired, Carl confidently submitted his bid for a new one. He had figured very closely.

But the contract went to another bidder.

When Carl and Ida got the word, they were dumbfounded. Without the mail job they would have to leave the ranch—it would never by itself provide for their needs and hopes. They must move again. But where! Not back to New Hampshire. But what was there for them in Idaho?

While they pondered, there came a chance to sell the ranch, and Carl jumped at it. Also, another mail contract was being awarded, the McCall-Warren, and if he lost no time he might be able to tie this one up. In haste he completed the ranch deal, trading the place and everything on it for a two-room house and six lots in McCall, with $500 cash to boot. Then he hurried off his careful bid.

This time he was low man. Immediately he went to Ross Krigbaum, a long-time freighter and mail carrier living near Old Meadows. From Krigbaum he arranged to buy an outfit. Ross took his note for most of the debt, and Carl got the Halfway House, 12 miles north of McCall around the lake, saddle and pack horses, unbroken stock, pack gear, harness, a stout wagon, and whatever else the good-natured Krigbaum thought to throw in.

Carl and Ida left the ranch in early morning, not the time to take sentimental last looks. Carl was eager to be going; Ida was not sorrowful.[15] In this canyon her life had deepened, she had borne care and worry, she had comforted the sick and troubled. She had become able to work unceasingly at hard or homely tasks without feeling martyred. And here it had been surely demonstrated to her that the man to whom she was married would never be defeated because he would never stop fighting.

After a few years it might be fun to see the ranch again, but for now it was a turned page.

As he went to McCall Carl found he still dreamed of the smell of raw wood and sweating horses, the whine of saws and the bite of axes, but if he had to go back to New England to realize his dream, he'd have to give it up. This present move was taking him no closer, he was sure.

They moved into the little two-room house with the porch across the front, and Ida measured her windows for curtains. On both sides were neighbors, and on the main street stores, a meat market, and an amusement hall. The people next door, the Clem Blackwells, had a hotel and bar. Carl already knew all about the blacksmith shop and the livery barn, and the lumber and flour mills.

Whenever Ida had time to look, there was the lake, endlessly diverting and capable of the most curious changes in aspect. In sunshine it reached away blue and innocent. But under a sullen sky it could pile up sullen waves. She had not seen it masked in ice, when the things that went on in its depths were its own secret.

Shaped like a gourd, the big end of the lake lay to the south, where the Payette river emptied it. At the narrows, midway, an eastern arm joined, and here was Channel Island, wooded, several acres in area, and uninhabited.[16] At this point the lake was said to be nearly 300 feet deep, although an underwater ledge a few rods away was only 15 feet from surface.

If the Browns' new home town had a rival, it was hardly Lardo, just west of the lake outlet, with post office, school and store. No, it was Roseberry, down the valley to the southeast. The town had been laid out by John Jasper in 1870. It grew slowly until about 1888 when an area influx of thrifty Finnlanders gave it a big stimulus. Thanks to certain provisions laid down by its founder, Roseberry had a completely different flavor from McCall. For instance "vending of intoxicating drinks and the maintenance of lewd or indecent resorts" was forbidden. Any such provision in McCall in 1910 would have eliminated considerable business. One Roseberry woman did give trouble, but her property was not seized—she was firmly warned.

The town had two "nice comfortable churches", a doctor and a bank, whereas McCall had none of these. Roseberry had a 23-room hotel, run by Winkler and McDougal, and an emporium where under one roof whiskers could be removed, phone business transacted and confectionery bought. Its sawmill was smaller than the one in McCall, but still it was very busy.

In neither town was there an undertaker, but neighbors *laid out* the dead, then sat up with the corpse day and night until burial. The neighbors also made the coffin, copying a store coffin kept in McCall, and women always padded the box softly with cotton before lining it with cloth.

McCall was still bold and unabashed. High sidewalks connected the stores, and here loafers sat dangling their feet and observing the women who went into the shops. In summer this single street was ankle-deep in dust. Through the winter it was plowed enough so sleighs could pass each other. In the spring mud was up to the wheelhubs, and if a wagon mired down and the horses laid into their collars too hard, half of the wagon might be left behind.

Cross streets ran somewhat at will, and hungry deer often wandered along them and into yards. In fact mountain goats, those wariest creatures, had been seen at Slick Rock, only 10 miles east of town; and bear were to be expected.

With the Blackwells on one side and two U. S. Forest men, Julian Rothery and Bert Williams, on the other, Ida felt herself fortunate. Clem Blackwell had ranches as well as his hotel and saloon, and there was his wife, Fanny. Rothery was supervisor of the Idaho Forest, which had been established only two years, and Williams was his assistant. Forest people, the Browns were to learn, were almost invariably people of character and attainments.

That there was no doctor closer than Roseberry or Meadows did not disturb Ida, not after the isolation of mountain cabins and canyon ranches. She knew how to do a tourniquet, and when not to give physic. In any emergency she could remain calm. She hoped to avoid midwifery, however, and was glad that in McCall this was usually taken care of by two resolute women, Valeria McFall and Grandma Shaw. These two were on call night and day and probably received very little for their unique services. Their names, though, were spoken with love.

In addition to caring for her two patients, Mrs. McFall was always expected to assume the family cooking, and surely to make some of her buttermilk biscuits. Mrs. Shaw loved gaiety, and in her earlier days had been known to ski 15 miles or so, pulling her children on a sled, to attend a dance. When the party was over she loaded the drowsy children and skied home again.

Left: A metal horse-snowshoe like Carl Brown used on his winter mail run. Right: U. S. Forest supervisor Julian Rothery at McCall in 1910; Ida Brown and baby Betty; Herbert Williams, a later supervisor.

Left: Edwardsburg, now Big Creek, where the Browns spent one winter. Right: Grandmothers Charlotte Brown and Elizabeth Harrington with Dorothy, on a visit from New Hampshire.

Left: Ida and Betty at the Shiefer ranch in South Fork canyon. Right: Betty, age 4, and friend at the South Fork house.

Left: Hannah Hoff, at the time she became Idaho Mother of the Year. Right: Theodore Hoff, lumberman, who came to McCall in 1910.

The lack of church services did trouble Ida, and in a short time she found herself helping other women start a Sunday school. It met in the schoolhouse on the south hill. Ida saw she was expected to go ahead. "You're a minister's daughter," her new friends told her, "so you'll know how to do this."

Next, the women thought they certainly ought to have some music. "You can play, can't you?" they asked Ida.

She could play some, Ida said. But on what?

That was the sticker. Ida thought. Then she went to Clem Blackwell, whose wife Fanny worked ardently in the Sunday school, one of the best women, Ida was convinced, that she'd ever known. To Clem Ida said: "We need an organ for the Sunday school. Will you give us some money for a start?"

Clem pondered. Finally he said: "I will if the organ stays here. I don't want it being hauled all over the country to dances and things."

Ida agreed to this condition, and he gave her $25. The rest took effort, and a lot of accosting and explaining, but in the end the women had raised $150. From the Sampson Music company in Boise they ordered an Estey organ. Its arrival by freight wagon from Evergreen was decidedly an event in town, but after it was in place an ironic thing happened. Some of the women objected to a saloon keeper's wife teaching a Sunday school class, so Fanny Blackwell sadly withdrew.

Meanwhile Ida's skill in charming money out of men had given her something of a name. Whenever a man saw her coming along the street he made an elaborate gesture of reaching for his pocket.

Again Carl Brown was a carrier of the United States mails, and again a freighter. Up the west side of the lake ran the road he would use, a road that dodged and sometimes climbed. At Lightning point, where a blasted snag stood, it swung high and overhung the water. When alternate thaws and freezes made this piece of road a glass slide, it was no joke. At times the whole road became impassable, and then Carl rowed a boat up the lake. In time he would secure a 20-foot steel boat with a "kicker," with which he could carry passengers and also pull a freight barge. His passengers would often include prospectors, who always seemed to be broke after a holiday in McCall. However, most of them paid later. At the head of the lake his station could offer overnight shelter and there was a Forest phone. Here he also stored grain for his horses.

Such roads as he had were pretty much his to maintain, except during fire season. If storms uprooted trees or piled slides in his way, that was his problem. Through Secesh Meadows lay a stretch of corduroy, for which he was thankful. It was bumpy, but it kept him out of the swamp.

The heavy freighting was a blessing, although it meant hiring extra help. Many different men would work for him, for long or short periods, and in most cases this founded enduring friendships. They had to be pretty young, tough and determined to keep up with Carl. To point out one such, there was Roy Stover.[17]

Stover's father, a miner, first saw McCall in 1899, and the Little Valley hot springs was once called Stover springs for him. A miner's life may be a roving one, and Roy sometimes went to school in four or five places in a single year. But to get to school at all was lucky. During a winter before the Browns came to McCall, snow lay so deep that McCall children, heading for the Star schoolhouse, sometimes failed to get there. Troubled about this, Clem Blackwell and another saloon man collected $400 and asked a preacher named Martin to hold classes at his house. Though surprised, Martin agreed, and 10 boys and girls came, each bringing two wooden boxes, one to sit on, the other for a desk.

For eight months, with seeming satisfaction all around, Martin heard lessons. Whether he was a good teacher was of small importance to the boys after they discovered that he had trained as a boxer while in the army in the Philippines. They got to see him in an actual fight that capped everything.

There were a few Chinese around McCall. Sing had a popular restaurant. However, Sing suddenly died, and his friend Toy, supposedly carrying out a Chinese rite, immediately bled him over the heart. A couple of doctors who happened to be in town wondered if there was any chance that Sing had been *murdered* by his friend. They did an autopsy and took out the dead man's heart. The kid Roy Stover was fascinated by all this. One of the doctors, as he remembers it, poked a finger into the openings of the heart and announced with authority that there had been no foul play, just too much nicotine. They put Sing's heart back, sewed him up, and he was buried at the edge of town.

A few days later Roy and another boy were driving in some cattle at dusk and had to pass the grave. Standing on his own mound, waving his arms was Sing. The horses shied, so the boys knew they weren't just seeing things. Then Sing started toward them and they were fit to die of terror. But when the ghost came near, they saw it was Toy, who had been out to leave food to nourish Sing on his long journey.

In McCall, an 18-year-old was a man, and when Stover and his friend Wayne Richardson were that age they set out on skis one winter day for a ranch at the mouth of the South Fork, to work for a sheep-man through lambing. On a stretch of road five miles short of Burgdorf, a stretch favorable to slides, one chose this moment to cast off from its moorings. The boys had a dog apiece, and some primitive instinct seemed to warn the dogs in advance. Anyhow they got out of the way.

The boys didn't. But when the ripping and grinding stopped and the terrifying calm that follows a slide enveloped the hill, Roy Stover knew he wasn't dead. He knew because something was scratching at the snow above him. His hand was sticking up above his head, and something now pulled his glove off. He heard his little female spaniel whining.

Snow like solid rock pressed against him, but after an hour and a half he worked his packboard around to where he could wrench off a strip to dig with. He had heard nothing from Richardson, and assumed he was killed, but when he'd freed himself he discovered a pair of legs sticking from a snowbank. When these legs began to wiggle, the dogs' hair stood up.

Richardson wasn't hurt either, but both pairs of skis were lost or shattered, and the only way to reach Burgdorf and shelter was to walk. The snow though softening was eight to 10 feet deep, but the boys dragged themselves through it. From Burgdorf they went on to Mackey Bar and put in the season.[18]

Julian Rothery had arrived in McCall in July 1910, shortly before the Browns. First as assistant supervisor, later as supervisor of the Idaho Forest, he served until the summer of 1912, resigning to go into private forestry in the East, but like many an unexpected friendship in an unlikely place, the Browns' and Rothery's appreciation of each other would continue and deepen.

Graduating in Forestry at Yale in 1908, Rothery had gone to the Cache National Forest at Logan, Utah. There he organized the forestry course for the state college. Transferred to McCall he was 40 miles from a railroad, had no telegraph service, and very sketchy telephone. Such trifles did not interfere with what he considered his main objective, getting acquainted with his forest. He roamed the mountains, knew trappers and prospectors, and later wrote a series of short stories of the Idaho wilderness that were published in the American magazine. Some of his trips took weeks.

In 1935, after wide experience, Rothery became inspector in the Division of Timber Management in Washington, D. C., a promotion in which McCall people, inferring they had had something to do with it, would take great pride.[19]

Rothery reached Idaho just in time for the appalling fires of 1910 that in his forest swept Brundage mountain and the Fisher and Lick creek drainages. Fire plans that he drew then formed the groundwork for the present intensive system of Forest fire prevention.

On August 31, 1910, he wrote a letter to his fiancee in Massachusetts which describes the terror of forest fires before the day of smoke jumpers and chemical-dumping planes.[20]

"I'll never write another account . . . so read this carefully. We have got 'em licked. Now for a while at least the air is clear, thank God! I don't know where to begin . . . A great canyon filled from brink to brink with a roaring sea of flame and covered with black billows of smoke shooting a mile into the air and booming like thunder while mighty trees thundered down and tongues of flame licked solid half-mile stretches in a single jump . . . A peep into Hell would seem like a trip through a cold storage plant in comparison. Flames would shoot up 300 feet in a single gush and spread sparks and huge burning sticks a mile or more. It burned huge green forests to fine cinders, it boiled water in the streams, it powdered great ledges and for all the world no worse vision of the infernal regions ever danced through the dreams of a delirious drunkard.

"McCall twenty miles away was as gloomy as twilight even at noon, and 40,000 acres of my empire went up in smoke and flame. It burned up houses and telephone lines, and the very earth itself. Twenty miles in length it strung out over the roughest country on earth, crossing great meadows or rocky mountains with a leap. Twenty miles my battle line extended, fighting like crazy men, campers, Indians, Chinamen, and we even opened the jail and took out the 'birds' and set them to work. Three pack trains ran from town with fresh men and supplies, and over that 20 miles yours truly went back and forth running the job, encouraging the men with a joke or two when I'd have given my last dollar to drop down on the bed in the windmill and sleep, or grab my mother's apron and cry.

"Many a night we dropped down and slept in the woods when they were bright as noonday from the fire. Some of the men deserted, but most stood to it . . . Through smoke and fire and freezing nights a bloody sun and ghostly weird moon glared down on our feeble efforts, and never a cloud for three weeks . . . Slowly we fell back, with every shift of wind, and seeing the work of days crumble in minutes. And trenches! We dug more miles of trench than the Japs at Port Arthur . . . eyes as big and red as apples, clothes torn to rags, often without food and water and little sleep . . .

"One ranger rode into camp smoking in 20 spots, the hair singed clear from his horse, covered with bruises and burns and exhausted from a two-day battle.

" 'Hello Rube,' I yelled. 'How's she coming?'

" 'She sure gave me Hell,' he said, 'but I'll stand on the ashes of the last tree in the forest and fight it out. I'll win tomorrow.'

"The wind dropped, and a snowstorm helped us, and in two days we had it under control.

"Tonight I sit in the office feeling fine and looking at a stack of bills. We bought all the grub and tools in two towns and our expenses must have reached $400 or $500 a day . . . It may break out tomorrow again, but tonight I am the winner . . . In my dreams I still fight fire. I hear the sullen crackle of the ground fire, or the howling shriek as it rushes through the crowns of our great timber trees and smell thick, choking, inky smoke which strangles, and feel the jar of the granite mountains as the burning trees fall and crash down the steep sides."

Though several of Rothery's fire fighters were injured, no one was killed.

During his stay the railroad was extended to New Meadows, but the four-horse stage continued from there to McCall.

Writing for the Forest Inspector 30 years later, Rothery recalled with delight Central Idaho of 1910:

". . . the last frontier, a rocky snow-buried land, with only a few old pioneers scattered away on the Salmon river bars, or in their prospector cabins. There were, I recall, five or six murders while I was there. Some old timer took the ax or gun to his pardner, or some intruder, though it would seem that Idaho was large enough to accommodate all.

"Perhaps the most significant development of my time was the awakening to the necessity of roads, trails and phone lines. The fires of 1910 burst out in a region generally so remote and inaccessible that no substantial effort could be made to control them, and in some cases they were never discovered, and only the next year would the ranger find the old scars."

Time was not yet when the National Forest and the good will of its supervisors would mean everything to Carl Brown. For now it kept coming to him and Ida how fortunate they were to have a man like Julian Rothery for friend and neighbor.

For Betty Brown, whose loves until now had been George Smeed, Cash Macey and especially Billy Mitchell, McCall was a window opening onto an exciting new landscape, one dotted with little persons her own size and age. The world contained so much she had never before seen. For instance there was something she described to her mother as black ice, which turned out to be coal. At four she had for the first time a level playground, and there were the pines back of the house for hide-and-seek. In her playhouse she had the old Edison phonograph which had been retrieved from the slide-sliced cabin.

Before the Browns were really settled, friends from the South Fork started visiting them. There was Sheepherder Bill Borden, somehow related to that well known family, who'd apparently never had anything to do with sheep. Well recovered from the hole in his chest, he could pack more on his back than anybody. More than limber Carl Brown. Once he carried a cookstove over the summits to Big Creek for Mrs. Edwards. On another trip, going in afoot with the Edwardses, he found himself packing young Napier more than seemed necessary. Finally rebelling he unloaded the child and said to Mrs. Edwards: "Ma'am, I think it would be better if we just killed this little boy and you went on home and made yourself another."

A stout drinker, Bill usually ran out of money before he could get himself out of McCall. One Sunday morning Ida, dressing for Sunday school, said to Betty: "If Sheepherder Bill comes here while I'm gone, don't let your father give him any money."

Returning, she checked with Betty.

But Betty cried, "What shall I do! Daddy told me not to tell you anything!"

"If he told you not to tell, then don't," Ida said, knowing the answer anyhow.

Sheepherder Bill prudently delayed his next trip to town, but by that time he had decided to go to Philadelphia for a visit. He was full of this plan, and explained it in great detail to the Browns. They thought it was indeed a fine idea, and when he left the house they assumed it might be a long time before they saw their friend again. Perhaps he would decide to stay among his relatives in the East.

But Bill got only as near Philadelphia as the outskirts of McCall. He was found there blissfully drunk. When sober he reconsidered his plan, and felt that having been delayed he might as well not make the trip. A few years later he was burned up when his mountain still exploded.

In 1911 McCall witnessed an event exciting and prophetic, the arrival of the first motor car in the village. Betty Brown may not have seen it, but Florida Boydstun,[21] daughter of the Lardo storekeeper, did. She saw the bright red monster thundering down the road from Meadows and in terror seized the hands of her two little brothers and dashed for the bushes. The car was a Buick, and it had come all the way from Council over the rutted roads of the day. Sam H. Hays of Boise, who about 1900 had acquired 143 acres of land along the west side of the lake, bought a seven-passenger Speedwell touring car in 1911, and this may have been the next automobile in McCall. The Hays family summered on the lake, driving up by a route necessarily roundabout—Boise to Shaffer creek to Horseshoe Bend to Gardena, up over Drybuck to High Valley, then to Smith's Ferry and over the hill to Round Valley, then keeping on the east side of the Payette to Crawford, thence to Van Wyck, then straight up the valley to Roseberry and on to McCall, entering from the east.

At some time before 1915 a man named Peterson ran an automobile stage from Meadows to McCall. A Winton Six, it had no top, no front doors, but it had gas lights and probably cost around $4000, and the road it negotiated would be a test of the best machines 40 years later.

In 1912 the valley saw its first motorcycle. This was a Yale single-cylinder that Bert Armstrong rode up from Boise. To make the village of Sweet had taken him one day, Smith's Ferry the second, and Roseberry the third. On hills he had to push the machine, but whenever the road was fair he made 25 miles an hour and 30 miles to the gallon of gas.

School plants, their equipment and their teachers have ever served as a fair index of the quality of a community. It was the second year that the Browns lived in McCall when Helen Wilson, a teacher, arrived and began influencing the place as she would for the next 50 years. She had definite opinions on politics, on the newest books, and on trends in education, and she did not conceal these opinions. She was Betty Brown's first teacher, and the schoolhouse where she reigned still stands, although it has been moved down the hill and across the road to house the city library and city hall. To Betty the building seemed enormous that first morning—it held 20 pupils in eight grades.

That Christmas Betty took to her teacher a flowered china plate, and 20 years later, on her wedding day, the plate came back to Betty as a gift.

Helen Wilson had graduated from Indiana State Teacher's College which for some reason was in Pennsylvania, but at the first smell of sage after she came west, she fell captive. First she taught in Nampa, then eager to live more dangerously she applied in McCall. There she lived at a hotel until small incidents led her to take rooms over what is now the Goodman Electric company. One such episode was a drunken logger falling downstairs with a lighted lamp, and another was the roomer next to her filling his coaloil lamp with gasoline. Later she built her home on the hill and became an owner of business property too.

McCall was then in Boise county, and after three years Miss Wilson ran for county superintendent of schools and served until 1917 when Valley county was split away from Boise. She went to Skagway, Alaska, where she became city superintendent of schools. But either the living there was not dangerous enough or her heart was still at the Lakes. Anyhow, she returned and married a mining man, mild, blue-eyed Ed Luzadder. Since he was at his mines much of the time, she continued teaching. The first year of her marriage she spent in Burgdorf, where one could live dangerously without even trying.[22]

School houses in 1912 in Middle Idaho were a social center, especially on long winter nights when there wasn't much one could do. In McCall no one could be expected to stay at home with children, certainly not a grandmother, and the children went along. When they fell asleep they were laid in rows in their blankets in some back room.

The Socialist hall at Elo, built by Finns, was a favorite place for dances, and there was always a big supper to top off the party. Whatever else was served, fish was likely to come in somewhere.

Carl Brown's mail contract would run four years. In the summer he had a stage with as many as six horses—after parcels post came in the loads were especially heavy. In snow he used pack horses or dogsleds.[23]

A summer morning, and Betty very excited. Today she was to go with her father on his regular freight trip. First they went by boat to the head of the lake, where Carl brought in the horses and harnessed them to the wagon. Betty was mounted astride one of the leaders on a blanket. She carried a short strap with which to tap the leader when Carl signaled her by rattling a piece of chain. Once his horses were used to the chain they really needed no other starter.

Betty rode until her chubby six-year-old legs ached too much to endure. Then Carl put her onto the spring seat of the lurching wagon. When it bumped into a rock or dropped into a chuckhole, Betty saved herself by clinging to the iron seat-rail. Or he laid a big hand on her to prevent her flying off.

When darkness overtook them, they had reached a little meadow where water and grass were plentiful. Carl unhitched, hobbled the horses and unloaded the bedroll and the grubbox. With Betty trying to lend a hand he cooked their supper over a fire. Then he spread the bedroll on a pile of beargrass and spruce boughs. Betty took off her shoes and crept into bed in her overalls. Over her arched the starry sky; woodsmoke from the dying fire gave her a sense of cosiness and security. She lay watching her father make the final preparations for night and wondered what her mother was doing now.

Carl took off his shoes and got in beside her. "It gets pretty cold up here before morning," he warned her. "Better get up close to my back."

When he wakened her it was dawn and quite chill. The renewed fire crackled and spit, and when she'd washed her face in the icy water she stood toasting by the flames. Carl fried bacon and eggs and made coffee. Some of Ida's lightbread and a jar of jam topped off their breakfast. Then while her father caught the horses and hooked up, Betty washed the dishes. Carl showed her how to scour the skillet with sand . . . wait until she told her mother about this!

She would have another day like yesterday with her father. Maybe two or three more days. How tall and strong he was, his hair dark and curling at the edges, and a kind of curl in his eyes and in his laugh too.

Whether Carl Brown liked or only accepted what he did, it was a livelihood, and he was doing pretty well at it. He and Ida never considered quitting to go elsewhere. At least he was his own man; he had independence. And life was better now for Ida. For the present he must keep on. Keep on until some unexpected chance might move him closer to his old dream of *using* trees, not just following roads and trails among them.

For two years the little house on Lenore street, with the Blackwells on one side and Rothery and Williams on the other, was home. Then Carl bought a larger house that sat on the east side of the road leading south from town. For some reason this was called the "transfer" house, and with it went a shake-roofed barn destined to stand another 50 years at least.

Probably an impending event hastened the move. On a June morning in 1912 Carl took Betty to the John Berrys' and told her she could stay until he came for her. This was fine, for she liked the Berrys. Late in the afternoon someone did come for her, but it was not her father and she declined to leave. Her father couldn't come, she was told, because he was busy with the horses.

This sounded reasonable, but she would still wait. She knew all about the horses, their names, which ones her father liked best. She knew about the two white ones. One was gentle, the other reliable enough on the wagon but a devil when a saddle was laid on his back. Even the men who broke horses steered clear of him. Once Carl had found Betty on a fence preparing to mount this horse. Carl's frightened face stopped her. "But this horse likes me," she protested. "I just know he'd let me ride him."

Mr. Berry was always saying things that made people laugh. Once her mother had told him that his porch roof was going to cave in if he didn't shovel the snow off. With a sunny air Mr. Berry answered, "Let the feller that put it there get it off."

Once John Berry got to celebrating at the nearest saloon and persuaded other revellers that they all ought to go down and take a swim in the lake. He somehow mounted his horse, which he had tied to the hitching rack outside, and spurred down to the water. The others streamed out after him. They ran to a wharf and leaped in, clothes and all. Not to be unsociable, Berry rode his horse in among them.

This same John Berry came to Ida's rescue one morning when winter was on the wane. Ida and Betty were alone, Carl up the lake. Ida had gone through deep snow to a small building in the yard, one of those with stars, diamonds or crescents cut high in the walls that sat behind every house in town.

Suddenly a three-foot cap of packed snow slid from the roof and landed squarely before the out-opening door.

At his place John Berry heard muffled calls. When he located the source, he came silently and sized up the problem. Sir Walter Raleigh laid down his splendid cape that a lady might pass dryshod. John Berry took his splendid shovel and freed an imprisoned heroine, then returned gravely to his own house.

Eventually Carl came for Betty. At home she found her mother lying in bed and beside her a little baby. Without committing herself, Betty looked the baby over.

Believing it wise to accept the gifts Nature offers, Ida was enjoying to the utmost her short vacation from housekeeping. What luxury to lie in the dim light and dwell, half dreaming, on the future of this little boy. He might have her father's resolution or her mother's passion for order. He might turn out a firm New Englander like his grandfather Warren Brown, who did not idly exhibit warmth or enthusiasm. She would like him to defend stubbornly what he considered right. Like his father he might choose close friends sparingly, take counsel with few, keep his own thoughts, go his secret way while appearing to conform.

Whatever his inheritance, this child, as all others, would draw in addition upon that mysterious spring that is filled for him by unknown agencies and influences in the moment of conception. Because he was so small, so motionless, she did not foresee the driving energy that would soon fill him.

His name: Warren for his grandfather Brown, Harrington for her father who was now gone, but who still seemed very close.[24]

The boy grew, a determined child. By the time he could sit alone in his high chair, only certain persons could put him there. Put in place by others, he flipped out. One of these persons was Chester Stephens, who often worked for Carl and was frequently at the house. If Ida carried the boy in her arms when she and Betty braved the mud to go to the post office, young Warren had only to spy his friend, whereupon Chester must carry him.

Chester had lost his mother when he was small, and when his father remarried he seemed to have no home. Taking over his own life, he became a kind of child bum. At 22 he was tending bar in Council. Two years later, in 1907, he came to McCall and for three years freighted into Edwardsburg. There he would often hear William Edwards say bitterly, "You Northerners ruined my father!" Figuring there was nothing much he could do about this, and being by nature gentle and unargumentative, Chester let it ride.

He did more freighting with wagons than with sleds; most of the freight could wait for wagon weather anyhow. He used two wagons and if the going got too tough, he put all the horses on one wagon and came back later for the other. Six horses could move 7000 pounds over most any kind of road. He carried grain for his horses, always wiring some in a tree to pick up on the return trip. With a grub box and a bedroll he slept out in all weathers.

In Warren it took quite a lot of whiskey to assuage public thirst. Once Chester took in a load of 54-gallon barrels that six horses could barely pull. A load meant as many as eight such barrels, with case goods and bottled beer besides.

The wood barrels permitted a good trick. With a chisel one raised the metal hoop, then drove a nail through where the hoop had been. With one man to blow through the bung at the top and another to hold coffeepot or waterbucket at the nail hole, good results could be obtained. Then the nailhole was plugged and the hoop replaced.

Once when he was using sleds, Stephens was snowed in at the Halfway house, one of his stops. He probably had shelter for his 16 horses, but the storm kept on, and after playing poker until nearly morning Chester went out to find his sleds just high places in the cold white.

Sometimes it took two tries, one on foot, to get even himself through. Once he was from seven in the morning until three the next morning making 15 miles. Then he gave up, put the locked mail sack in a tree and walked the rest of the way to Burgdorf. Here the mineral pools were always hot and a man could thaw out his stiffness. By this time there was a woman at the place. Fred Burgdorf, now past middle age, had married. His place, still the only stop-over on the only route to Warrens and the country beyond, probably netted him and big Jeannette an exceedingly good income from its various services.

Though Chester Stephens often saw bear and elk, he never carried a gun. Young elk wasn't bad eating, but bear steak was not his choice. Once he took refuge from the storm in a cabin where no one seemed to be at home. Half starved, he found a kettle of stew still warm on the stove. He was eating stew with relish when the owner returned.

"What d'ye think you're eating there?" the man asked.

Chester tasted slowly, pleasurably again. It still seemed mighty good. "It must be elk," he said.

"Nope. It's bear."

To Chester it still tasted good but not quite so much so.[25]

CHAPTER SEVEN

In McCall Carl and Ida Brown had never been happier although they had little time to dwell upon the fact. His business, which Carl pushed with exhausting drive, was not yet producing security, but he had paid off Ross Krigbaum and was slowly building a stake. He and Ida had many friends, fast ones. Old cronies from the hills, hustling McCallites, and people like Fred Mock of Nampa, who had loaned him $1000 on not much but his good name.

He knew he was a fortunate man, even if he hadn't found his niche in the workingman's world. He sometimes wondered how he'd had the sense to pick the wife he did, but there she was, beautiful, capable, keen, with an unquenchable sense of humor. He had a daugther close to his heart; now he had a son too. And this village, so different from the town where he was born, and the lake that carried his freight—these things were becoming his. Perhaps for always.

56

Setting a dinner plate for whoever comes also makes one feel part of the country, and Ida was always doing this. People, mostly men of course, from the mountains and the canyons were always dropping in, usually at meal time. On a summer afternoon Boston Brown and Sheepherder Bill came to town. They intended to drop in first at a saloon, briefly. More drinks later than they realized, they set out for Ida's. However, they didn't quite make it—they collapsed in the weeds at the edge of her yard and fell asleep. Their sleep was not too sound, for they reared up at intervals and yelled Yippee, or they advised listeners to Let 'er Go Double.

Some of Ida's more staid neighbors were shocked and were determined to do something. But Ida earnestly explained that the two men were old friends, they were doing nobody any harm and shouldn't be bothered.[26]

During the summer months when her husband had to be away, Ida did not worry, though she was well aware of the passage of each day. Winter, however, provided unaccountable delays and therefore some uneasiness, but she did not let this show in her face or make her temper brittle. She had become something of a fatalist. In this primitive land you used all the common sense you had, you tried to stop accidents before they happened, and if disaster did befall, you kept your head. Her calmness in an emergency was known and depended on.

On a cold, gray afternoon while Warren was still small, this calmness got a stiff jolt. From the station at the head of the lake came a phone call.

"Where's Carl? His team ran in just now. They're still hitched to the sled, but there's no load on, and we can't see Carl anywhere."

Ida said in a tight voice that she didn't know. Carl had left several hours earlier, intending to follow the road along the west side . . .

Suddenly she realized she was talking into emptiness—the line had gone dead.

Through the cold, whipping breeze Carl drove two horses, with Roy Stover's wagon box fastened to the sled, and over him Roy's wagon sheet to keep out some of the wind. In addition he wore a long, old fur coat. Nobody else had cared to undertake the trip; he was quite alone.

Almost from the start the road had been glassy. Freezes, light thaws, another freeze had made the layer of ice ever thicker and smoother. For the first few miles the sled kept upright, but Carl, perched on the load, rode tense and alert. Now the horses approached the lake face where the road climbed to go around Lightning point, the jutting shoulder that dropped straight into the water. The horses themselves appeared nervous, but they kept going and they neared the top. Here the sheet ice sloped out suddenly. The sled began to skid, Carl sticking to the load, the load swaying. The horses skidded too, everything heading for the edge.

The load teetered, Carl felt himself going.

The sled caught, and with the weight gone, the horses clawed their way around the turn and shot down the other side. Still frightened they began to run, gradually calming, but keeping on toward the place where shelter and grain always rewarded them. When they stopped, two men ran out. Then one ran back to the telephone.

The men started out through the sunless afternoon, down the road between high snowbanks. Presently against the confusing all-white they spied an apparition. It staggered toward them, Carl Brown in his frozen fur sheath.

They got him to the station and warmed up with everything they had, liquid and solid.

The wagon sheet and the old coat had probably cushioned his fall and actually helped keep him afloat amid the lake ice. Anyhow he had scrambled ashore, and kept on around the road. It was a matter of keeping on the move or freezing.

Somebody was sent to McCall to tell Ida. By the next morning Carl was nearly as good as ever, but Roy Stover never forgot his lost wagon sheet.

It was simpler when the lake froze solid and Carl could drive a loaded toboggan across, avoiding the road. Toward spring a long used lane of lake ice would compress under hoofs and runners until it was stronger than the ice on either side. One morning Carl drove along this thicker lane, when a sudden wind, an almost balmy wind, snatched his hat away. He stopped the team, got off the load and started after the hat. An ominous crack! It came from all directions, seemed to focus right under him. Carl changed his mind about needing his hat.

On a wintry late afternoon he was approaching one of his camps on the shallow North Payette on snowshoes, leading a packhorse that carried lock sacks. To let the horse go to the ice-filled stream for a drink, he looped up the rope and gave it a slap on the rump. The horse went down to the water, but it didn't stop to drink—it plunged in.

The mail, the holy mail! Carl Brown dropped everything and plunged in after the horse, but it kept just too far ahead to seize, and when it climbed out on the opposite side it kept going. Down through frozen brush and timber, Carl running after, the horse running faster. Then some obstacle stopped it.

Jerking angrily at the rope, Carl hurried back, fought his way across the stream. On the other side, just for an instant, he dropped the rope. The horse took off again, this time along the bank. Though his clothes were freezing, Carl pursued. Again he caught the horse, didn't drop the rope for anything.[27]

Somehow he got to shelter, built a fire and dried out. If he said anything to the horse, it was probably

59

his one supreme epithet, in clipped New England English, you bastahd!

Two years after the Browns' destiny was altered by the loss of the Warren-Edwardsburg contract, this was readvertised by the government. The man who had underbid Carl had drawn harsh winters and was unused to a job with such desperate demands. From his bondsmen Carl bought his outfit and assumed the contract. To carry it out meant more of everything, including more help. It would mean depending on more men and further developing a gift he had already demonstrated of securing loyalty and cooperation in tough times as well as good.

Christmas 1914. New Years 1915. The season promised to be a happy time for the Browns because Carl could be at home. Even when dry things cracked with the cold, McCall at Christmas was a precious time. But from Whitefield came sad tidings. First, Carl's sister Daisie, the invalid, had died. Warren Brown saw his daughter buried and felt thankful that he had been allowed to outlive her, to see that she suffered no want. But less than two weeks later he lay beside her, although in nearly 60 years he had never been ill.

An upstanding man, a rock of responsibility, he had lived out his years. Ida, who wrote the letters home, would miss Warren right now more than Carl would. In his son's mind he would live on for a long time, his energy and shrewdness, his business ways and initiative often recurring to Carl in his own times of difficult decision.[28]

There would not be a great estate left, Carl guessed. In the last few years his father's investments had suffered for want of an earlier wisdom.

CHAPTER EIGHT

The years 1913 to 1916 in McCall were full of drama, some of it unappreciated then. Two McCall men, both robustly individual, both demons for work in different ways, both community minded, and both possessed of competent, conscience-ridden wives, united to form a business that became the life of the town. McCall got a railroad. The lake got its first big-scale caravansary.

Theodore Hoff, a Minnesotan who had been lumbering in McCall for several years, took into his firm the New Englander Carl Brown, who had always dreamed of working with wood.

Theodore and his wife Hannah had been reared in stout Norwegian-Lutheran tradition. Theodore was the oldest of the 13 children of Hans Hoff, and most of the family eventually followed Hans and Theodore when these two came west in 1907. The elder Hoff had done some lumbering in Minnesota and had by no means put it behind him.

Hannah Hagebak, a girl with unusual dark eyes and dark, heavy braids of hair worn around her head, had graduated from Normal school and taught a while before her marriage. When she came to Idaho she and Theodore already had two children.

It was August 23, 1910 when she descended from the stage in McCall, and she was presently appalled. The town had no doctor, no public nurse, and to her teacher's eye, the school was no school at all. But a woman of Hannah's character and upbringing took what came and made the best of it. Though she cried for two years, she cried in secret.

Hans and Theodore had bought the McCall flour and lumber mills, which sat side by side, and operated them for two years. Then both mills burned. It was more than a financial crisis for the Hoffs—they lost many of their dearest personal possessions, things brought from Minnesota and stored near the mills until they should have a proper house to hold them.

With their whole working outfit gone, Hans decided to withdraw, but Theodore, a forceful, square-built fellow with black curls and sea-blue Norwegian eyes, decided to rebuild and go on alone. He heard that Charlie Campbell, owner of the Circle-C cattle ranch below New Meadows, had a mill he might sell. No, Campbell didn't want to sell, but he referred Theodore to a mill at Mann's creek above Weiser.

Hoff took the train from Meadows to Evergreen, walked to Mann's creek, bought the mill, arranged to have the machinery hauled to Evergreen, walked back to this point, by rail and stage returned to McCall, and was gone only a week. So much for decisive Hoff. In McCall he had been obliged to leave two big mares ready to foal, mares used for logging. In his absence they did as expected, Hannah overseeing things. Hoff's own child, due any moment, thoughtfully awaited his return.

Now he reexamined the boilers of the old mill and found them still usable; and a local clay with which the fireboxes had been lined had proved as durable as firebrick. Moreover, even the sad pile of burnt rubble gave back returns, for Ben McCall, one of Hoff's men, proved a wizard at fishing out warped shafts and gears, working them over with balingwire and ingenuity, and putting them back into use.[29]

It was now June, 1913, and by August Hoff had not only rebuilt his mill with lumber from New Meadows but was turning out lumber himself. Good timber was available close in at 50 cents to a dollar a thousand, and homesteaders who needed cash were glad to sell stumpage. Logs were no special problem. The new mill had double circular saws, a 52-inch bottom saw, and a 48-inch top saw, and not only cut both lumber and railroad ties but did some planing. Although ice in the log pond allowed it to run only about eight months out of twelve, it cut between five and six million board feet a year.

The reestablished payroll, the only one in McCall other than that of the U. S. Forest, gave the town a strong lift, and business grew faster than Theodore and Hannah had dared hope. Even Hannah began to feel that a place where you had borne a child, survived a disastrous fire and could have in your community a teacher like Helen Wilson, that place could be truly home.

Since there was no bank in town, the mill's cash drawer was simply a shoebox under the counter. Legal tender was mostly gold, especially 20-dollar pieces, and silver, too heavy to carry easily. Whether or not this made any difference, Hoff was never robbed, never even threatened. He presently took in a new partner, Bert Bills, but neither of them ever used a penny out of the shoebox without accounting for it.

Bills was to remain only a few months, and he is best remembered for a magnificent draft team he had. A man without family, he loved these horses so much that people said he was married to them. When he left McCall the horses went with him.

It was now April 1914, and with Carl's mail contracts to be completed in a few months, a new chapter in the lives of the Browns was preparing to unfold. Carl was ready for it because he had waited so long.

Whether Hoff approached Brown or it was the other way around is unimportant now. The two men were probably drawn together by each other's very predominance, a quality essential to success in a setting where things can change overnight. At any rate, a partnership in the mill was discussed and agreed upon, to take effect in the fall. Unconsciously each man intended to control whatever operation he undertook, and some instinctive caution shaped the agreement so that each should have his own defined area of management. Hoff would continue to run the mill; Brown would take over the business end and the logging.

Shortly before Bills decided to withdraw and go elsewhere, he had arranged to buy the timber on a tract east of town. Stumpage had been estimated, and was to be paid for before the logs were moved. The estimate was 200 thousand board feet. Now when Carl looked over the tract, he was convinced there was twice that much. To forestall later argument, he gave Bills a check for $400, payment in full. In late October or early November, he began work in this timber. Before snows stopped them, with one helper, a man who shoveled snow and loaded, Carl got half of the logs cut, skidded and decked. Scaled, the Bills timber came to 500 thousand board feet, not 200 thousand, and Hoff & Brown were the gainers in that proportion.

Their equity had cost the Browns $3000, and while this left them not a great deal but dreams to go on, Carl's secret dream come true and Ida's secret dream for Carl realized, they felt happy, and looked forward with eagerness.

Two years earlier a bright balloon had mounted the sky in the proposal of outside interests to built on the west side of the lake a mile or so from Lardo, a very large inn. Estimate said it would require as much as 285 thousand feet of lumber, and Theodore Hoff had contracted to deliver this at $12 a thousand. When the time came his four-horse teams started delivering. Four horses could haul a thousand feet at a trip.

Financially the bright balloon began to wobble in course. By the time Brown joined Hoff, only half of the lumber had been paid for. The partners must have assumed that eventually they would get their money, and perhaps the gradual dispersion of this hope dulled the final shock. The remainder of the bill was never paid, so that in effect they received only $6 for lumber that today would bring around $90 a thousand.

But it would have taken more than this to dash Carl's spirits. At 18 he had known what he wanted to do. At 37 he was granted his wish. The great woods that had been silent except for the passing of his horses or his sleddogs wove a different spell now, and he didn't even mind having to live at times in camp. He might have to cook for himself and his helpers in a decrepit cookshack or old cabin, but this didn't matter. He was working at last with big trees and with big horses that he loved and with big men he had learned to handle.

The railroad came. What it would do for the lumber industry!

It was not a continuation of the Payette and Idaho Northern (called Pins), now reaching New Meadows, but the Oregon Short Line, a branch of the Union Pacific out of Nampa, and it had had to fight its way up the brawling Payette to Cascade, then up Long Valley to McCall. The rails were laid, the station built.

The day the first engine puffed into town hadn't been declared a holiday. This wasn't necessary. Everybody in McCall was out celebrating anyhow—the census could have been taken. In the woods Carl's loggers stopped; at the mill Theodore laid off his crew. That morning Carl hitched to his light buggy the registered Hambletonian he had secured from the stables of the copper magnate Marcus Daly of Montana— after all a buggy was a family necessity and a good horse an investment. He loaded the family in, the children in their best, Ida with one of her own unique hats atop her pinned-up hair. Riding behind the Hambletonian she probably recalled rides with Carl Brown fifteen years earlier, and a trip into Vermont to hear Sousa's band play The Stars and Stripes Forever. Riding into Vermont could bring one, apparently, to a place and a moment like this.

Engineer Ole Anderson brought in that first show train, and even if the story about him was made up, McCallites have always liked it. It is said Anderson suddenly shouted from his cab to the thick-clustered admirers below: "Look out! I'm gonna turn 'er around now!"

A belch of steam, a whistle, the jangle of a bell, and the crowd scattered like terrified quail. Rocking with mirth, Anderson nearly fell from the cab. He was enjoying himself today, and he would for the next 40 years on this same run.

When they had seen and heard everything at the station, Carl drove south to a place along the rail line where there was a machine that was said to lay railroad ties and track. He had never seen such a thing, but ties were enormously important in mill economy and he ought to know everything about the use of them. Though no fixit man himself, he was fascinated by machinery big or small. He treasured machines of all kinds, to own them, to some extent to operate them, but *not* to keep them in condition. You turned that over to someone else. You paid him to keep a mechanism in top running order, and if the thing didn't work, that was a heinous offense. Machines, like horses, were to obey orders.

The summer the railroad came, the Browns left the transfer house to return to Lenore street. Their new home had grass and shrubs, a real yard. On a certain morning there, three-year-old Warren couldn't be found. Ida's calls brought no answer. Maybe he had gone to the mill with his father—that was where he always begged to go. But she couldn't go looking for him anywhere today. Betty searched too, and Betty at nine was as good in a difficulty as any grown-up person. Outwardly Ida kept calm, but inner warnings said it wouldn't be long now. Dr. Ross of Nampa, who was summering in McCall, had been notified.

It was hours before Warren was found, asleep under a low-growing bush in the yard. Perhaps he had been there all the time, catching up on his energy.

By evening Ida lay tired and happy, with a little golden child at her side. This was Dorothy Caroline, and it seemed likely that she would be unlike either Betty or Warren. Resting, Ida dreamed. In this child there might be a love of beauty, especially music—already there was something different about her hands. What would be her nature — would she love everybody as the Harringtons did, or would her spring of tenderness be more like the Browns', pouring forth when she was ready, not before. The golden hair, the dark blue eyes, shadowy with the languor of birth, perhaps here was an iridescent child, for whom life must shimmer.

Ida slept. Tomorrow meant new problems that she must be ready for. With her community chores and her family she was already a busy woman. Another child meant more work and, also, more discipline. In discipline she and Carl believed—with Ida to administer it. She had small patience with this new theory about delaying punishment until anger cooled. If you waited, how did a child know what he was being punished for? No. Strike while indignation was hot.

For some infractions she applied a small stick. For some she strapped — lightly. Or she withdrew the promise of a trip or other reward. If by accident or intent the children caused loss or annoyance to others, they had to make amends in a manner suited to their age. Betty and her little friends, playing Crossing the Plains, agreed that they were all starving. Food must be had quickly. Seeing a big rooster of somebody's at large, they ran him down and killed him. But it turned out the rooster belonged to a widow with four children. When Ida heard about it, she spoke firmly. And it took Betty a long time to hoard enough nickels to pay for her fun.

A few years later when Warren was old enough to have a gun, Sheriff Wilson came to the house one day.

"Where's Warren?" he asked Ida.

"At John Cook's."

"Has he a .22?"

"Yes, he has."

"Where was he yesterday?"

"He and some other boys were out shooting rabbits."

"That wasn't all they shot," the sheriff said. "They shot insulators off a lot of telephone poles."

When he came home, Warren admitted the truth. His father settled this one. "If it had been an accident, I'd have paid the bill. Since it wasn't, you'll have to."

Once when Warren reached the teasing stage he tried his mother out with this: "What will you do if I don't mind you?"

"Young man," she said, "as long as you live in this house you will do what I tell you."

The winter of 1915-1916 wasn't much worse than others, but when snow deepened along the valley so that the train couldn't get north of Cascade, everything seemed to go wrong. Mail and freight couldn't move, but that wasn't the worst problem. Hoff and Brown couldn't ship lumber. No lumber shipments, no payroll money coming in. With wages cut off mill-hands and loggers were going to be in straits.

Carl Brown came up with a solution. The snow was too deep for logging anyhow, so he would offer to run a mail sled from McCall to Cascade. The post office accepted his offer. For three months he drove six horses on a big double-runnered, two-seated sled, completing two weekly trips, 30 long cold miles down the snow-bound valley to Cascade and back. Snow never seemed to be done falling. He had to put snowshoes on the horses. Often he mushed ahead of the horses on snowshoes himself.

Freight and passengers brought in extra cash besides the $50 the post office paid for each trip to Cascade. All that he took in Carl turned over to the mill, to apply on payroll. This same year he took on the Lardo to Warren mail route again, hiring help when he couldn't go himself, and again applying the pay against expenses of running the mill.

CHAPTER NINE

In April 1917 came the declaration of war, called the Great War or the World War, since no second world war was dreamed of. Among Carl's former employees who went were Chester Stephens and Roy Stover. Idaho Forest Supervisor Herbert C. Williams went too. Stephens and Stover came back; Williams gave his life.

The conflict in Europe must have seemed a long, long trail from McCall. Because the area produced lumber, meat and some strategic minerals, no great outside pressure was put on men to drop everything and volunteer. If they could get away and thought they ought to, they enlisted. However, on the women everywhere, the Red Cross impressed its needs, and in McCall women began making themselves white kerchief headdresses—and they were invariably becoming—to wear while they rolled bandages and did welfare work. Among these women in McCall were certainly Hannah Hoff and Ida Brown.

Consciousness grew of the unstinted compassion of the Red Cross wherever men died, or thought they did, to preserve democracy. Color, race, made no difference. The Red Cross summoned to its overseas service high calibre men too old or unfitted for the armed ranks—they too gave all they had. Such workers might show up in No Man's Land alongside medics. At home in store fronts the dedicated, almost holy faces of Red Cross nurses looked out from a hundred thousand posters to comfort parents of American boys gone to war. A Red Cross worker returned to the states by disability spoke in McCall.

"For whom do you suppose a dying man in a field hospital asks?" he queried. "For his sweetheart, for his wife, for a child?"

He waited. There came a little sound of weeping.

"He asks," the worker said, "for his mother."

Ida Brown, who was again with child, found tears in her eyes.

In May, 1917, their fourth-born came to the Browns. This was Margaret Josephine, from the first like only herself. This time in her contented, cloudy dream, Ida saw an impulsive, warm-hearted child, confident of her welcome anywhere, loving others and expecting to be loved back.

Born in a different house, one across the street, Margaret was to complete the family, something the family didn't know. As before, Carl and Ida were content that the infant was obviously a perfect little machine, ready to start growing. Indeed Margaret proved a bouncing healthy child, who investigated everything as soon as she was able to get about. Movement and activity effervesced in her like bubbles in champagne.

From the beginning she was a clear little girl, transparent about it even when naughty. Later, when she was old enough to be left in Betty's charge, she might disobey but she would not deceive.

A lesser event of the Brown year was also exciting. This was Carl's first automobile. A modest car, an Oakland, it was still a mark of distinction in a town where because of no paving and the terrific spring runoff, automobiles were few and stayed in their garages nearly half of the year. Around Thanksgiving, after the first heavy snow, they retired, not to emerge until summer was looking in over the mountains and the roads were dry.

Like all cars of the day, the Oakland was black. It had a boxy high-riding top with side curtains, a horizontally-split windshield that could be opened for more air, a horn that squawked like ten setting hens in chorus, and no back compartment. Its overall length was not much more than 12 feet. Extra luggage was to be carried in folding racks attached to the running boards; and the spare tire—tire only, not wheel—was cased in waterproof and bolted at the rear. As in all automobiles then, the number and shape of the isinglass windows in the back indicated a car's make.

Collins hill was the test of all new touring cars. If they could pull this, they could qualify. How much driving Carl already knew is doubtful. Nevertheless with 12 or 15 children, including three of his own, he set out for Collins hill. Before the rise began he squared off to get all the running start possible. In the car was dead silence, the children as awed as he. Now he was ready. The Oakland snorted through first and second, then into high gear, hitting its top speed. But as the pitch increased, he had to go into second, the gears clashing. Again speed failed, but with more grinding of gears he got into low without killing his engine—that would be fatal. In the seat the children were pressed against him and behind they leaned over, breathing on his neck. He had the gas lever as far down as it would go—they weren't going to make it! But the Oakland strained a little harder, the pitch slowly leveled, they panted over the top.

No children had fallen out or off.

Proudly Carl turned and sailed home with his passengers.

Immediately his sympathies were aroused toward a class of travelers he'd never noted before, the hitchhikers. On every road he met them, and he picked up every one. As long as they could be stuffed in or hung on he kept adding them, and they adhered like sugar to a hot doughnut. When 11-year-old Betty went anywhere with her father, she was always being embarrassed by having to sit on the lap of some man she'd never seen before.

One cold day Carl picked up a man waiting beside the road and took him to Donnelly. The fellow shivered constantly and looked so miserable that in parting Carl pressed some money on him. Sometimes a passenger wasn't even shivering and still felt money in his hand. Carl's explanation for giving to another rider was half apologetic—"but the fellow said he was a Mason."

Though he loved it, Carl was no easier on his car than on his horses. He expected service of it. In behind the front seat he threw peavies, stretchers and logging chains. If a standing tree blocked his way, he all but made the car climb it. If a tree was down and he had a saw amid his clanking hardware, he sawed out a section. If not, he forced his way around the obstacle, straddling small trees, scraping hidden rocks. His policy, as when he carried the mail, was go through, never back.

A story persists that one night he could hardly coax the Oakland home. It didn't respond to anything he tried. Disgusted, he said to Ida that when you paid a garage man to fix your car it ought to perform. Willingly. The next morning Ernest Watkins, saw filer at the mill, took a look at the car and told Carl he'd lost his gas tank somewhere in the woods and had apparently coasted in on gas in the carburetor.

Anyhow, it was satisfying to own a car.

On his first attempt to carry mail to Warren by car, Carl had two passengers, Larry Phelan and his niece Grace Exum (later Grace Hoff). Dropping into a particularly bad chuckhole, the car broke a front spring. This caused the motor to shift so that the steering-wheel would turn in only one direction. The only way

Left: Carl Brown serving his first legislative term, 1923. Right: Margaret and Dorothy Brown, ready for the legislature.

Left: Ida Brown, when she was nominated by Valley County for Idaho Mother.
Right: Betty Brown at 13.

The Browns' first home in McCall. Carl, Ida and Betty, and deep snow.

Winter logging. Carl and a team of Percherons.

Lovely Payette Lake in winter. A skier has just passed, leaving the print of his skis and poles.

Before the days of power logging. Carl Brown holding his hat.

Loading railroad ties, often the mainstay of Hoff & Brown. From left: Elmer Phillips, Carl Brown, Thompson, Clarence Olson, Theodore Hoff, Hans Hoff, Unknown, Earl Casey, Orval Hubbard, Bill Newman.

to achieve an opposite turn was to reverse with the wheel cramped, then straighten and go ahead.

Turning, reversing, advancing, they used up the day and still had miles to go. Somehow they got a message to Otis Morris in Warren to come out in his Ford for Grace, but it was then only two hours short of midnight. However, in the famed tradition, the swift courier did not fail in his appointed round and finally arrived.

In 1914 Hoff and Brown had secured a Union Pacific contract for railroad ties, and the partners continued to depend on this business as a mainstay. One such contract called for 250,000 ties. Red fir, available by short haul, made the best ones. With the tie business increasing and lumber in good demand, the mill required more men, and more houses had to be built for them. Along Main street, new shops and businesses gave a more permanent look. Homes pushed their way slowly up the nearby hills and out from town, and on choice lake sites, Boise and Nampa people built attractive houses, mostly for summer use, all with local lumber.[31]

At the mill sawing and planing continued each fall until the millpond—one end of the lake—froze over. This might occur in December or in January. The mill closed but some of the men could be shifted to the woods, where work continued normally until about the first of March. Then the deep snows brought an end to logging too.

During one such winter of heavy snow, Frank Morgan, moving antimony ore from Yellow Pine, lost a valuable mule on a high summit. Floundering in the snow, to which he was unused, the mule, according to report, became crazed and "beat out his brains against a tree."[32]

In 1918, the fourth of Theodore Hoff's brothers, Martin, came to McCall and began to work in the mill. The tendency of Hoffs to stay together and follow the same type of work would continue for years. Martin was a bachelor, but he made his home most of the time with one of his brothers, Brownie (Melvin), Henry or Peter, who were already employed at the mill. Martin's first job was helping the engineer keep up steam.

And this was no simple task. The mill burned sawdust and wet scraps, and sometimes steam got so low work had to stop. If this occurred on Saturday night, some of the men would rush home, change clothes and get to a dance. It came to be noted that steam always fell when a dance was on, but if Theodore Hoff had had any suspicions of this, he'd have dealt vigorously. He was not only his younger brothers' employer, he made himself their Lutheran conscience.

Brownie Hoff had begun at the mill when he was hardly more than a boy.[33] Except for time out to go to school, he never stopped working at the mill. His first teacher was Helen Wilson. He finished high school in Boise, then attended business college, and in Portland the Oregon Institute.

The summer he was 14 he earned 25 cents a day shoveling sawdust from the mill conveyor, a not too grueling job for a boy, for he could spend a good deal of time in the lake, swimming. The next year he got a tremendous raise, earning 25 cents an hour for pulling logs into the mill with a cable choker. The third year, beginning to develop the strength and weight of the big man he intended to be, he was turn-down man on the deck. After that he was to become an apprentice sawyer under two old-timers, Ben McCall and John McMurren. By 1921 he was sawing full time on the night shift, later was made head sawyer, key position in the mill.

CHAPTER TEN

Payette Lakes Inn, built of Hoff lumber, though it was only half paid for, was a sign that McCall was growing, that its "Alaska type" era was fading. The Inn was also to become a half-mystic symbol. Unquestionably a sort of enchantment was built into the structure as it rose. From the very first days when McCall people flocked to the Inn to dance and dine, it began whispering to them. These people might seem as ordinary as oatmeal for breakfast, yet seated in the Inn's diningroom, they began to feel warm and glowing inside, as if they hid unsuspected romance in themselves. They felt as if they might suddenly become figures in drama. The gentle lights and music, the shadows and murmur of the trees outside the windows made everything seem like a German fairytale, and themselves playing parts in it.

F. C. Cottingham, builder of the Inn, had given it a modified chalet air, with many dormers and little white-railed balconies and flowerboxes. There was nothing else on the lake remotely similar—perhaps not in all Idaho.

Including the basement, it had four floors, the upper two for bedrooms, 50 of them, each to be furnished with kerosene lamps and a tiny wood stove. On the main floor were lobby, big dining room and kitchen, with a sunparlor that looked toward the lake and required 60 pair of window drapes. To the south was a 300-foot esplanade, and on the lake shore below a pavilion for summer night dancing.

As soon as the outside walls were finished, Cottingham and his wife May moved in, to do the interior finishing themselves. Boards were laid across the main floor ceiling beams to floor the bedrooms. An artesian well had been developed, and a tower set up for pressure. On each level one bathroom was completed. Through the winter Cottingham became a cabinet maker, constructing bureaus, beds and chairs. As soon as the dining room and kitchen could be used, the serving of meals began.

The Harold W. Arnold company, which had engaged Cottingham, was a non-profit social club with memberships at $100, and this included somewhere in the lake area a building lot. But either the directors sold too few memberships or they priced them too low, for when the bills came in, funds refused to cover them. To protect his own claims, Cottingham remained as manager of the Inn, staying far longer than he intended—fourteen years.

When he left, in the summer of 1928, Mr. and Mrs. D. L. Crain took over. They employed two dishwashers and brought with them four schoolboys and three teachers for help. Their two little girls lived on the beach or on horseback, and indulged their passion for pets to the degree that by summer's end they had 25 cats and eight or 10 dogs. Though they had to work harder than they ever dreamed, the Crains loved the Inn.

The following summer they would have bought the place, but arrangements could not be worked out, and besides the coming Depression was casting its cold shadow ahead. The next summer the Emmitt Pfosts took charge. Guests still registered, and there was an occasional convention or banquet. But pressures tightened and by the season's end it was clear that the Pfosts' hard work was not going to pay off. The new governor, Ben Ross, appointed Mr. Pfost commissioner of law enforcement, and the Inn, which he had contracted to buy, he turned back.

The Browns loved the Inn and always went there on Ida's birthday, which sometimes coincided with Thanksgiving. Summer excitement was past, most of the rooms closed, but the diningroom could be had for private parties. Helga Cook or Grace McRae would work out a potluck dinner plan, and tell the others what to bring. Carl got out a log sled, lined it with hay, gathered up laprobes and blankets. He hitched up one span or even two of logging horses, and these were really horses—to Carl any horse under a ton was a pony. Then he went about picking up families and food. Sometimes he had 30 people on a sled.

While the women set dinner on the Inn's tables, the men lighted fires in the two big fireplaces and the kids capered about. Dinner, when all was ready, was too big to eat in a hurry. Every woman had brought the dish she made best, and it must be noted by all the men and praised. Nobody's cake or pickles or vinegar pie or macaroni salad should be overlooked. A man like Carl Brown tasted and complimented everything.

When dinner was at last disposed of and the tables cleared, it was time for cards. Men and women played Five Hundred, or men played poker by themselves. The children played Flinch. Before anyone realized it, however, the cozy afternoon by the fires had flown. The lamps were lit, the remains of the food came back, with a new big pot of coffee, and after that dance records were produced and the old square phonograph wound up.

For Ida it had been a lovely day. For Carl too. The big Belgians, driving them himself. The rich, tasty dinner. Cards. He liked playing for money, but even without stakes it was fun. And now dancing.

Here was good body movement, which his muscles always relished, but this movement had special, irresistible allure, partly the melody, partly the rhythm. Dancing took him out of himself, into another world. No need to think about the steps; they were part of him. It was like drifting down a shadowy stream; life had no problems any more. There was only depth and peace, stolen moments with moonlight and poetry, love and imagery.

If his dance partner glimpsed his face she might even think he was unaware of her. And he might be. Of course if she bobbled or babbled or if she had the bad habit of trying to lead, his dream was shattered. Any woman who ever danced with Carl Brown remembered, and she was likely to refer to it afterward.

Inevitably there was the last record, the last dreamy note, the grinding of the needle until someone stopped the phonograph. Time to get the horses and sled ready, to take people home to their beds. Now everything was loaded, and Carl drove along the dark lake, hearing an occasional sound from the other side. The runners purred against the snow, harness chains jingled, sleepy children murmured. From the snow-weighted evergreens a little breeze fluttered as they passed. Carl drove the gentle Belgians with one hand. With the other he pressed Ida against him, and they hummed the last dance tune together.

But like a beautiful woman gone bad, the Inn seemed foredoomed. Its descent began. When it finally closed, late in the '30s, it was hardly more than a honkytonk, avoided by the respectable. After that it became a haven for hoboes, bats, maybe wild animals. The window panes were broken, doors sagged or were gone. An evil air seemed to surround it, and to those who had been happy and light-hearted there, the sight was indescribably sad. The wonder was that somebody meeting somebody there some night didn't burn it down.

Finally in 1959 a Boise valley church group would rescue the Inn and restore it to usefulness if not to its old time magic.

During all this time the popularity of the lake as a warm weather retreat was increasing. When summer people came from the baked plains of southern Idaho, they came to swim, laze, dress as they pleased, and to be left alone—except by other summer visitors. There was no great mixing with the year-round McCallites, and in turn the villagers would say, "Sure, the summer folks are okay; they bring business. But how nice it is when they go home and leave the place to us." In time, becoming more aware of the summer dollar, or less provincial, they would refrain from saying this openly.

The Browns still felt a strong attachment to Nampa, and increasingly to Boise, and their summer contacts were often a renewal of treasured friendships. They did not consciously cultivate friends—that would be ridiculous. McCall was still the most important place in the world, and whatever was good for McCall they were for.

While Cottingham still ran the Inn, the peninsula that jutted into the lake between the east and west arms was set aside for public use. W. B. Boydstun was largely responsible for this move, and as the lake front built up and many of the beaches became private, his wisdom was more and more appreciated. He served in the state highway department and labored unceasingly for better roads. He owned farms and did a real estate business. His name, like a sturdy thread, runs all through the history of town and valley.[34]

CHAPTER ELEVEN

Spring 1920. The war was over, and whatever restrictions it had put upon trade and people's spending and eating habits, the great urge now was to get on with living. Rising above personal sadness and the somewhat sonorous quality of collective national mourning, nearly everybody looked forward to activity and new developments. Taking up the slack, country-wide business began an acceleration that would hold three-quarters of the way into the new decade.

In McCall as elsewhere the wave was felt. Hoff and Brown noted the pleasant rocking of their craft on the business tide, and Carl went home and said to Ida that the time had come to build the house they had so long dreamed of. The growing children needed more room. And extra people—Carl was always bringing them in five minutes before a meal—were getting a little hard to take care of. Besides, New England relatives were becoming frequent visitors, curious, apparently, to see what had so enthralled Carl and Ida Brown.

In 1916 Charlotte Brown and Elizabeth Harrington had both visited. Elizabeth was not only a regular loving grandmother, making trousers for little Warren from his father's worn ones, but she knit mittens for Brown and Hoff children, and any others with cold little hands.

On one point Elizabeth was forthright. That was plumbing, and she was not referring to kitchen sinks. At times she said to her daughter: "In McCall when you wish to go to the bathroom, you just about have to go to Donnelly."

So there was to be a new house. Did Ida think of any other place she would rather have it built? No. Did Carl? No.

First they must have a lot. The north side of Main street had begun to fill up, and the lot they chose lay at the west edge of town, on the lake side of the street. It was wide, and it ran down to the water, so that no one would ever cut off their view. On both sides were houses already built by Newt Williams. Carl hired Fenton Cottingham of the Inn to do the building, showing him the plans he and Ida would like incorporated.

Now that the decisions were made, they were suddenly very impatient to have the house completed. The children were even more impatient. Meanwhile, a slight complication arose.

Hoff and Brown had secured a very competent millwright, Joe Kasper, under whom the mill had been running double shifts to meet the lumber demand. The Kaspers had lived in all sorts of places and under varying conditions—in Mexico, Canada, Minnesota, Montana—and Mrs. Kasper herself came from a long-established family in British West India. But when the Kaspers found there was no available house in town *with plumbing*, they were shaken. Alarmed that the Kaspers might decide to leave, Ida and Carl offered them their house, which now had plumbing—they'd soon be getting into their new house, and after all summer was here and you lived outdoors most of the time. And so on. Reluctantly the Kaspers and their four children accepted.

The only house Carl could find had just two rooms, quite like their first home in McCall, when they had only Betty. And as then, there was no plumbing. However, this was minor, everything considered, and all would have gone well except that the Kaspers had unwittingly brought with them whooping cough. At least there seemed no other explanation. Promptly Ida's children developed it, and she spent most of her time that summer driving them around in the durable Oakland. In the car they seemed to cough and strangle less miserably; and she could keep them away from others. However, they threw up by day in the car and at night they threw up in their beds. And when not wheeling dismally round and round the village, just to keep moving, Ida washed clothes, bed clothes and the interior of the car. A time to remember, but these trials seemed only to cement friendship with the sympathetic Kaspers. The Brown children began calling the Kaspers Uncle Joe and Aunt Edith and felt like cousins to the young Kaspers.

Now the house was ready; furniture, rugs, curtains ordered from Boise had been delivered. For days Ida had been sorting and discarding. Dishes, bedding, books, pictures, anything that harked back to New England must be moved. One thing she was not going to throw away, Ida knew, was the featherbeds from

Whitefield. What would they do for unexpected guests without these to make down? And Warren—he had never given his up and was indignant if anyone in making the morning beds smoothed out the hole he had burrowed for himself.

At breakfast on Friday, Ida said briskly that she was all packed and it would be a good day to move.

"So it would!" Carl said, amiable and equally brisk. Then he took a look at the calendar. Friday. Move on Friday into a new house, one planned so long?

"No, I guess I can't, either," he said. "Just too busy today."

On Saturday they moved.

The house stood wide and high, with sheltering big gables, and an easy flagged entrance. Across the front ran a big livingroom with windows on three sides and a fireplace. Beyond that was a diningroom to seat 15 or 20 people. On the left an office or small library opened, and at the back were the usual stairways, bath and closets. A kitchen and a bedroom had windows looking onto the lake. Upstairs there were more bedrooms and another bath.

In the basement towered something that Ida at the Shiefer ranch had never seen in any dream. A furnace. Naturally it was a wood furnace. For fuel, Carl hauled over a great load of tie-ends. And since Ida was the one presumed always to be at home, she found herself elected furnace-tender. And since McCall had few mornings without at least a small fire, Ida came to know the tie-ends well.

One night after a strenuous day with them, she said to her husband: "Some evening you'll come home and look for me. You'll call and call. But there won't be any answer. Do you know where you'll find me? In the basement, a victim of tie-ends."

Carl did not forget this warning, and when the first wood furnaces were converted to oil, the fireplace upstairs claimed Ida's wood.

As their older employees took on responsibility, the mill partners both gave time to community affairs. Carl helped organize the Elks, whose charitable works moved him—and he didn't mind their high-jinks. Later he would become a Mason, joining in Boise. He avoided joining Ida's church, under Congregational jurisdiction but generally called Community church, an avoidance that may have required neat footwork at times. However, he often attended, and his financial support was generous and cheerful.

At one time, without seeming to know exactly what he was getting into, he became a kind of police judge. On cold Sunday mornings while the two younger children tried to dress inconspicuously by the diningroom register, Carl would be sitting in the livingroom, separated from the girls only by transparent space, dealing with last night's drunks and peace disturbers. However, he felt so much sympathy with the guilty that he was embarrassed and soon dropped both title and duties of office. In fact he soon forgot that he had ever held the honor.

With no Lutheran church near, the Hoffs could rarely enjoy their own services, but they attended and warmly supported the Community church. Even with six children Hannah Hoff found time to help with benefit dinners and money-raising programs. Both she and her husband served on the school board, a pretty thankless job at any time. In an era that seemed to be marked by startling innovations in manners and social standards, the Hoffs spoke firmly for sobriety and common sense.

Through their growing-up years McCall children never lacked for stirring things to do, or had any excuse for feeling bored, or failed to get into scrapes. Betty Brown and her pals rode horses a good deal. Sometimes they rode to Slick Rock, 10 or 12 miles uphill through timber. On one side the mountain-size granite slab reared into the sky without foothold for trees or kids. At its base ran a creek, and across the creek was a patch of woods with an old cabin, a good place to tie horses and spend the day fooling around. However, Betty would have to start her gang back to make it home by dark. About things of that sort her mother was adamant.

On winter afternoons they could beg a ride with Hank Hoff as he drove his sled back to the woods for one last load of logs. When they returned and had to sit on the frozen logs, Hank provided each with a gunnysack stuffed with hay. There was always the chance of accident—no use denying it—but Hank told the kids what to do. "If you see you've got to jump, jump *up hill*. And I'll tell you when!"

Dorothy too rode the logging trucks. If she had to go alone, she didn't mind too much. But her choice of thrills was to ride the carriage at the mill. She did it by the hour. The violent rush, the scream and roar of the biting saw seemed to satisfy some childish craving, and while it looked dangerous, there was probably more excitement than peril, otherwise she would have been stopped. The men liked to see her coming and were disappointed if she didn't show up to ride.

Margaret too small for the daring adventures of her sisters found her own entertainment. She especially liked to go out with other children onto the tethered logbooms and skitter across their bobbing surfaces. One day when she was seven, however, she slipped between two wider-spaced logs. This might have been the end of her, except that when she "came up for the third time," as people used to allege everyone did, an older girl, Ruth Cook, seized her by her good strong hair and pulled her out.

At eight Margaret broke her leg skiing and dropped this sport but she swam and hiked. Even in the winter she hiked, over bare trails, over snow. The Brown blood hadn't thinned any.

From the age of 12 Betty could wash and cook commendably. If Carl and Ida had to go to Emmett on business, or on to Boise for clothing or furnishings not available in McCall, Betty could take charge. When she entered high school she found life pretty wonderful. Girls she liked exceedingly; of boys she was shy. She loved dancing, which helped; and she loved parties.

Theodore Hoff was then chairman of the school board, but his children were not allowed to dance. However, after basketball practice, or after games, the high school kids hung around the gym until the oldsters were gone, then turned on the phonograph and danced. What a delicious sensation, after a thrilling game; but it was more than that, *for Mr. Hoff might come.* Think what Mr. Hoff might do if he came and found them dancing! He might have them all expelled from school.

So as they danced, they listened intently. At the slightest warning they were ready to douse the lights and flatten into the shadows.

At this time there began between the Brown family and a woman they called Aunty Harland, born Elizabeth Jones in Wales, an enduring affinity. A widow, Mrs. Harland had come alone to McCall, but was joined later by her 14-year-old daughter, Catharine, who was Betty Brown's age. The girls became inseparable friends.

Whenever Ida needed extra help she could usually get Elizabeth Harland, and if she had to be away, Aunty took over. Aunty knew exactly what Carl wanted for his breakfast, and she had it on the table at six sharp. Sometimes after a rush was past, Carl would develop a streak of thrift and say to his wife: "With the girls to help you, can't you let Aunty go now?"

But if any confusion then ensued, due to Ida's community labors or if the girls got too busy with whatever absorbs school girls, Carl would find himself going wryly to bring Aunty back. He liked to crowd her a little, to see what she would say. Once he told her she was too generous with her older children. Ida advised him to let Aunty alone, but the little Welsh woman could speak for herself.

She asked Carl: "How generous do you think you could be on $20 a month?" That was the amount he was paying her.

It was an April day in 1920 that she arrived in New Meadows, coming from La Grande, Oregon, where it was warm. That was why she wore summer clothes and a flowery hat. However, at New Meadows snow lay on the ground, and for the trip to McCall she was handed by stage driver Frenchy Yriberry into a horse-drawn sled with a Ford top on it. At the Krigbaum place cold sleet began, and Frenchy buttoned on the side curtains. The sleet turned to snow, and by the time they reached the site of the present ski run, a thousand feet higher, the snow was so deep the road was a trough between high banks. Here they were joined by four men who had been cruising timber, among them Carl Brown and Forest Supervisor Lyle Watts. The sight of a strange small woman in summer finery in this Arctic setting startled Carl, and of course he couldn't foresee the time when this little person would become indispensable to him and his family.

At first Mrs. Harland stayed with the Geelans, who had a store and hotel. To relieve winter boredom, men had set up a toboggan slide that ended at the lake edge. Only men had been riding it, but women were secretly eager to try. Some of them persuaded the newcomer to try it too. When she got up courage and boarded the sled on her stomach, she wasn't expecting the bump at the bottom. Down she went. She hit. She flew from the sled, soared, crashed. Stars exploded in her head. Everybody was laughing fit to kill, so she somehow pulled herself together and climbed the bank, then struggled to the Geelans to get supper as usual.

The next morning she couldn't get out of bed without help. She was too timid to go alone to the new osteopath, so Mrs. Geelan firmly took her there. The doctor said she had slipped a vertebra and had only missed breaking her neck. However, the sturdy Welsh went right back to the hotel and to work as best she could.

Later Mrs. Harland was to lose her older daughter and a son, so the love of the Brown children, who called her Honeybunch about as often as Aunty, must have been very comforting.[35]

Warren Brown had as much fun[36] as his sisters, though it was different in kind. By the time he was ten, however, he had discovered the world of the entrepreneur, and thenceforth he would live in it considerably. This is not the world of the capitalist. The entrepreneur manages and directs; he organizes and assumes risks. The capitalist, on the other hand, avoids risks, holds to what he has.

Like his father at an early age, Warren saw the advantage of being at the right place at the right time with a desirable service. On Saturday nights when there was a big dance in town, he took a shoeshine outfit to the barbershop, where miners and loggers eager for night life always hied themselves. Shined shoes were almost as important as scraped chins and short tonic-smelling hair. With generous tips, Warren often had $10 to take home.

The summer he was ten his father, remembering his own stifled yearnings at that age, permitted him to work on the log pond. By the time he was 14, Warren was hiring out to others, making men's wages. To be unceasingly busy, to surmount difficulty and to outdo was by this time a set pattern. And it was this pattern that soon starred him in a sport that put his picture in papers across the country.

CHAPTER TWELVE

In the summer of 1922 Carl Brown found himself unintentionally projected into county politics. He registered as a Democrat but had never thought of seeking office. Nevertheless, a fellow Democrat filed his name and paid his fee to enter the primary for state senator. Carl didn't withdraw his name; he simply let the matter ride. No other Democrat showed up for the primary. Before the general election he did nothing more than state his political beliefs if they were asked. These beliefs included the importance of solvency in state government and thrifty use of taxpayers' money. As to business, he felt that those who enjoyed the benefits of sound economy should be willing to pay for them via some tax route or other.

He won in the general election, and since the legislature always met about the time work in the woods closed, he might as well go down to the capital and see what it was all about. He stayed at the Owyhee hotel, and Ida joined him there for some of the social goings-on of the session. The children remained in school under the eyes of Betty and Aunty Harland, but Dorothy and Margaret made at least one trip to the city. Ida had made them black velvet jackets and white kilted skirts, with which they wore high-buttoned shoes of white kid. They wore these outfits to several affairs, and Ida knew that no legislator's children were more attractively dressed.

The social life in the capital during the legislature was not all that Ida enjoyed. The sessions she attended sparingly, but she sat a good deal in the hotel lobby to catch the talk that ebbed and flowed around her. Through the doors of this the best hotel in town passed the same kind of lawmakers as congregate in any state capital, though they might handle smaller deals. She saw a few crooks and schemers, some dolts, a sprinkling of misfits who didn't even care what went on, but also many men of honesty and intelligence with only one object, the good of Idaho.

With her shrewdness and good memory, Ida learned to identify the men Carl talked of. Sometimes she was able to guess what kind of bills they would support, and to read a meaning into the groups that ascended by elevator to rooms above, rooms surely smoke-filled.

She was disappointed to find no women in the legislature, although Elizabeth Russum was serving as superintendent of public schools.

Carl did not let the legislature disturb him. He sought to protect his county's interest and uphold what he considered good bills. He introduced no legislation, made no freshman speech. When his voice was needed, he discussed briefly, but that was all. One thing was certain, he felt within himself no stirrings of political ambition.

Meanwhile in McCall the usual winter activities went on, for with the better roads that automobiles demanded, and with a dependable railroad, McCall was no longer winter torpid. At the annual carnival which included dogsled and ski racing, there was now a queen contest. Betty Brown, a high school junior, and probably a little mournful in secret about her size, assumed that the five-foot girls would be preferred. But Betty's name was put up for queen, and her friends supported her with vigor. Toward the last, when it didn't look too good for Betty's chances, a big bunch of votes came in from some unknown source, putting her in the lead. Those votes were bought by Theodore Hoff, chairman of the school board, who didn't know that the nice daughter of his partner stayed after basketball games and danced on school property.

Besides honors and a crown, Betty was presented with a diamond ring. It was a moment never to be forgotten, a moment to be recalled on the blue days that every teenager knows. By today's standards the diamond was not enormous, but it was then, and Betty would never get over the thrill.

The McCall high school occupied but one room and could offer only three years' instruction. But Helen Wilson had moulded her clay well, and good high school teachers had followed her, so that what the youngsters got had quality at least. For their last year in high school Betty and the two older Hoff boys, Harvey and Irwin, would have to go elsewhere. They applied for admission to the high school in Boise and were told to enroll.

It must have been a nervous morning, that first one, for all of them. Hallways full of students, big classrooms, not a soul they knew. And there were *rules* which they hadn't had a chance to learn and might be infringing. Worse than rules there were *customs*, unknown but felt, and things you just did or didn't do.

Carmel Parks had joined them so they were now four.

The Jim Harrises, friends of Carl and Ida, had agreed to board Betty. She felt at home with them, and her parents sometimes came down. School was exciting, she seemed to be getting along pretty well in her subjects, and she didn't have time to be homesick. Besides she had the three boys for company.

Small schools *can* produce good minds willing to work. Each of the McCall students was on the honor roll at some time during that school year, and for one month they were all on.

Irwin and Harvey had come down with new suits, but early in the fall their suits were stolen from their room. However, the boys didn't seem to mind wearing Levis to school—others wore them. And a rumor got around that not only were both suits seen in a hockshop somewhere but that the two Hoffs were taking dancing lessons.

The next year they enrolled at St. Olaf's College, a Lutheran school in Minnesota, strong in the liberal arts. Theodore had once visited the school and admired its campus. Besides, to both Hannah and Theodore, only a church school was to be thought of.[38]

The fact that McCall was not giving four years of high school troubled both Hoff and Brown. Shortly after this, they headed a private subscription to teach the extra courses required to accredit the school. For a number of years their $150 stood annually at the top of this list.

With 1924 barely in, Warren Brown, coming 12, had begun dog-racing. For some time he'd had a shepherd named Rex that he drove to school as soon as snow came. Unharnessed, Rex would lie outside to wait for noon dismissal. Or he trotted off and returned at noon and again after school to take Warren home.

Ted Geelan staged the first dog races on a course a mile long between Lardo and McCall. Warren won his first honors driving Rex over this course, finishing in four minutes. Only 15 seconds behind him came Bunny Hoff, aged five, described as "about the same size in all directions." Along the way Bunny fell off three times but his dog Tip always waited for him.

The next races required two dogs to a sled, but no boy owned more than one, so in each team one dog had a strange driver. Warren drove Rex with another dog, but time was not nearly as good, a fair indication that dog-boy relations do matter.

The following year competition had sharpened and Warren had to be satisfied with third place.

By 1926 the races had spread to cover two days and they attracted considerable outside interest. Snow was four feet deep on the level this February but fans from Boise and southern Idaho did not let this discourage them. One train load of sports coming for the winter festival had their liquor aboard, and somehow missed the whole affair. Their train was ready to start back when one fan came to the surface to say thoughtfully, "We must be just about getting into McCall."

For two months Warren had been taking his dogs out on the frozen lake every night after school. He worked them until they had all the edge he knew how to put on. He thought he had a chance to win this year, but on the first day of the races, a professional dogteam man, Smoky Gaston, showed up. In the first lap Gaston took the lead and held it with seeming ease into the third. At that point Warren's hard work began to show. His dogs surged ahead to win by a margin so narrow—10 seconds—that the judges at first gave Gaston the victory. On a recount they changed their decision. Eighth-grader Brown had done 10 miles in 48:20.

This gave Warren the Ted Geelan cup and first prize of $300. And it was announced that if his mother and his teacher, Clarence Oylear, would relent about his missing school, he would go to Ashton, in southeastern Idaho, for the much-publicized races to be staged there 12 days later.

Except for William Deinhard, one of Carl Brown's good friends, 13-year-old Warren went alone by train with his dogs to the town at the foot of the Tetons, six hundred miles from home. Officially Deinhard was representing the McCall Chamber of Commerce, but he was always close at hand if the boy should need help or counsel.

Warren's team consisted of dogs of several colors and breeds, from a blooded pincer police to a plain mongrel. His lead was a 90-pound half Airedale, half red Irish setter named Tuck, a wonderfully keen dog who responded instantly to signals and never fought the other dogs. So willing were all of them that Warren had to keep the sled tied to something while he put on their harness. And once ready, he had only to call "All right, Tuck," and they were off. He used no whip, only his voice. Carl had provided his sled with one special feature, runners of bandsaw strips. These took a fine polish and resisted scratches from dirt and gravel.

The 22nd of February opened in Ashton in spring-like warmth. On the main street 16 dogteams lined up to start two minutes apart on the 15-mile course. The sidelines were crowded with 10,000 spectators, described by one newspaper as including "eastern bankers rubbing shoulders with lumberjacks from the Payette."

The sun came out, shone fitfully, retired. Clouds turned the sky gray. Before the first team was half way along, a blizzard struck. Snow drove into the faces of the spectators, but they stayed—it was too exciting.

The race took two hours, and in that time 10 dog-sled records were made and broken. Warren Brown was not to make the best time—the best was for Howard Salley, a veteran musher driving Labrador retrievers. Warren's nondescript dogs that he had trained himself came in 7 minutes and 42 seconds behind Salley.

But it was 95-pound, freckle-faced Warren at the finish, against a backdrop of excited faces and snow-flecked fur collars, that the newspaper pictures played up.

". . . leading one dog and guiding the sleigh with the other hand. Several yards from the finish line the dog he was leading started as though to break through the crowd. This caused the lad to let loose the sleigh handle. Old Tuck, leader, turned as if to inquire. Brown yelled at him, 'Get on there, Tuck! I can handle this dog!' Old Tuck straightened in the harness and led the team across the line while the boy raced across with the unhitched dog."

Pictures and stories appeared in the Saturday Evening Post, the Chicago Sunday Tribune, the Los Angeles Times, the National Dog Journal, the American Boy, and others.

Warren and his dogs and Bill Deinhard set out for home. At Nampa when they left the train, a hundred people, including old friends of his parents, were there to congratulate him. Women insisted on kissing him—"I had to take it," he told his mother later. By the time he reached home letters and wires were pouring in. From former employees of Carl's, from bankers, from families that had moved away. Sometimes several members of a household wrote in the same letter. Ex-Governor D. W. Davis sent a picture "which is appearing in many large dailies in the East;" and Governor Charles C. Moore, who had witnessed the race, sent word that it was the best in Ashton history.

To anybody in McCall, second place for Warren in such an unequal match was the same as victory. Ida had sent him a wire of congratulation and had met him at Nampa. Carl paid cheerfully for the meat and milk the dogs consumed, and for harness and express, but he was probably too rigid with pride to say much when the boy came home.

Warren seemed unaffected by attention. How he felt about contending against experienced dogsled men and coming out with credit had to be surmised. The one bit of show-off he allowed himself was to slip under his father's plate at breakfast the morning after his return the sum of $750. After all, his father had put out cash for a number of things. Of course Carl made him keep the money, and so frugal and hard-working did he continue that by the time he was ready for college he had saved enough to keep him there two years.

What Aunty Harland thought of Warren's feat was no secret—she told all who would listen. Besides she had a sort of stake herself in the race. She had regularly baked the dogs' training "bread," a mixture of horsemeat, vegetables and cracked corn. Warren had taken to Ashton a 2½ foot stack of this bread baked in slabs as big as the oven would admit.

The following year Warren went again to Ashton, but now professional competition had become so harsh that the best he could make was fourth place. First went to a former Alaskan government musher with a team of Irish setters.

The summer that Warren was 14 he went to work in the woods on Brundage mountain for Harvey Meldrum. Meldrum was a barrel-chested young fellow who two years before had come to McCall to do contract logging for Carl at Fall creek. Meldrum's wife Minerva and their two children were with him. Carl often came by their camp and if he saw something to do, he seized a peavey or a pikepole or a canthook and went to work. If little Luella saw him coming, she's run to Minerva crying, "Hurry, Mamma, make some tea. Mr. Brown's here!"

Besides tea, Minerva's castiron stove turned out lemon pie—lemon pie in camp—and Carl liked pie.

In 1923 some timber was still being felled by two men on the ends of a six-foot saw. A v-notch was first chopped into the tree in the direction of desired fall. Then from the opposite side sawing began. When the tree began to quiver, it was time to get out of the way. Now the stricken giant's movement quickened, the great swing began. The crash. After the tree was limbed and cut into sections it was dragged to a skidway for loading onto a sled or a wagon, depending on the time of year. A wire cable was then hooked to the middle of the log, the other end to the loading bar of a crosshaul team. The horses pulled and the log moved up over small skids to the bunk or to the top of the load, as the case might be.

This summer Minerva boarded Warren and his friend John Newman. The boys slept in a little bunkhouse and liked to carry the Meldrum baby, Wilbert, to their bed, to play with him. Harvey paid Warren top loader wages, $6, though the boy protested he wasn't worth that much. Yes he was, Meldrum insisted, for the willing errands that saved Meldrum's own time if for nothing else. There couldn't be a better boy, he and Minerva said to each other.

The two following summers Warren worked on his own contract for Hoff and Brown, skidding logs in the woods, again on Brundage, for $1.50 a thousand. To get underway he had to buy a team of big horses and their harness. Then he had to buy grain for them and hire an old lumberjack to swamp logs. He paid this man $6 a day.

Each morning at four the two of them harnessed up, and sometimes they didn't unharness until 9 p.m. The harness was heavy and awkward for the boy to lift, and besides one of the horses kicked if anything touched its leg. To throw the harness on, Warren had to stand on a box or stump.

At dusk one night Ernest Watkins was coming along the lake. When he heard the sound of an ax in the timber, he thought he'd better investigate. It was just Warren chopping away as long as light lasted.

Each of these summers Warren skidded a million feet, but his expenses were so high there was little profit left. At least he was paid in cash for his work and he had acquired experience as a logger and contractor, experience in rather heavy chunks. In later years it seemed to him he had worked himself too hard, later when he had a boy of his own.

Warren was trying to see into the future. In the fall of 1929, when he was 17, his friends John Cook, Bill Parks and Jim McCall registered at the state university, where they would live with Mr. and Mrs. Clarence Oylear—Oylear had been Warren's teacher in McCall and was getting his master's degree at the university. Warren urged his folks to let him go along too and take his senior high school year in Moscow.

He would have to go somewhere. Ida and Carl decided Moscow might be a good arrangement.

CHAPTER THIRTEEN

Betty was through high school; the next step was college. On a cloudy September morning she and her mother set out by car for the University of Idaho campus. The car had the usual leatherette side curtains that could be unsnapped and stored under the back seat. Unfortunately they had been unsnapped and not stored. By the time the travelers reached Craigmont, a pouring rain was beating in on them.

Was her daughter to arrive at the state university looking like a drowned kitten, Ida asked herself. Hardly. She pulled up at the general store in Craigmont and bought several pairs of cotton blankets. These she hung by safety pins across all open spaces in the car, and thus Betty arrived at Ridenbaugh hall, the only women's dormitory on the campus, in first class condition.

It was well she did, for flocks of massive buildings and strange impinging personalities made her feel lost anyhow.

To greet her at the hall was a woman who would become her warm friend, and whose standing at the university was to eclipse that of many a faculty male of higher rank. This woman was Permeal French, dean of women, a post she held for many years. In a comparatively new, small university that drew students who had never traveled, knew little of society manners and thought education was to help one make more money, Dean French performed a task of monumental importance. Out of good natured hoydens she made ladies; out of their green boy friends she made gentlemen. A woman of uprightness, scholarship and dignity, she tolerated no casual standards. Like Deity she was feared and loved.

Despite the kindness of her housemother, Betty became homesick to the point of actual illness. She couldn't eat; in one week she lost 10 pounds. She wondered if she could stand it until Christmas.

When she did get home, there was all the old, dear activity. Making wreaths; taking door-wreaths to friends, especially older ones; making pans and pans of candy; going to church programs and dances, where she knew everybody. At first she seemed very happy, but when it came time to return to school, she was suddenly all too quiet, Carl and Ida thought.

Back at school she finally wrote her mother a letter whose real message lay between the lines and it said to Ida, something is wrong. Ida wrote Betty to finish the semester, then come home if she wanted to. A girl old enough to go away to school was old enough to work out her problem herself, Ida thought. Just give her a little more time.

So Betty returned home. By fall she felt ready to give college another try. This time she joined Delta Delta Delta, and whether it was the closeness of the group or just another year's maturity, she found she could support life away from home quite tolerably. In fact she began to enjoy it.

New Years, 1927, had arrived in McCall with appropriate noise and concussion. If it was not the rip-roaring celebration of the turn of the century, cherished in memory but not much imitated now, it was still hearty. The village had neither hospital nor ambulance yet, but it was assumed that Carl Brown would pick up in his car any unwise reveller who needed quick stitching up or a chance to die between sheets at the hospital in Cascade.

However, it was not revelry that felled Bill Harp, lean and blondish, not very big, a long-time employee at the mill. And he would recover from what hit him and work on for 33 years longer. He was skidding logs in the woods that January day, when a tree rebounded and struck him. What happened after that is typical of the McCall lumberjack's toughness and tenacity. Harp was loaded onto a truck and taken to the mill, where Dr. Roscoe Ward, rushed from Cascade, eased his pain. However, he'd have to go to a Boise hospital as fast as possible, Ward said. So he was made ready for the trip, Hannah and Theodore Hoff driving him in their car.

In Boise Dr. Fred Pittenger found that not only was Harp's arm shattered but that his liver—as Harp remembers the diagnosis—needed straightening out. When it was straightened, Dr. Pittenger, assuming that his patient intended to live, turned to the arm. He sawed bone, he grafted bone, he pinned and sewed. And while McCall was still sadly awaiting Harp's death, the man came home, fretting to get back to work. Today, except that the arm is an inch short and doesn't rotate much, it is perfectly good.

Since the arm and liver affair, Harp has had one leg broken four times. A horse insisted on "acting stubborn," and had to be hit on the nose with Harp's fist, and the nose didn't give. A wagon rolled across his other arm, and it too rotates less than well. By count he has had 24 bones broken in the service of lumber, yet he *has never been sick*. Since his father lived to be 89 and his mother into her seventies, Harp, just under 80 and still full of ginger, expects to continue for some time. When Carl Brown looks at his man Harp he has to concede that his mother had something when she spoke of the rough life of the logger.[39]

CHAPTER FOURTEEN

Carl Brown was never the political thinker that his father had been, although he was probably a shrewder judge of people. For one thing, politics in New England had undergone the seasoning of a century and a half. Out here the story was quite different. Carl regarded politics on a local level as pointless, yet a two-party system meant that to accomplish ends one worked in one party or the other. And this had to begin somewhere.

His feminine opposite on the county Democratic committee was Helen Wilson Luzadder. And they warred. She had her opinions; he had his. However, if Helen ran into storms, it was to Carl she turned for help. Help generally meant financial help. Their frequent squabbles over some small matter of patronage were the delight of the card-players at the Washwoman's club, so called because it met on Mondays. There Helen Luzadder played with Ida, Jessie Moloney, Helga Cook, Grace McRae and a few others.

Politics on a national scale was something else. Carl was not returned to the legislature after his initial term, somewhat to his surprise. A Republican, R. B. Halferty of Donnelly, campaigning mostly on the issue of better highways, defeated him in 1924. So in the spring of 1928, when 10-foot snows brought work in the woods to an end, Carl decided to take Ida and go on a trip that would combine business, pleasure and maybe a little political entertainment. The southern lumber market needed study; and he was curious to observe whether the strong Baptist South would accept Al Smith, a Roman Catholic, who seemed likely to become the Democratic nominee for President.

The trip did not look to be an unreasonable expenditure. Hoff and Brown had been able to add new machinery and improvements, to acquire timber and ranch land; and they enjoyed a pleasant relationship with their bankers. The warming, spreading sensation that goes with an accession of strength felt fine.

In college Betty was doing well; Aunty Harland could manage the household and the other three children, who would be in school or on the ski hill all day. Ida was delighted with the thought of the trip and went to Boise for new clothes.

Like his father Carl enjoyed meeting big men of big ideas, and he hoped on the trip that he might manage to meet Al Smith personally.

From all three points of view the trip was a success. Carl crossed paths with Smith several times while the latter was in the South, and Smith questioned him about the state of western political thinking. By the time he returned home, Carl was sure that even among the Baptists, Smith's political soundness would outweigh religious prejudice.

Home had a fresh new look when the travelers returned, and moreover a sharp suspicion beset Carl that it was well they had gone when they did. There were portents of trouble in the air.

Herbert Hoover was elected. He had hardly settled at his desk in March, 1929, when the stockmarket crashed. Upon any industry dependent on good or reasonably good times, the effect was stunning. Lumber did not escape. For Hoff and Brown the first shock was the failure of the Union Pacific to contract ties. Next came the cancellation of lumber orders on their books. Over night the whole business atmosphere darkened like an eclipse.

On every level people talked gloom and fear. It was bad enough in small towns like McCall, but in cities it was far worse. In McCall nobody shot himself or jumped into the lake; but elsewhere they did.

Whether it was because of the general apprehension or something more personal, and the matter is no longer of vital moment, Theodore Hoff and Carl Brown now decided to end their partnership. Their fifteen years together had been a stirring period, for themselves and for the community. Each had acquired more depth and undergone seasoning; financially they were in good shape; their wives had worked on the same community projects; their children had become warm friends. The time seemed to have come to separate, and it would be untrue to say that these two determined and completely different men ended in perfect amity their long and useful association.

As one reflective Brown said later, partnerships are made to be dissolved. Obviously some are. In theory a partnership is set up to meet a certain need. If the need ceases to exist, is there any obligation to continue?

Given his choice, Carl Brown elected to stay with the mill. As part of the settlement effected, Theodore kept a planer that the firm operated at Horseshoe Bend and took over cattle ranches the business owned. It was his intention to run these ranches, which lay in the area, and so the Hoffs said only a tentative goodbye to McCall.

Carl had friends who feared he hadn't the experience to operate a mill by himself, especially in these unpredictable times. He had non-friends who hoped he'd fail at it. It would be absurd to say that every soul who knew him liked Carl and his family. No determined and successful person but has his detractors. It is human nature. However, it is possible that those who willed him to fail were not themselves doing anything special for the town.

The first thing Carl must have was a mill superintendent. The man he was sure he wanted was already on the payroll, Leslie Ulmer, stocky, round-faced, with friendly blue eyes and a quiet manner. Ulmer was a Pennsylvanian whose father had moved west hoping for relief from chronic asthma and had settled at Horseshoe Bend.

Young Ulmer learned early that money is elusive. At eight he was earning 25 cents a day doing something with sawdust at the Horseshoe Bend mill. He went to Boise for high school, then came to McCall in 1925 to work in retail sales for Hoff and Brown. His thought was to stay possibly six months. Soon, however, he was moved into the mill to serve wherever he was most needed, and he never left. He had a steadying presence that Carl Brown knew he could lean on, and Ulmer liked Carl's attitude that a workman who makes a mistake *but has tried*, is still all right. He approved of Carl's theory that if a fellow stings you once, that's his affair, but if he stings you twice, that's your fault. He approved but he smiled. He could remember times when Carl went to collect an overdue bill, perhaps a long overdue bill, and came back not with the cash but with an order for more lumber.[40]

The name of the firm would have to be changed. Carl decided on Brown Tie and Lumber company. The matter of continued credit at the bank in Boise was something yet to determine. As long as the small bank at New Meadows could carry them, Hoff and Brown had banked there. Then they moved to a bank in Emmett, finally to the Boise City National. Carl went thither to state that he was now on his own and hoped the directors would extend to him the same line of credit, $40,000, that Hoff and Brown had enjoyed. There was no delay; the bank was pleased to continue. This confidence on the part of the directors affected Carl deeply. He interpreted it that his honesty and competence beginning 20 years before in the paying off of a heart-breaking debt was accepted.

The printed words, Brown Tie and Lumber company, the sight of them on paper, stirred Ida and Carl deeply. They knew times were bad, unlikely to improve soon, but at last they were on their own. Whatever they had was theirs alone. Back in New Hampshire business titles Brown This and Brown That had conveyed security. To be sole owners of an establishment called Brown was exciting but sobering.

On him, Carl knew, the future of a small town now largely depended. As an employer and head of its one industry, he must be right, or close to right in all decisions; where time pressed critically, he must be quick. Mistakes, if he made them, he must retrieve at once. He was aware of an increased concern for the welfare of his men, and he hoped sincerely that they would trust him to do his best for them. If he assumed that Theodore's four brothers would leave, he assumed wrong. Martin, Henry, Pete and Brownie, they all stayed; and Carl put Harvey, Theodore's son, into a foreman's job. In fact, no one quit.

Carl allowed himself one small vanity: pencils marked Brown Tie and Lumber company. If the mill went broke, these pencils would be turning up somewhere for years, to remind people that he couldn't make a go of it. He knew this.

To Ida the combination of their heavy new responsibility, the business slack and the general gloom meant one thing: the family would cut down, spend only for necessities, shun any sort of show. Serious minded Betty undertook some adjusting of her own. She had finished her sophomore year at college, and now she stayed out to teach the 3rd and 4th grades in McCall. With her pay she did a curious thing, curious but not to be misunderstood. She turned over her salary checks to a friend, Herb Clare of Cambridge, so that he could finish college. The next year Herb worked and loaned to Betty. They exchanged signed notes, all very businesslike. This attack on a money problem might have looked small in relation to the size of the Brown Tie and Lumber budget, but at least it showed a Brown figuring out something to do and doing it.

Archery Lesson. Carl and his first grandchildren, Frank Brown and Stan Harwood.

Warren Brown, 13, and the dogs that made headlines on frozen Payette Lake.
With Aileen Ray, movie actress.

Carl Brown, legislator who introduced no bills.

Thus it was 1931 when Betty finished college. Among her friends there she had loved a few people warmly, but gone overboard about nobody of either sex. In her sorority she had an outlet she was ever to need, someone requiring her help. In a girl's house it is money that is needed, or clothes, or class notes; or a shoulder to cry on; or taking over somebody's all night job on the house float because this somebody is tired or sick or having heart-break.

For Brown Tie and Lumber, the year 1930 was a bad one. Prices slumped, no money circulated, bills weren't paid. For Carl the life-saver was the new tie contract with Union Pacific that he went to division headquarters at Pocatello to sew up. He assumed the reason it was awarded him was his not defaulting on earlier contracts when prices fell. Many small northwest mills were closing, and Carl would soon have a year when he could run only a few months.

In January 1933 Franklin Roosevelt's New Deal took over, and by Inauguration Day many banks had closed, among them the Boise City National, where Carl had $3200. However, many people saw hope in the spending plans of the new administration. At the mill men were thankful just to hold their jobs—and Carl kept every man that he could find work for.

Perhaps it was the nervous tension in the air that suggested to McCall women that they form a club open to all. In such a way they might do something to lift public morale. With hard money almost unobtainable and unemployment rising, people must be encouraged to believe that nothing was so bad it wouldn't come to an end. Thus the Women's Progressive club was formed. Ida Brown helped get it going but declined office, other than to agree to be chairman of the civic committee.[41]

Christmas treats was one of the Club's first projects —in hard times children's little dreams should come first. Later the women started work on the cemetery,

105

they instituted clean-up week and they set up a community gymnasium. In time some of these projects would be adopted by special groups, but the Progressive club founded them. Two of its best ideas turned out to be the annual garden show—this in an area where flowers have to start in the snow and bloom fast—and the McCall public library. Girl Scouting it also took to its heart.

A mile or so south of McCall lay a forty-acre tract covered with yellow pine and scrub. It was state land, but since McCall had no graveyard, people had started in an earlier period to bury their dead there. One morning a woman came to Carl Brown with tears in her eyes. She said a tree had fallen across her daughter's grave on the state forty. Carl pondered . . . a tree right across a young girl's grave . . . the neglected grave of an old-timer from the South Fork . . .

He arranged to buy the tract, paying for it as he could, then deeded to the village of McCall enough of the land for a cemetery. The spot was well suited to the purpose. The gentle slope faced the sun, which in the lake country is always beneficent. The yellow pines could be left, and everything else could remain about as Nature preferred it.

Besides accomplishing real gains, the Progressive club took women's minds from their troubles. They could feel one with each other, on the same level, united against the same enemy.

At the mill Brownie Hoff had decided he might as well enlist in the army. He went to California, took his physical, waited. The same day that he received word of his acceptance he had a letter from Carl Brown saying he needed him.

Perhaps he weighed the prospects of adventure against the memory of the home mountains, the lake, green summer solitude and white winter silence. He knew quite well what he would be returning to: a boss who expected work to be done right and done fast, a man who could be hard-boiled *if necessary*, but whose firmness left no bruises. Oh yes, Carl respected his men, but they knew how far they could go. So, Brownie thought with amusement, did his children.

Brownie started home.

CHAPTER FIFTEEN

In Cascade Betty was teaching school and enjoying life. Life included a well-built young man named Stanley W. Harwood but called Ted by everyone but his mother. In 1905 Ted's father had come from Buffalo to settle at the town of Thunder City, three miles from the present Cascade. His mother's brothers, the Logues, were already running stores in the area. Despite his poor health, which was the reason the family came west, Mr. Harwood filed on a homestead and at the same time took on stage-driving between Smith's Ferry and Van Wyck. The hardships of this work on mountain roads in every kind of weather were too much, and Mr. Harwood died of a heart attack. His wife Bessie had no choice but to stay with her four children on the homestead and prove up on it.

Several towns that were thriving in the valley when the Harwoods came presently disappeared, leaving little trace. In their 1907 heydey, however, a booklet was put out by the Long Valley Real Estate agency describing their charms and facilities.

Crawford, in a cove on the banks of the Payette river, a mile from present Cascade, was the center of the longest-settled and most densely populated part of the valley at that time. It had roads north to McCall and south to Boise, and the Intermountain State bank —dim letters on an old, small frame building there still say BANK. There was a hotel, meat market, livery stable and school, even a doctor.

Van Wyck, at a spot now under Cascade Reservoir, had a Baptist church, an Odd Fellows hall, stores, hotels, a dental "parlor" and a newspaper. Its two-story school was brick, with arched windows and a bellfry. In Van Wyck, the real estate booklet said, "dwelt the dove of peace."

Roseberry, which has been referred to earlier, was thriving and remained so for another eight years, until the railroad passed it up in favor of Donnelly, to which its bank was transported. Its other buildings were moved away or torn down.[42]

Thunder City served as a gateway to the Thunder Mountain mining country. It was surrounded by virgin timber in which sheep and cattle grazed on Forest reserves. It had a mill, livery stable, two stores; and a Miss Sadie Alvey ran a confectionery with a nice line of ladies' furnishings. F. S. Logue was U. S. commissioner for the district, receiving entries for government land and taking final proof. The Thunder City hotel was known to travelers from every state in the union, its proprietor Thomas L. Armstrong, declared.

Thunder Mountain has since come to intrigue people greatly, first because its activities sounded like the Klondike revived, and second because of what happened to Roosevelt, the only town in the area.

A letter by an unknown woman who cooked at the Sunnyside mine describes a Christmas there in 1899 or 1900.

The celebration was held in Lee Lysonbee's saloon, and among the six or seven women was Josie, but the other women agreed she ought to be invited—it wouldn't rub off. The miners were all shaved and cleaned up and had brought food with them to add to the baked ham and the dishpan full of taffy the women brought. The Christmas tree was decorated

108

with apples, toilet soap and popcorn, which were given out as presents. The bar was closed and people visited and ate and danced until daylight.

In 1905 an earth slide dammed Monumental creek, creating a lake that slowly inundated Roosevelt. At that time the town contained about 50 buildings, including stores, restaurants, lunch counters, saloons and the post office. Hard as the place had been to get to from November until June each year, it had everything that could be packed in. Dance halls had pianos, and one Madame of a house of joy stormed as the waters rose around her place of business because nobody would help get her piano out. At least two pianos were rescued, however, one said to be now at Yellow Pine. In 1959 skindivers from Grangeville found deepening silt on the bottom of the lake but little else of interest. A few roofs still showed above the water.

For widowed Mrs. Harwood and her children on the homestead, life was not easy, but neither she nor they spent time in useless regrets. The children got their schooling and Mrs. Harwood married again. Ted attended the College of Idaho for two years, but when his stepfather John Lambie died, he felt he must quit school and go to work.

When Teacher Elizabeth Brown came to Cascade he was employed in the C. C. Anderson store, one of the interesting bachelors of town. He had met Miss Brown previously, and he found himself seeing her as often as possible. Undisturbed, Betty went right on teaching for two years. She loved her students; she involved herself in their problems. One snowy weekend she decided to take two of them to McCall with her, just for fun. She was driving Carl's Chevrolet, old but by no means retired, and they were making good time up the frozen valley. Suddenly the car struck icy ruts. Some of the wheels didn't match the ruts. The Chevrolet flipped over.

Betty pulled herself out of the car. No, she didn't seem to be hurt much, just bruises. And the kids scrambled out, shaken, not hurt, but excited. Betty felt pretty glum. What was her father going to say about her driving, and about what she had probably done to the car. Robert Wilson, Valley county sheriff, now came along and took her and the youngsters to McCall. First Betty phoned the kids' mothers, so there'd be no anxiety. Then she went miserably to the mill to find her father. Nobody had seen him. Maybe he was at the Dog House. Putting off telling him would make it no easier. So Betty went to the Dog House, a place pretty much reserved for men. And there she saw her father, relaxing for once over a daytime game of pinochle.

She stopped at his elbow. He looked up.

"Dad?"

He held the card he was about to play. "Well, Betty, how's everything?"

"Dad, I turned your car over on the way home. I had to leave it there. I don't know how much damage, and I had two kids with me—"

"Was anybody hurt?"

"No."

Carl played his card. "Two ten," he said mildly.

In the Sigma Chi house in Moscow Warren Brown, a first semester junior, was seriously ill. A doctor called it trench mouth, an affliction first observed when doughboys came home from the European front. It had never been completely routed and was supposed to flourish where crowds ate and dishes were poorly washed. Nevertheless the most aristocratic old ladies were not immune. Something in Warren's system was allergic to the treatment, and instead of improving he grew steadily worse. His fraternity brothers became so alarmed they thought he might die and after calling Carl they took him to a hospital. Carl went as fast as he could drive it, felt equally alarmed and phoned a Portland specialist to come.

Under this doctor's care Warren improved enough to be taken home, but he was still sick. Convalescence gave him time to think. He decided not to return to college. His own savings were used up; a degree in Forestry wouldn't be worth to him what it would cost his folks to keep him in college—at least he'd do without the degree now.

Perhaps he resolved something else during those weeks, what to do about a certain Alpha Chi he'd first met on a blind date at the university. Jayne Jones of Malad had gone to college one year in Utah, then transferred to Idaho. Here she showed her capacity for intensive work by carrying a course in English and dramatics and at the same time acting as secretary to J. G. Eldridge, head of modern languages.

When Warren's phone call came she checked with the sisterhood. They okayed Warren, so she said Yes and went to a dance with him. They kept on dating. He invited her home for Christmas in McCall. Tinsel and Yule fires, church programs and Christmas trees, snow falling against home lights slanting through windows. She and Warren got in a good deal of skiing, under their own power, or pulled by horses. Warren was adept at both. As a kid he had often skied in from camp with a rope fastened to his father's car. Carl never looked back. If Warren took a spill, walking home wouldn't hurt him.

Jayne and Warren rode the empty logging sleds out to the woods and the loaded ones in. She returned to school knowing at least what McCall was like at Christmas.

Betty finished her second year of teaching and told her parents that she and Ted Harwood were engaged. If Ida and Carl felt that she was going to be taken from them—and she had shared their hardest years—they could take comfort in thinking she wouldn't be very far away. Thanks to Senator Bob

Halferty the road to Cascade was the best it had ever been.

It was Sunday morning, June 25, and the clock in Carl Brown's living room gave the hour as nine. Betty, attended by his sister Dorothy, and Ted by his brother George, took their places before Miss Gertrude McCheyne, an ordained minister who had come to the local church from England. Betty wore a soft green dress trimmed with cocoa lace, with no veil. With times uncertain, it had seemed foolish to spend money on glamor, so the wedding was kept simple. Only the families were present. After the ceremony and a breakfast served at Sylvan Beach by Oma Webb, who was highly successful with food, Betty and Ted left to visit in Portland, in Seattle, and in Kirkland, where Aunt Josephine Libby and Uncle Kenneth Brown now lived. In Olympia they stayed with the Fred Logues, Ted's relatives.

This used up a week and they felt they must hurry home. They slipped into McCall quietly—if Warren knew they had arrived there would be a crashing chiravari—and went on the next morning to the home that awaited them in Cascade.

A year later they moved to McCall, where Ted joined the staff of Williams and May, general merchandise. Later he bought a store of his own, subsequently selling it to C. C. Anderson but remaining as manager.

It was time for Dorothy to go away to college. Again it was the University of Idaho and the Tri Delt house. From childhood, just as her mother had dreamed, music was important to her. In McCall there was little outlet for vocalists except funerals and church choir, but Dorothy had sung and sung obligingly. Because of what was now called the Depression, college classes were small and life lacked traditional glamor, but Dorothy was too taken up with her music and art studies, with a minor in psychology,

112

to be bored. With boredom she had no patience any-how.

She tried out for the singing Vandaleers. The di-rector liked her voice, and for the next four years she sang and traveled with this group. On tour it was fas-cinating to stay in the homes of other students or friends of the university, and to discover that nice as they were, these homes didn't satisfy her as her own did.

When the Vandaleers went to Spokane, the nearest broadcasting studio at that time, she appeared on radio. But she was hard-headed and knew just how much of a voice she had. Her lyric soprano was sweet, but it wasn't big. "I know. I don't have to be told," Dorothy insisted.

Apparently she finished college with an undam-aged heart, and she was overwhelmed when her par-ents decided that regardless of any penny-pinching it would require she must have a year's study in the East. That fall she enrolled in the Fashion Academy of Rockefeller Center in New York for further art and music. She stayed at the Rehearsal club, where lived ambitious girls from everywhere, some of them eventually to shine in the stage and concert firma-ment, some to return disappointed to their little towns.

Before she left McCall for the great, wicked city, her mother's friends warned Dorothy with candor that anyone as unsophisticated as she would run into situations she'd never heard of. One that she dearly loved warned that it wasn't just men that were dan-gerous.

Whatever her discoveries that winter, and when after ten months she decided to return home, it wasn't disillusionment about the human race or about her personal hopes that spoke to her. She had simply con-cluded that while opportunities to deepen and broad-en endlessly were here, what *she* most wanted was to be found elsewhere. It was back in Idaho. She'd had plenty of time, some of it wistful, to think about the community where she'd grown up. Oh to be again in a setting where people *cared*. To be again where if somebody's house caught fire and burned everybody rushed to help put out the blaze and then thought up things to aid the homeless. The New York fires just weren't that kind.

For the rest of her life she would be influenced by this year, that was true. But she had had her fill. Returning home she worked in the mill office for a year. Then she took charge of the cottages and supervised activities at Sylvan Beach.

CHAPTER SIXTEEN

During 1932 B T and L operated only a few months; there was no lumber market. But 1933 saw definite recovery. Much of the stimulation was due to the Roosevelt administration's new CCC (Civilian Conservation Corps), which placed several camps in the McCall area. The corps recruited mostly from low-employment sections of the country, to put young fellows into work units. In the West these boys were likely to work on roads or trails, and they ranged unbelievably in experience, skill and gumption. Some came from hardworking families that had never before known financial anxiety. Some came from tenements so crowded that the boys had never slept in beds—they rolled up in blankets on the floor.

For the dormitory camps, lumber was required immediately, and Brown Tie and Lumber had it. There was no other producing mill left in the area. Within the same month that the CCC was born, the New Deal set up another employment project, the Public Works Administration. PWA crews, as well as those of CCC, would require local foremen.

114

Carl Brown had had one more or less accidental term in the legislature and had been county Democratic chairman, a job usually pushed onto somebody good natured or ambitious enough to bother with it. Patronage in a small county was no consuming problem, and Carl's tiffs with Helen Luzadder over its details had not been very serious. However, he was also Democratic national committeeman, and with Democrats at last in the White House, Carl found himself in the middle.

For the administration of the CCC several agencies were responsible: defense, state forests, the national forests. The government provided enlistees with food and clothing, but fresh meat and vegetables had to be bought locally. Upon Carl devolved suggesting the names of suppliers of camp needs and also the recommending of foremen for these camps, and foremen and laborers for the Public Works set-up. For the managing and directing jobs, it was implied, men from industry were to be preferred.

So Carl Brown wrote out lists. These were okayed by the federal and state forest heads on his simple statement that the men were willing and capable. Quickly things began rolling. Lumber and supplies were hauled, the camps rose. Enlistees arrived, were put to work. Almost immediately every kind of business in the area felt the pleasant shock of money again changing hands, whether much money or little.

The forests decided where the CCC roads were to be built, but unquestionably they leaned on the counsel of Carl Brown. From experience in his mail years and later at logging, he could say where to put a road *to best tap native resources,* and that was the object. He understood about following natural grades, how terrain influenced flood danger, and how needless powder work could be avoided. He could advise on camp locations and facilities.

Patronage, which is as old as the two-party system and as inevitable as the weather, always offends somebody. But on the lists Carl made were Republicans as well as Democrats. Accordingly he was criticized from *both* sides. Why, there was Warren Brown, his own son, a CCC foreman. But on the other hand, there was foreman Theodore Hoff,[43] who was certainly no Democrat.

Warren *had* to make good. He would have anyhow, whether or not his father had anything to do with it—it was his nature. But he seemed to spend 24 hours a day proving it. He had never worked harder.[44]

Carl was freely and openly criticized on the location of some roads built by CCC. They went too close to timber he hoped to cut, yet it was a government agency that decided the routes. Probably his critics if put in the same position would have done about as he did, or observed fewer scruples. His test of any man he employed was his honesty, and it seems unlikely that he would have recommended those who loafed or chiseled, or that he wouldn't have removed those who did. As to his taking undue advantage of a wonderful situation, there is nothing criminal in shaking a tree where the plums are ripe when it's your turn to shake.

Those in charge of the CCC squads handled them with varying competence and military precision. A few marched their men to work like POW's, and frowned on any friendly overtures from non-trainees. Some citizens feared the CCC—its purpose was sinister; it might turn into a military arm some night and take over the country. Nevertheless in a time of great unemployment it provided work in a presumably healthful atmosphere, and a chance to develop skills of a sort and see the country. Many an Eastern enlistee decided the West was the place he wanted to live. For the duration he was not unhappy, and when he was allowed to go to town he kept pretty well out of trouble. The CCC had its place.

Meanwhile in McCall as elsewhere there were provident, hard-working people whom work projects

116

could not benefit, who had to seek government relief. Some applied for the sake of invalids or old people or because of small children. There were others who preferred to suffer. In his pocket Carl Brown always carried some silver dollars. It was easy to slip a few into a man's hand. He himself seldom smoked, but he always carried cigarettes to pass to men who did smoke and now couldn't afford to.

Of Ida's and Carl's secret giving during these hard years, there is of course little knowledge. Stories persist, however. For instance, about a widow who had a flock of children and a nearly bare cupboard. One night she came home from work to find a box of groceries on her table and warm blankets on the thin beds. But there was nothing to show who had been there.

CHAPTER SEVENTEEN

Jayne Jones and Warren Brown were married May 15, 1934, in the home of Jayne's parents in Malad. Margaret Brown, 17, was bridesmaid and Phillip Fikkon, a fraternity brother of Warren's, was his attendant. This wedding, like Betty's the previous year, was simple, with only relatives as guests. The blue-eyed copper-haired bride wore a floor-length white lace dress in princess style, with long sleeves. After a luncheon, Warren and Jayne left for the coast. They went by Salt Lake and Las Vegas, which was not then fabulous. They saw Los Angeles and Portland, then turned toward home.

At first they lived in a small house near Carl's, which Warren had bought as a surprise to his bride. A few months later they went East to pick up cars and a truck that B T and L needed. This was their chance

117

to visit New England, which neither of them had ever seen. Only Betty had been back to her parents' home.

In an atmosphere where customs and usages were already old when the republic was born, their reactions were mixed, perhaps confused. They both read widely, they were history conscious, and they sensed the depth of reflective living that filled New England old houses and haunted its old streets. At the same time they felt the hedging, the limits and boundaries of traditional thinking. They were happy that they had come, happy in secret that they had been born beyond the farther mountains.

In Boston by odd chance they stopped in front of the Quincy House, and saw on the ground the very fir flagstaff that Warren's grandfather, that earlier Warren, had shipped from Washington territory as a present to a Colonel J. W. Johnson. Now the flagpole that had stood for more than six decades was being dismantled.

Warren repeated to Jayne other stories his father had told him. How Warren Goodhue Brown and his brother Alson had built themselves a ship, The Brown Brothers, costing $120,000 to bring spars from Puget Sound, a first cargo shipped in 1876 followed by six more.

Once the brothers chartered a vessel that lay at anchor in a Washington harbor and which must sail in 60 days. Warren Goodhue left Boston by rail for California, hurried north by stage to Roseburg, Oregon, by rail again to Puget Sound. There he engaged loggers, rushed them to the woods. They hewed timbers, the timbers were hauled and loaded. Within the set 60 days, everything was completed. This was an early day kind of rapid action for which Warren the younger had a decided taste himself.

The young folks left for Detroit where Warren bought a truck, loaded a car on it, then bought another car for Jayne to drive. Their trip home was one to remember, and another reminder of how fortunate their living had been. Through the plains states, now unhappily the Dust Bowl, the air was often too murky to see the car hood. None of this made Payette Lakes less beautiful.

Logging horses, the kind that Carl Brown had watched in his father's woods, that had been an essential part of Carl's life for twenty years, were to go. Time and machines had outmoded them. In their place logging trucks would roar down the mountain roads. Operations in the woods would employ a few for a while, but eventually these too would be seen no more.

To Carl it was the end of an era and saying good-bye to something almost personal. A truck now didn't brace itself against the load when the brake failed. It didn't miss you, raise its head when you approached, or notice a friendly slap. It didn't give you everything when you shouted.

B T and L took an agency for International Harvester and would now use its trucks. Around 1927 Little and Paul, a Boise firm, had done some truck-logging for Hoff and Brown, and Carl knew trucks were feasible. But it was only now that he felt he was ready for the change-over, ready financially and operationally. Ready sentimentally? No.

It was Margaret Brown's last year before college. In 1923 McCall had erected a building to house grades and high school. To build a separate high school at that time was regarded by many as simply throwing money away, so this new structure had to suffice for the next twenty years. For Margaret's last year Carl and Ida decided to send her to Nampa.

There that fall Margaret required a bit of surgery on her foot, and one afternoon when she wanted very much to attend a wedding, a problem developed. How could one enter a church with dignity when hobbling?

119

The brother of the groom, a stranger, who obviously had an eye for a good looking, animated girl, offered to *carry* her in. Whether or not this was more dignified, Margaret looked the fellow over and did not refuse. Thus they became acquainted. He was also a high school senior, and they finished at the same time. The next year both set out for the state university. The young man's name was Homer Davies.

On campus Margaret pledged to her sister's sorority, where Dorothy was a junior. Probably it didn't bother Margaret to be preceded by a competent sister and an artistic one. She seemed to assume that when special talent was required of her she would be supplied with it. She majored in a subject appropriate for any Brown, physical education, and thought seriously of going into Girl Scout work or social service if— well if. She also took voice.

In 1936 Carl Brown was persuaded to run again for the legislature and was elected. Legislators liked to arrive in Boise about New Year's day, with lodgings already engaged, so as to be on hand for the political jockeying and horse-trading that preceded organization of the houses. However, Carl arrived there ahead of everyone else, and in no happy frame of mind.

Just before Christmas, Ida had met with a cruel reward for her unflagging devotion to the church and its annual Christmas program. She was helping practice the children at the hall which the Musical Martins had built for summer dancing and which would presently be turned into a community gym by the Progressive club.

This afternoon it was cold, cold, both outside and in, and the children, trying to focus their minds on their songs and little plays, were shivering. The Musical Martin heat registers gave out nothing. But Ida was not one to be intimidated by a furnace. You went to the basement, stoked with whatever was provided, you opened drafts, you unset dampers. No need to call some busy man from his work to do these simple tricks. Confidently Ida started down the basement stairs.

It was dark there. A board was gone.

When her calls finally brought help, Ida was carried home. A doctor found that her leg was broken below the knee in three places.

Carl took her to Boise to the hospital. Then he secured one of the penthouse apartments atop the Boise hotel, new since his last legislative service, and only two blocks from the capitol. In time Ida was released from the hospital, consigned to a wheelchair, and established in the apartment. Her doctors had not dared tell her she might never walk. She only knew that being immobile was almost unendurable. She had lost none of her usual vigor and ambition; waiting for bone to knit, nerves to resume their message-carrying—!

By phone Ida began searching the town for a masseuse and found one. This woman's patient, old-country arts sped the healing. She got Ida up. There was one thing to make the recovery pleasanter—Betty too was staying at the apartment now. Betty too was expecting to go to the hospital.

Despite his worry over Ida and his conscientious attendance at sessions, Carl found time to think of the future of lumbering. Away from the mill and the woods, perspective was better. He knew he should buy timberland. Now, before general economic recovery. He must watch the situation closely.

Later in the year he was able to purchase from Boise-Payette Lumber company a tract that lay on the divide between Meadows and McCall, along both sides of the present highway, 1100 acres that had once been selectively logged. Carl was sure he could still cut as much as 6.6 thousand feet per acre, and the tract also contained some species of fir just reaching proper age to log.

Each year the trees would increase in size and value, and he would hold them for the rainy day that even the wisest lumberman can't be expected to foresee. His $15,000 was well spent—he was positive. The output of the mill this year had increased to where the payroll had climbed to $110,000, more than twice what it was in 1931, its low point. And he had better be ready to buy other timberland if the right thing showed up.

In the legislature he again did nothing that diverted attention to himself — there were already enough laws. He spoke infrequently and co-sponsored some bills. His committees remained about the same: fish and game; forestry; highways, bridges and ferries; public lands.

After the legislature adjourned, Ida still remained at the apartment gathering strength. Betty waited too.

On the morning of March 13, 1937, Dr. Hal Dedman was summoned to St. Luke's hospital. When he left, Ted and Betty Harwood were the parents of nine-pound Stanley Carl Harwood. On getting the news Carl Brown rushed to Boise and took Ida in her wheelchair to view their first grandchild. They found Ted already there.

Carl looked the child over. "The homeliest baby I ever saw," he said sadly, but the young parents felt that even this was a distinction—little Stan was already the mostest at something. Now the nurse looked at the baby more closely. To Carl she said, "Anybody would know he was your grandchild."

Carl looked startled. He said no more about homely babies.

Ernest Watkins dropped in to see the new child. "Look at those feet!" he exclaimed.

But the boy had a right to large feet, large anything. Nature had decided to make a big man of him.

It was a month and three days later, April 16, when in the same hospital there arrived a second grandchild for Carl and Ida.

Jayne and Warren, accompanied by Dr. O. J. Hawkins, had had a wild night ride from McCall, barely arriving in time. Such rides are not amusing to doctors, but the young couple, afterwards, are likely to regard the split-second race with the stork as something rather ingenious they pulled off. At the hospital all went well. Frank Elliott—for Jayne's father and Warren's grandmother — understood at once what was expected of infants. He gave no trouble whatever until after the usual week or ten days when his parents took him to the apartment which Jayne's mother had rented for the event.

Frank cried all the first night there, and Warren and his mother-in-law never even undressed. Only Jayne slept. But Mrs. Jones didn't mind—it proved she was really needed, and besides she and Warren had a chance to get better acquainted.

These little cousins, Stan and Frank, would grow up side by side, completely different in looks and personality. Each would follow his own path, but in one thing they would compete, that sport for which McCall was becoming famous, and they'd begin as soon as they could stand up on skis.

It would be unfair to McCall not to pause here to say that it has had its day in the moving picture world. In 1937 MGM producers of "Northwest Passage" hit on it as background for an Alaskan drama, for here were rivers and lakes, snow, primeval forest, packtrains and miners. And Indians were available. It is true no Brown was asked to appear in the film, but B T and L undoubtedly loaned properties and assistance and advice any time such were asked for, and Ernie Watkins was drafted from his saw filing to serve as unit manager for construction sets.

During the summers of 1937 and 1938 one might brush on Main street against stars and starlets, rangers, bad men, dance hall girls. The noise of sound trucks often disturbed packstrings of mules bound on actual, not fictitious business in the hills. Some reminders of McCall's day in filmdom persist, especially at the north end of the lake—bits of frontier buildings, perhaps only a piece of false front, settling softly into the mold of time. The Quentin Mack house in McCall has chimney stones from an MGM fort.

In 1940 Twentieth-Century Fox came to film scenes to use in the picture "Hudson Bay."

In 1937 Carl Brown gave to McCall a gift whose dollar value though considerable had little relation to the blessings it was to provide. Three miles west of town lay 80 acres of Brown land that humped itself into a ridge of the proper steepness and contour for a ski course. It would be close in and accessible from Highway 15, which creased its north edge.

The United States Forest Service had recreation programs, but it could not spend money to improve any but Forest-owned land. Accordingly, Carl Brown deeded the 80 acres to the Forest, and the Forest created a course for novices on one side, a course for competent skiers on the other side, with a ski jump between.

This benevolence a few months later brought to Pat Hays, Carl's firm office manager, an unexpected problem. On income tax forms the gift was neither charity nor educational. The only possible slot seemed to be *advertising*. The internal revenue department may have pondered that one, how a business concerned with wholesale lumbering could require so much local promotion.

CHAPTER EIGHTEEN

The fourth McCall Brown at the University of Idaho finished in 1939. Margaret and Homer Davies had known each other through four years of college, and had not gone separate ways. Through the summers Davies had worn his tires thin getting to McCall from the hardware business of his father, Benjamin G. Davies, in Nampa. With help Homer had built a 13-foot boat—built it in the basement at home where fortunately the door jambs were removable. He hauled the boat to McCall and he and Margaret spent happy weekend hours in it—it had a motor—and when he was in Nampa working hard it made her think of him.

Homer was graduating too, and a grocery chain executive in Florida offered jobs to six Idaho seniors, including Davies, who was a business major. Not that he was tired of hardware but that he didn't intend to pass up other opportunities that might prove golden, Davies left promptly for Florida. By October he had been tried out in 13 stores in about as many towns. Only one thing marred this exciting life: paying advance room-rent and staying in each room so briefly, he was rapidly going broke. Slightly embarrassed, but also determined, he told his boss he'd have to have more money or quit. He got the money. Before October was out he was a store manager. Quite sure that Margaret was not hopelessly bent on being a teacher, an artist or a social worker, he wrote her to come. Naturally he was too busy to go.

It took Margaret little time to decide, and only a little more to get ready. Accompanied by her mother, by Homer's mother, and by Dorothy as driver, Margaret set out by car. With her was the bridal dress of sheer white wool with jacket, and a hat of the same material designed and created by a Boise woman, Mabel Kinkaid.

On November 30, Margaret and Homer were married in a Congregational church at Vero Beach, a Spanish style, white stucco church. Dorothy was her sister's bridesmaid; also she sang. Homer's attendant was a long-time friend, Glendon Davis.

The visitors did up a leisurely week of sight-seeing, but so demanding was the grocery business that Homer and Margaret had to return from their Miami honeymoon after but a single day.

If Carl and Ida yearned over this their youngest, separated from home by so many miles and time zones, their yearning was wasted. The young people were neither worried nor lonely. True Margaret missed the lake and mountains, and all that went with them, but she honestly liked Florida, and there was so much to see and do when Homer had the least bit of time.

Then there was something else. Before many months had passed she became aware that she was to star in a new role, and she was delighted. In September 1940 Richard Warren was born to the Davies. To make things perfect, Margaret's mother was able to be there. By the following spring the Davies decided to return to Nampa, where Homer joined his father's firm.

In McCall Ida and Carl gave them the two-acre State House Landing site on the west side of the lake, about two miles from Lardo. In early days it had been a stopping place for travelers, ore shippers and trappers, and was one of Carl's first buys. Sheltered by tall pines, it sloped gently to the water, ideal for a summer place. Whenever the Davies did any digging around their new domain, they turned up bits of the past, old spurs, horseshoes, rusty buckles and rotting strap leather.

From now on Margaret returned to McCall for a part of every summer. The old lake-centered activity was little changed, and Homer could drive up for weekends. Friends always came by. Stay-over friends. Morning always disclosed a casual flock of beds on the Landing lawn.

Late spring, 1940. B T and L installed modern bandsaws to replace its circular saws. Business brightened. Railroad ties, the old standby in bad times, sold at $40 a thousand. Carl even recovered $3200 lost in 1933 when his Boise bank closed. The whole country was responding to better times—war times, alas—and the two political parties now geared for their national conventions.

As a former legislator and national committeeman, and as a man able to contribute to the state party coffer and pay his own expenses to Chicago, Carl Brown was a natural for delegate to the Democratic circus in July. Although some people, including Ida Brown's husband, suspected that she had always been a Republican at heart, Ida did not refuse to go with Carl to the convention.

They arrived by train, found their rooms on the 16th floor of the Stevens hotel. Already everything was in systematic confusion, and to Carl it was complete fascination to watch important and self-important characters boil in and out of the seething scene. The streets, the restaurants, the lobbies, the whole city was full of it. There was no peace or quiet anywhere, save possibly in the churches.

Carl took enough time away to buy a new Plymouth, but that was all. For Ida the high point was not the speeches or whether the presidential two-term tradition was to be ignored, but the voice of Kate Smith singing a new song, "God Bless America." The haunting melody, the easy words, the full serene roll of sound—this was rapture, and she would never forget it. Secret sorrow, suppressed yearning—the voice swept away anything like that. No other voice had given Ida this uplift, this peace. It soared above ugly

127

convention rumors that buzzed like unwholesome insects, rumors of deals, payoffs, double-crossing, even fraud. To Ida a national consciousness that produced an Irving Berlin and a Kate Smith couldn't be very bad.

Carl and Ida discussed the two-year term matter. In his eight years in the White House, Franklin Roosevelt had been unable to develop anyone else that he, the President, thought could win the election. In Europe nothing had withstood Hitler. His tanks and subs and bombers were taking whatever stood in their way. And now ominous clouds were rising over the Pacific. The President himself declared he didn't like to break with precedent but—

In a radio speech he said: "Lying awake as I have on many nights I have asked myself whether I have the right, as Commander in Chief of the Army and Navy, to call on men and women to serve their country or train themselves to serve and at the same time decline to serve my country in my own personal capacity, if I am called upon to do so by the people of my country."

"He's a great man," Carl affirmed to Ida.

The pressure of the two terms had not threatened Roosevelt's health; and to change horses in midstream with war a possibility seemed to Carl, and probably to almost all Democrats, not only unwise but unthinkable. Astute James Farley, national chairman, whom nobody fooled very long, appeared to want Roosevelt.

There had already been three days of blistering Chicago heat when after dinner Ida left the elevator on the 16th floor of the Stevens for her room. It seemed to her she had never spent so hot a day—how cool McCall would be tonight . . . the breeze off the lake, the soft lapping of the water . . .

She was greeted by the hostess on their floor, who handed her a telegram. But when she got to their room with it, Carl was already on the phone.

July 16 in McCall had been a hot, sleepy day, with no wind, everything dry from days of brilliant sunshine, dry and ready to crackle at a single spark. Late in the afternoon several men were standing across the road from the mill, talking. The day shift was still at work, the mill running with measured, reassuring scream and rumble. Suddenly in the furnace room, unseen, a boiler backfired. Sparks must have shot into a pile of dry sawdust, for it leaped into flames that instantly were shooting up the wooden walls, snatching at oil-soaked timbers above.

The men who were talking saw nothing, heard nothing unusual. Then before their eyes, in one great clap, the mill seemed to explode in fire. Out of nowhere roared a wind. From the mill heat the planer shed began to smoke. Long tongues of flame leaped the narrow road to the dry roof of the Payette Lakes Star. The air cracked like gunfire.

A hundred feet from the Star stood Bill Deinhard's hotel, beyond it a row of wooden business buildings, the heart of town.

It was only seconds until the town knew. On the run came a Forest crew, then volunteer firemen, some CCC fellows. They got a hose connected to a hydrant, the only hose available. In the searing heat from sheds and blazing dry scrap, the hose burned in two.

People were running screaming, their cries lost in the roar. In the nearest houses they began tugging frantically at furniture, throwing things into the yards. Men seized sheets of plywood, using them for shields to get in close to the blazing buildings. Women ran with wet blankets, rugs and gunnysacks, anything for men to throw upon roofs and walls. Power and phone poles crashed, snarling their lines, adding new danger. On a railroad spur a car of dynamite waited its chance—nobody remembered its being there.

Joe Kasper tried to get into a blazing shop where his tools were kept, tools he had been years gathering.

Ted Harwood yelled for him to keep back. Joe started in, and Ted had to seize and hold him.

The mill roof became blackened rafters that fell in; lumber sheds were gone. The Star building collapsed. Ding's Club, Dewey's barbershop, Lowe's cabinetshop and three houses of Bill Deinhard's were blazing beyond help.

Suddenly, as fast as it had risen, the wind died, the roaring diminished. Scorched and blackened firefighters caught their breath but kept on until it was clear the fire would spread no further. It looked as if the town was to be saved.

Saved. Saved for what. The mill was gone, and it was on the mill that every home and every business depended. What would men do for work, what would families do for groceries.

Warren Brown was at Smith's Ferry. Carl was days away. It was as sad and disconsolate a night in McCall as anyone could remember.

Carl repeated to Ida what he had learned from the phone call, which was little more than the bare facts. When Ida could grasp his meaning she was stunned. Slowly she asked, "Was anyone hurt, anybody killed?"

"Betty says no one was hurt very bad. Some severe burns, but nobody seems to be in serious condition. *But everything's gone*. Everything, Ida. All that we've worked for. I haven't had time to estimate—"

"What burned besides the mill?"

"They saved most of the lumber in the yards. The Star, several other places, and the old Hoff house. They thought the whole town was going."

"I guess we ought to start right home," Ida said. "We'd have sure not bought that car if we'd known—"

"We *can't* go. Roosevelt isn't nominated yet!"

"All right, then we'll stay, but I can tell you one thing, Carl Brown, we're not going to stay and go on talking and talking about the fire!"

Carl didn't answer. He had begun putting figures on paper. The loss, he told Ida, would be between fifty and seventy-five thousand. Insurance wouldn't cover half, maybe not a third. But they must think about the men who'd be out of work. A hundred men. Maybe more than a hundred. And what about their families. This fire meant the end of the town.

But of course Ida was right. They couldn't talk about it and stay. He'd simply force himself to think about all the issues the convention had brought into focus, and the possibilities ahead. He'd tell Ida about Henry Wallace, a good earnest fellow—why was he getting boos as well as cheers? The lady theosophist yarn would amuse Ida . . .

Would the Boise First Security want to extend enough credit to cover rebuilding, and if he *could* borrow, how long would it be before he'd turn out lumber again. If it was quite a while he'd lose a lot of good men he'd depended on, men who'd grown up with the mill. Without a payroll, what would McCall families live on? What was Warren thinking. The bank—

No! He was back at the beginning, and Ida was right. If they were to see the convention out—and he meant to—they'd have to think about that, not about the fire.

Oh yes, Henry Wallace. The president said he wanted him for running mate, or he *seemed* to be saying so. If Wallace had corresponded with the lady theosophist, the letters weren't about anything but religion—theosophy was religion, wasn't it. They did say Harry Hopkins had managed to buy the letters and lock 'em up.

"Ida, he said, "I heard the President was disappointed when he was assured over and over that Wallace had never registered at a hotel with this lady— you know, the one with brains. Roosevelt said, just as if he meant it, that the American people understood romance and they'd forgive Henry, but that they didn't understand theosophy and would probably never forgive him for that."

Now Ida did smile.

Roosevelt was nominated on the first ballot; Wallace made it too.

The acceptance speeches were over. The fantastic noise-making whether spontaneous or triggered from subterranean floors was over. The perspiring mindless milling slowed down. With the hot crowd, Ida and Carl melted out of the amphitheater. The present had become the past. Ahead lay campaign and election.

As she packed Ida gazed mournfully at things she wouldn't have bought had she known. They loaded the new car and turned their faces west. Now with the convention behind them, Carl couldn't keep away from the subject of the fire. Finally Ida cried miserably, "If you want to know everything about it, stop somewhere and call them. But don't keep asking me what *I* think."

In silence they drove into town, a moment they had been trying to prepare themselves for. The place looked so small, so defenseless. Now ahead they could see the first signs of the disaster, burned posts standing.

"Ida, do you want to go home first, get rested, then come back later?"

"No," Ida said, "I want to see right now how bad it looks."

Suddenly sounds came to their ears, the blessed sound of axes, men's voices. Now they saw that on the spot, amid charred ruins, Warren was directing a crew of men. Some cleared away debris. Some were hand-hewing timbers. They left the car, went to Warren.

"We're getting these timbers for the foundation of a temporary mill," Warren explained. "We should set one up at once and get our tie contract finished.

We've got a million feet of logs in the pond and more coming in. Why should we wait?"

It was a bracer! A temporary mill, of course. Then they'd rebuild. They'd get the money somewhere. This was home, and they'd been through worse things than fires!

Carl knew a better site, too, farther around the lake on the east side. Better place for a new mill. They owned the land already, 20 acres that he'd bought a while ago, never dreaming it would be needed for a new mill. Some was in lumberyard, but that didn't matter. All of it was in the city, and paying city taxes.

And he already had a man who would know exactly what they ought to figure on in a new mill. He'd often said that when the time for expansion came— well this was it! The man was Joe Kasper.

Warren was reminding him of the mill on Spirit lake in northern Idaho that had been closed, forced by the Depression to quit. It was about what they needed now. "We could start Joe up there to look it over, and if it's what it sounds like, I could be up there the next day with enough trucks to haul it here."

Definite plans, men at work, Warren going ahead with confidence. Carl and Ida got in their car and went home.

"Nobody that's ever lived here will want to move away," Ida said sighing with relief. "Now maybe they won't have to."

"A lot still depends on the bank," Carl said soberly.

CHAPTER NINETEEN

Carl drove to Boise. To bank president Lynn Driscoll he stated his estimated needs, his other assets, his contracts; he outlined business possibilities with a new and larger mill. He would need, he said, $220,000.

If the directors deliberated long, the fact has been forgotten. But the confidence expressed in him Carl Brown would never forget. It opened a door onto new developments and new relations; it almost closed a door on old anxieties and the dogging fear of failure.

"Ida and I have taken it tough some times," he thought as he drove home, "but we've tried to deal straight. This is our reward, if we needed one. It isn't just the loan. It's knowing how others feel about us."

Joe Kasper found the small mill to be as they hoped. They bought it. As fast as the machinery was dumped from the trucks, he was setting it up.

The August air vibrated with robust activity. Saws whined, hammers rang and winches growled. Carl and Warren had every man at work for whom any useful labor could be found. The ground was cleared for the new mill. Construction began. Kasper's plan called for more space, and all new modern machinery. The mill would require more men, turn out more product, and do it faster. It would be sprinklered this time, and adequate hydrants installed in the yards. Measures like these would bring down the nearly prohibitive insurance rate of $7.60 a hundred on a one-year basis that they had paid on the old mill.

In the excitement and anxiety of the fire, another event had received decidedly less attention than it warranted. This was the arrival of a third Brown grandchild, a first granddaughter. Several months earlier Warren and Jayne had moved temporarily to a trailer house at Smith's Ferry, so Warren could better oversee a logging job. Their same Dr. Hawkins had no longing for another wild midnight ride to a hospital, and had told Jayne to go to Boise early. Her mother again came from Malad and took an apartment, and the two with three-year-old Frank had had a lovely week together.

Diane Louise, blue-eyed like all other Browns, arrived safely but had hardly assumed her place in the family when the call came that the mill had burned. Her father rushed to McCall.

It was really three months before Diane came home to the lake, for during the delay of mill construction Warren undertook a jippo job for Boise-Payette Lumber company at Smith's Ferry, and the baby was brought to the house trailer. Infants are said to like *closeness*—humans and things close, so there will be no danger of falling. Diane's first world was indeed very close and compact.

CHAPTER TWENTY

In 1938 Theodore and Hannah Hoff decided to go back to their first love, lumbering. At Horseshoe Bend, 25 miles north of Boise, where their planer had burned, they bought a mill and ran it for two years. Then bright prospects attracted them to the Willamette valley in Oregon. In Albany they carried on a successful business, but however Theodore may have felt about this more sedately moving life, Hannah longed for the vigor and naturalness of wide-spread Idaho. In this peaceful Oregon valley where people raised hay and fruit on small tracts of land and knew all about their neighbors' affairs, she thought she would smother. Oh, for great hills shouldering the sky, harsh in midday sun, velvet and mystic at dusk.

And so in 1941 the Hoffs returned to Horseshoe Bend, a place that was becoming a habit. They bought out the man who had bought them out, and settled down contentedly.[45]

Like Brown, Hoff saw the importance of buying timberland before it was gone. He bought land when, he suspected, he should be buying bread and butter.

CHAPTER TWENTY-ONE

New Years Day 1941. Work on the big new mill had proceeded well, but its machinery would not start rolling until May. In November Franklin Roosevelt had defeated Wendell Willkie in the most breathless campaign the country had ever listened to. He would become the first three-term president in the history of the republic, a prospect both exciting and frightening. In the papers Carl and Ida read of the inauguration plans. They read, that was all. Carl had no thought of going to see his president installed in office. It was true that business had a very favorable feel and that no worries pressed inordinately. He had no doubt that B T and L would presently recoup its fire losses, and meet the expenses of the expanded program. But the international picture was so oppressive he felt that to spend money *for pleasure*—and it would take plenty—was inappropriate if not downright foolish or wrong.

They had received and dwelt on the special invitations from the Inauguration committee, squares of cardboard one ought to frame—thick, off-white paper, the colorful embossed seals, formal words in formal script. One invitation was signed by Joseph E. Davies, former ambassador to Russia.

In the midst of a business talk, Lynn Driscoll at the Security bank in Boise, said to Carl, "You're going to the inauguration of course, you and Ida. Ida especially will love it."

"No. We are not going. We haven't even considered it."

"You *must* go."

"No, it wouldn't look right—on account of the fire. It wouldn't seem right at all."

The fire of 1940 that destroyed Brown's Tie and Lumber mill.

The Brown Tie and Lumber Mill in McCall, rebuilt after the fire.

Idaho State Forest photo

Left: A state forest employee marking a yellow pine for cutting. Right: Weiser Forest lands. Trees marked with white spots will be reserved from cutting. Piles of slash will be burned for fire prevention.

Ansgar Johnson Photo

Yellow pine logs being loaded from a state forest sale. Scaler with his stick at right.

"That's nonsense. You've got things in good shape. Warren's as steady as a rock. That man Pat Hayes in your office knows more about the business than you do. You and Ida owe it to yourselves. It's a pay-off for your good party work. And the chance may never come again. You're going, that's all."

Carl was undecided when he went home. He and Ida talked. The first three-term president, a solemn tradition broken because of the times. Perhaps there would never be another three-term executive—

Ida packed; Carl got ready. In Boise they shopped for the clothes that Dorothy assured them they would need. Ida's purchases came up to the hotel room. She dressed, to give Carl a little private showing.

The white satin floor-length formal shimmered with sequins. Ida carried a little more weight now than in her days at the Crown cabin, and the extra length was right for her compact figure. Her skin was still firm and responsive, her gold-flecked eyes always bright—especially when she was amused—and only a little gray showed in her heavy hair.

Over her shoulders she drew the new evening cape of American Beauty red.

Carl said: "There won't be another woman in Washington as beautiful."

"If you don't get busy on your things," she told him tartly, to conceal her pleasure, "you'll never get there to see me."

"Oh, my things will be up. Dinner jacket, fancy pants, exactly the right shirts, shoes, gloves and ties."

And when the boxes were opened he paraded too.

He also was heavier, more authoritative, and distinguished still by his air of deference that won women and sometimes misled men. His eyes were as keen and his color as fresh as when he was Skinny Brown of the South Fork, but his face had deeper lines of maturity.

They laughed together, two children escaping from school for a day.

137

CHAPTER TWENTY-TWO

For the trip Ida Brown kept a diary. Here is part of it:

January 16, 1941. Arrived at 8:50 in Washington and had to wait until noon for our room. Rainy, snowy, slippery. Carl and I went to see "Hudson Bay," starring Paul Muni. Part of this picture was filmed at Payette Lakes . . .

People are gathering from all over America for this occasion. In the evening we went to the lounge with some Idaho people, Congressman Compton White and his daughter Jean, 17. Friday Jean Rothery came in. We went to an antique showing with the lady that was so lovely to Dorothy. Went to dinner at Jean's, had a most delightful time. Anne is a big girl. Jean and Julian look grand.

January 18. Carl got up early to go to work as gov. offices are not open on Sat. Had my hair fixed and manicure . . .

Took a drive over the city. Lincoln Memorial, by the White House, and all the gov. buildings. Had dinner with Ralph and Mrs. Olmstead in Arlington. Played cards, came back to the city about 12 o'clock. No dancing. Everything closes at 12 o'clock Saturday night.

January 19. Had late breakfast. At 1:30 we went down on the docks to lunch with Jean and Julian . . . wonderful fish meal, and then took a ride beside the Potomac through the War College grounds and all over the city. At 4:30 went to Carleton Hotel to a tea. Met Franklin Roosevelt, junior. Had a nice long chat with him. Looks like both his mother and dad, strong and dynamic.

As we left the hotel we met Eleanor Roosevelt coming. Most charming personality. She was dressed in a dark dress with a lovely grey squirrel cape and black hat with black and white wings.

Compton White called and wanted us to go with him and a cousin to another tea at a lovely home in the country. Met Paul McNutt and wife.

In the evening we went to the dinner for the Electoral College honoring Franklin Roosevelt and Henry Wallace . . . in the ballroom of the Mayflower hotel, with 1500 attending. Lovely palms and beautiful ferns and flowers. Each table accommodated 10.

Our table was on a raised floor near the table for the guests of honor, so that when they came in I wasn't more than 3 ft. from them. Mrs. Roosevelt was lovely in a heavy cream satin gown, a long ermine coat with a big white fox collar. Mrs. Wallace wore blue and when her husband stepped off the platform in back of her you could see he was worried for fear he would step on her train. Mrs. Josephus Daniels came in a wheel chair but was helped up the steps and walked to her seat. There were about 1500 at this dinner. Lovely music . . .

We were first served some light wine and then a lovely dinner. Terrapin soup, champagne and all the trimmings. I might say this dinner was $10.00 a place and well worth it for once. Mrs. Roosevelt made a very cordial and appreciative talk. Nelson Eddy sang "God Bless America." Mickey Rooney came and talked. They had wonderful guest artists and a most wonderful time for a country maid from Idaho to enjoy.

January 20. Inauguration Day, a clear, cool day with a brisk wind. First we had a terrible scramble to get a cab as they were all busy, but we finally arrived at our seats . . . close to where the ceremonies were to take place. Carl and I were visiting with some nice young people . . . she asked if we knew Ross Pope of Boise. So you see the world is a small place after all.

As the President came out the crowd stood, but as it was a cold day the men did not leave their hats off. But I was impressed as the minister started to offer prayer nearly every head was uncovered for the length of the prayer, showing that the U. S. have not drifted too far from the respect due the teachings of our forefathers.

These services were very impressive to me . . .

We were invited to a buffet luncheon at the White House immediately following. We were a long time getting out of the jam & a long time finding a cab. We had cards for everything. A card for the windshield of our car, so that we could get in close to the White House. A card to get into the White House. None of these cards were transferable.

We went through several smaller rooms, the hall where there were many paintings of former Presidents and their wives . . . then up a stairway into the rooms where Mrs. Roosevelt was receiving. She was dressed in an afternoon dress of red. We passed another stairway with a heavy grilled gate of iron and a guard standing in front . . . it led to the President's private apartments.

139

We went to the East room . . . a delicious luncheon of ham, tongue in real thin slices, delicious vegetable salad, rolls, ice cream and cakes, and the best hot coffee. Lovely pink rosebuds, maidenhair ferns and freesias, beautiful silver and dishes . . . a lovely setting for all the gay party . . . 1000 attending.

At 4:45 Mrs. Roosevelt with some others gave a tea for between four and five thousand. As we left the White House Nelson Eddy and his wife were directly in front of us. He is a grand looking man and I wanted to touch him just to see if we were both real . . . his little wife looked up and smiled graciously . . . he had on a frock coat and spats.

From here we went to the reviewing stand and sat near the President and his party. Really, for quite country people from Idaho, I felt we were favored.

In the evening we went to a dinner given for Mr. and Mrs. Flynn. He is successor to James Farley as National Chairman. There were several hundred at the dinner . . . at the Mayflower.

Ida reported well. She got names, descriptions of food, decoration and dress; she indicated the numbers attending. She told what inspired her, a rounded person, and it probably inspired others similarly. She was untroubled that she and Carl were not special guests —they were but two in 1500 or in 5000. She was grateful that they had seats in the reviewing stand close to the President and his party—"for quiet country people from Idaho I felt we were favored."

CHAPTER TWENTY-THREE

On May 15, 1941, with full crews working in two shifts, the new mill began turning out lumber. It was a day for rejoicing in McCall—the very sunshine was brighter.

There was another day for rejoicing—if parents can rejoice on losing their last child to another. In July Browns journeyed en masse to Boise for a wedding in the Congregational church on State street, across from the capitol, where Carl Brown gave his daughter Dorothy in marriage to Arlen C. Beyerle.[46]

It began in Sun Valley. Dorothy was employed there one year. A sturdy young stranger arrived from California specifically for the skiing. Now he could have done nothing which in itself would interest a Brown more. Besides, he had steady brown eyes in an olive no-nonsense face; strong hands; and a nature fascinating to one like Dorothy. He understood certain surprising things: the affinities of color, the subtleties of line, and the moods that line and color in alliance can invoke. He knew what makes richness in rooms where people have their being—richness, or serenity, or innocence, any number of things. His mind seemed complicated, not immediately transparent; and Dorothy, when from time to time she looked into it, would look with care, so as to come up with the right answers.

Of German extraction, Beyerle had heard only German spoken in the Dakota classroom of his early school years. However, he was definitely far western in his upbringing. In California he finished grade and high school, and by this time his English was careful and scarcely accented. He next attended college and a private school in interior decorating.

His father was a painter and decorator, and to this work Tuck Beyerle turned when schooling was over. For the next five or six years he bought, re-designed and re-decorated older houses and sold them. However, he must have allowed himself time out for vigorous sports. Pursuing sport at Sun Valley he met—Dorothy.

After the wedding the Beyerles spent a few days in McCall, where Carl took the artistic young man over to where they were building a planer and discovered that he knew what a hammer was for. Then they went to Berkeley, but this did not mean that Dorothy would settle into suburban domesticity, for later the same year Beyerle joined the staff of the United States District Engineers as chief administrator's assistant, and by 1942 he was giving full time to this work. Following America's entry into the European conflict, he was sent to Prince Rupert in British Columbia, about 50 miles from Ketchikan, where he was put in charge of arranging property leases between his government and that of Canada. The property was for military purposes, Prince Rupert being the closest coastal port to Japan. Later he enlisted in the U. S. forces. When he was ordered to remain where he was, Dorothy joined him.[47]

The bombing of Pearl Harbor shocked McCall far more than the declaration of war in 1917, for which the country had been in a measure prepared by the U-boat sinkings of American vessels. Moreover the town was now closely linked to the outside world by rail, plane, highway and radio. Now excited young men rushed to the nearest recruiting stations to sign up and soon disappeared into the maw of fast-changing events. All too soon a few would be heard of by way of a piteous device the Japanese employed. This was permitting prisoners to identify themselves and say a few words over a radio hookup reaching the United States.

Their measured phrases, the anxiety in their voices —who could say whether they were being forced to utter these words about conditions as the price of speaking.

In McCall as elsewhere, radio listeners with spare time kept pencil and paper close, to dash down the home address of a prisoner and the gist of what he said. Then they mailed the information to his family, in case they had missed the broadcast. Some parents, some young wives clung to these wisps of intelligence through months of silence, finally being forced to conclude that "something had happened after that."

Mrs. Les Ulmer, who assisted at the Star, wrote to a Mrs. Steiger in Los Angeles about a message from

Mrs. Steiger's husband, an officer, captured at Corregidor. Mrs. Steiger wrote back that she had received 200 letters, seven recordings and hundreds of phone calls, but not one of the cards her husband said he had sent her. The effect of the messages on America was probably not precisely what Japanese intelligence assumed. It could not have realized how sympathy for the families of these prisoners and the exchange of letters about them would bind Americans together. Your boy became my boy.

CHAPTER TWENTY-FOUR

New Years 1942. Many men had gone. Women took over their jobs and were always tired; anxiety became a habit. However, nature cheerfully started replacing at once the manpower that war siphoned away. In January the second child of the Homer Davies, Philip Evan, was born in Nampa. Homer and Margaret were wholly pleased that it was another boy. Two would be company for each other, etc. By summer, Philip would be big enough to go to McCall and give his grandparents a new thrill.

To the mill office at this time came Margaret Peck, whose husband worked in the United States Forest office. She had lived in McCall long enough to have a pretty good notion of the man who now employed her, and by degrees she was to discover some of his secrets, the less guarded ones. For instance his distaste for fullsome publicity. She observed his nearly unfailing courtesy, his reluctance to speak until he knew, and his way of according respect to every man who worked for him, so that this composite fellow began regarding himself as a pretty good sort, but able possibly to do a little better. Mrs. Peck liked loggers, found them very genuine. As yet they weren't expecting the government to assist them at every turn. Also they were past the riproaring era when a man blew into town on Saturday night for 24 hours of joy and spending, notwithstanding which he was on the job Monday morning. On the job and needing a loan. A loan he could usually get out of Carl.

Like the Brown women, Mrs. Peck found herself belonging to every organization in town *on a work basis.* In Sunday School she had girls aged seven to 10. A little later she would get the same group in Girl Scouts, then again in Job's Daughters. Grown to womanhood, they would show up in the Eastern Star. In the office, Margaret Peck was the contained, efficient secretary, friendly enough, but wherever her employer's business or private affairs were concerned, a sealed and double-locked cabinet.

The war was not cutting into business. All lumber had to be sold subject to government priorities, but the government took plenty. Ordinary citizens could buy lumber only for something essential to the war effort, a provision strictly enforced. This year B T and L added to its timber land on the ridge between McCall and New Meadows 7702 adjacent acres, and the following year nearly twice as much (13,463 acres), making a total of over 22,000 acres to be selectively cut when ready. The land lay in one piece with jogs.[48]

McCall women tried to comply with defense department urgings. They collected aluminum; they stamped their cans flat and turned them in; they salvaged scraps of all kinds and gathered clothing to send to poor Russians. Like other women, Ida Brown saved meat drippings and waste fat to make soap. Much of the time only toilet soap could be found in the stores, and it was useless for laundry purposes, even if in despair the laundress added kitchen cleanser. Edith Vassar made her own soap, and so did Jessie Moloney, her husband Bill helping her stir. The Moloneys hadn't gone to California this winter.

The first McCall man to die in battle, Editor Albin Seaquist of the Star reported, was Clarence McPherson, who was posthumously awarded the DSC with oakleaf cluster. His wife had lived in Warren and on the South Fork. The war was coming closer now.

In April the Yacht club burned, leaving a dismal gap on Main street, and lumber to rebuild called for too great a stretch of imagination for the priority people. The $50,000 loss was not all: $10,000 worth of privately owned boats burned too. A list of the boat owners suggests the popularity McCall had attained as a pleasure-boat harbor: C. W. Gamble, J. L. Driscoll, Bessie Falk, Lester Albert, Dr. Arthur Jones, J. C. Jordan and Alfred Fraser, all of Boise, and Denny Hogue of Nampa.

Without pinning itself down as to when, the Star declared: "The Club will rebuild."

The summer of 1943 saw the initiation on the Idaho Forest, under Supervisor James W. Farrell of the new fire-fighting technique called smoke-jumping, i.e., parachuting a man and equipment into close proximity to a forest blaze. The first experimental jumps had been made in Winthrop, Washington, before 1940. This year, 1943, on July 12, an Idaho man, Rufus Robinson, made an actual jump to a fire in the Nez Perce Forest at Martin creek.

Smoke-jumping invites catastrophe, foreseen and unforeseen, yet in the 17 years of it on the Ida Forest, now the Payette by union with the Weiser, headquartering in McCall, there has never been a casualty *due to the jump*.[49]

It was late in the year, November, when misfortune befell Ida. She and Carl were driving home from Portland. Near La Grande, Oregon, they struck an icy

145

turn. The car skidded, and Ida seized the doorhandle on her side. The door flew open, pulling her with it.

When Carl could get the car stopped, still on four wheels, he found her lying crumpled by the road. Beside himself, hardly remembering the details afterward, he got her to a hospital in La Grande. There they found that she had six broken ribs and a fractured skull.

Carl called all the children. Betty, Warren and Margaret came at once. Dorothy caught a boat from Prince Rupert to Portland, but there her plane reservation to Pendleton was canceled. War priority, she assumed. Anyhow she made it to her mother as fast as she could by other means. Until Ida left the hospital just before Christmas, five long weeks, Dorothy stayed with her.

She and her mother were not particularly alike, but Ida understood her better than anyone else, and influenced her more. The chance to visit seemed one tiny compensation for Ida's misfortune.

Improved if not recovered, Ida was taken home, and for Carl Brown the sun shone again.

War restrictions seemed always to increase, never to fall away. They were in most instances not actually painful, but they were inconvenient for women trying to do their men's work and their own. When illogical they irritated.

Grocery deliveries were so limited to save gas and tires that it seemed simpler to carry things home. No new phones could be secured without a priority. Shoe stamps came, a double dilemma for parents of lively children and for store clerks and waitresses. Shoes wore out before new stamps were issued, and all stout, long-wearing, unfashionable shoes went off the market, or so it seemed. Bed-ridden and inactive people gave away their shoe stamps and enjoyed the good sensation of generosity. Families expecting blessed events sought to get this addition recognized with a stamp book.

Gas and tires came first, then meats, fats, some vegetable proteins, dried fruits, and sugar were restricted. Sheets, dishes of certain types, aluminumware, cotton cloth and clothing were often unobtainable. Store managers who were very brave—or reckless—might admit to favorite women customers that a small shipment of nylons was expected. Sometimes they did come. Sometimes they were high-priced and the weave not very attractive.

Rationing boards were accused of unequal treatment of petitioners. Small people developed big antipathies; nerves splintered. The May Hardware in McCall urged its customers by way of Star advertising to release their tensions by going fishing—with May's tackle, of course.

More news of American war prisoners trickled in. Norman Whitton and Kenneth Johnson had been captured by the Japs on Wake; they wrote from Shanghai prisons. Late in the year Boyd Hayes reported from a prison camp, but his letter had been written *in April*.

The mill had lost some men to the services, and in a few instances women actually took their places. For instance, there was a woman night watchman. One night she thought she heard a duck quacking at the lake edge and suspected somebody was jobbing her. Nevertheless, it was a real enough duck, wild and fat, that had come in contact with a high tension wire and been knocked out. When it recovered, it couldn't remember where it was.

Another woman employee was asked what she had been doing this morning at the mill. "Shooting the bull and feeding the hog," she said.

Women became proficient meat cutters; they drove delivery trucks that only men had handled before. One garage had a woman mechanic. Where farm and ranch help was scarce, women took over unquestioningly.

This year B T and L did a record cut of railroad ties, 300,000. If war materials were to roll, roadbeds must be maintained.

In December Homer Davies enlisted in the United States Navy, and was commissioned an ensign. Facing Christmas alone, Margaret brought her two little boys to McCall, to an apartment.

Jayne Brown became head of the McCall Red Cross War Fund, and Betty Harwood became Valley county chairman for the same drive. The county the previous year had ranked highest in the state in per capita giving, and now Betty and her lieutenants readied to outdo their own record. No one responded more warmly than the Finn population centered south of McCall, who held their own Red Cross auction. One specialty at this sale was wool socks. Sometimes a single Finn hand, probably a woman's, had sheared the sheep, carded the wool, spun, dyed and knitted it. One such pair of socks sold and resold brought $1300.

At Lake Fork, also strongly Finn, Mrs. Bill Ax turned in for her small district not the $75 quota but all of $193. The county total, on a quota of $4800, came to a wonderful figure when all the returns were in: $8189.91.

In this year, there passed to his certain reward, W. B. Boydstun. He came to Roseberry in 1890, to the lake in 1903. Particularly in better roads and better schools, he had left a mark on the community.

As the year closed in, McCall felt more tightly knit in spirit, each more concerned for the other, than it had ever been. People's chief worries were their boys, or their neighbors' boys in service, and the course of the war. Parents of 15- and 16-year-olds looked at them wistfully and wondered if they would have to go too.

It was a blessing not to be overlooked in nightly prayers that McCall had a war-essential industry and a steady payroll. Some improvements had been made at the mill, and experiments were always being tried to hasten the thaw of ice in the lake log-pond. The faster the thaw the sooner the mill resumed.[50]

CHAPTER TWENTY-FIVE

In England it was June 4, 1944, early in the morning hours. In McCall it was still yesterday. Supreme Commander Dwight Eisenhower started across the English channel a striking force of tremendous size and fire-power, backed up by 4000 boats and 11,000 planes. In an order of the day to troops under his command the general said: "Let us beseech the blessings of Almighty God on this great and noble undertaking." As soon as the first authentic word that this was it reached McCall, its people sat tied to their radios.

There had been more deaths reported. Private Willard Gribble was missing and word came later that he had been killed—he was with Patton in France. Mrs. Morris C. Crawford heard from her husband that he was well, and she also received the Purple Heart awarded him. Then came word that he had died.

Three McCall women had enlisted: Winona May Furrey, daughter of the Roy Mays, a yeoman 3rd class; Jean Evelyn Lansing, daughter of the Ralph Lansings, with the WAVES; and Mrs. Gordon Hood, a WAC. Editor Seaquist of the Star was putting in 10 hours a day, five days a week, in Carl Brown's mill. In addition he set type, ran the press and wrote news. Keeping up his readers' morale through news and cheerful editorials would have seemed job enough.

Word came that Newcomb McCall, a captain in the airforce, had been awarded the Distinguished Service Cross for bravery above the call of duty. And this was

149

not all. The following year the captain admitted to his grandmother, Martha Newcomb, that he was an aide to General Robert Fredericks, 7th army in Italy, and that there were some other citations, like parachute wings and golden star for combat jump, the purple heart, the bronze star for participation in American defense in the Pacific theatre, four stars for European service and an infantryman's badge. Newcomb McCall's comment, "Dear God, what a collection."

The winter brought word that Seabee Eugene Maki had been killed in the Philippines. His two brothers, Eino and Edward, were also in the service. John Kangas, another Finn, a waist gunner on a flying fortress, was reported missing in action.

CHAPTER TWENTY-SIX

Perhaps the constant struggle to be prepared for bad news plus myriad other tensions made McCallites turn for relief to rumor that "the monster" was active again in the lake. In July 1944 Walter Bowling saw what he though was four large fish disporting themselves, then discovered that they were connected separate humps of something 35 feet long that moved with an undulating sweep. It seemed to be covered by a protecting case or shell.

A Nampa woman, Mrs. George Van de Steeg, saw it about the same time, with binoculars. A theory circulated that the monster made its home in a section of the lake warmed by subterranean hot springs, and that it ventured to the surface only after warm weather made the upper waters pleasant.

A week later the supposed fish was seen by five different observers, and a man from Twin Falls took a picture of it—the whereabout of the picture seemed unknown. Some thought that what they saw resembled sturgeon often taken from the Snake river, though these fish were generally smaller.[51] Credence was added to the sturgeon idea when P. J. McDermott, a former conservation officer, stated that 20 years ago some fertilized sturgeon eggs had indeed been planted in the lake.

After that Matt Heikkola, a mill employee, reported watching the monster not for just a few seconds but for a good half hour, as it disported itself at the Narrows. Finally the creature selected a professional observer and exhibited himself to the editor of the Star. Walking along the shore near the mill, Seaquist noted a great commotion in the water, like a stream before it goes over a dam. Moreover, he saw something new, specific color, a greenish yellow. Others had mentioned iridescence, if the creature was in full sun.

If any of the hardy-minded Browns glimpsed the monster they did not go to the press with it. They seldom went to the press anyhow. Moreover Carl and Ida had something else to think about just now, a sixth grandchild. The Tuck Beyerles were still living at Prince Rupert, Tuck with the district engineers; but Dorothy, intending that their first-born should be American in every sense, had come home. Thus Karyl Lynn was born in Boise, September 21.

Homer Davies, who had been serving on a destroyer in the Atlantic, the USS Alden, stopped in McCall for the briefest of visits with his family. He came; he was gone; Margaret was hardly sure he had been there at all. His new berth was communications school at Harvard.

In McCall teachers were hard to get and harder to keep. Men teachers had virtually disappeared. The gap was filled by the return of qualified women teachers who had retired. When these were used up, the call went out for permit teachers. Grandmothers responded. Still there weren't enough, especially in the country schools.[52]

At the time that temporary consolidation with Donnelly was effected, Betty Harwood had consented to serve on the school board, but now they needed her for a high school teacher as well. Young Stan was in school himself, so Betty consented. At the same time she resigned from the board.

CHAPTER TWENTY-SEVEN

On January 4, 1945, after the longest run it had ever made, the mill closed for the winter. Lumber sales were still government controlled, but regardless of the fact that under such conditions local advertising had small value, businessman Brown encouraged the Star by taking space to say that he *couldn't* sell lumber. Not anyhow to buyers not holding rated certificates from the AAA county war board, or an approved certificate from the War Production board.

Karyl Lynn Beyerle was nearly four months old. Dorothy, as an employee of the government at Prince Rupert, had arranged for her own return there, but nobody had arranged for Karyl Lynn. And this took doing. When Karyl was cleared, Betty and Ted drove Dorothy to Vancouver to catch a boat. Dorothy didn't attempt a flight this time. No sense in risking another cancellation, not with a little girl in your arms.

Ensign Homer Davies hurried to McCall for what was hardly more than a look-in on his family. However, this now included a third sturdy boy, Glendon Homer, born the previous October. Three boys would be more company for each other than two, etc., etc. If Homer had hoped for a daughter this time, no one could tell it. He and Margaret managed a little holiday in Boise by themselves. Carl and Ida had also put in some of the quiet months in the capital, where their circle of friends always widened—Carl's business associates and former legislative friends, people who spent their summers in McCall, and others who regarded the Browns as genuine and unique.

They appeared to be experienced and wise, even if they had lived in a village, people who could be gay and communicative as well as serious. Carl particularly liked dancing, although Ida's Baptist conscience still spoke to her on this subject. Cards they both enjoyed.

Sometimes they were guests of Margaret Cobb Ailshie, who had visited them at the Shiefer ranch and now published the Statesman. Carl enjoyed the Arid club, a good place to meet business friends, where he had been a member for some time. The club's name was not to be taken literally. At a luncheon and bridge party given in the elegant Crystal ballroom of the Hotel Boise by Mrs. Charles Gosset, wife of the governor, Ida won high score. Other women of social importance at the capital also entertained her, but none of this went to her head.

They weren't forgetting the war or being extravagant. They were, however, leaving responsibility to Warren. No one believed that the war could go on much longer. Something colossal somewhere was about to give, to go crashing headlong. Now in succession and rapidly, the battle of the Bulge, the battle of the Ruhr. Montgomery freeing most of Holland and driving into Hamburg. Only 250 miles separated the allies in the West from the Red army in the East. The U. S. third army with units of the French army was advancing upon Hitler's last redoubt in Bavaria.

Before the first of April Carl and Ida returned to McCall. Carl was at home when shocking word came of the death of President Roosevelt. As national committeeman Carl had not opposed a fourth term, although he knew that the chance of the President's collapse with the war approaching final fury was horribly possible. The recent pictures of him, even though only the best were allowed printed . . . To Carl, Roosevelt was one of the greats; he would always be that. He was thrilled when he read the eulogy of Winston Churchill to the House of Commons: "There died the greatest American friend we have ever known, and the greatest champion of human freedom who had ever brought help and comfort from the New World to the Old."

In St. Paul's Cathedral, preserved by miracle in devastated London, King George, the Queen, and Princess Elizabeth attended a memorial service in the President's honor.

A newspaper account said: "Marines standing in the gallery over the great west door blew 'The Last Post.' The bugle notes flew up the great dome to throb and echo there with their quick calls to our everyday world, and the long enigmatic questioning at the end. Nowhere do the bugles call so searchingly as they do in the great dome of St. Paul's."

In McCall, as it was all over the country, apprehension accompanied shock and grief. The Ladies Aid of the Community church, seeing no other way to convey its sorrow, postponed its carnival.

The greater shock, accompanied at first by more fear than rejoicing, was reserved for a day in August. Over Hiroshima on August 6 flew a lone B-29 carrying a small bomb—small that is by later comparison. The plane released this bomb. In the midst of the horror that its fall created, President Truman issued to the Japanese government an ultimatum, surrender. Officially at least, the ultimatum was ignored. On the 8th, a second bomb, improved, was readied.

A plane, the Great Artiste, flew over Nagasaki. Again an object was dropped. There was a giant flash and a blue-green light across the whole sky. Then came a blast wave which shook the Great Artiste from

154

nose to tail. Four more blasts came up, like the boom of cannon.

In great boiling rings rose a dreadful ball of fire, then a shooting pillar of purple that mounted 10,000 feet, and all this in 45 seconds.[53]

On August 10 President Truman again warned Japan. More of these atomic bombs—the country was beginning now to recognize the term—would be dropped unless there was immediate surrender. The Japanese government agreed, provided the Emperor retain his sovereignty, to accept certain terms. On August 14 these terms were arranged, and the most powerful fleet the world had ever known moved into Tokyo bay. Paratroopers and marines landed on soil that had known no invader for more than a thousand years. On September 2, surrender documents were signed.

In McCall the first joyful news had been signaled by the ringing of the bell in the Community church. People were partially prepared by the news of the two bombs, and the continued clanging of the bell assured them that surrender had really come. Some rushed to the nightclubs, but more hurried out to meet their neighbors on the street, to press hands and rejoice together. At the mill men dropped their work and went to town, impelled by the need to be with others, especially anybody with a boy in the Pacific theatre. Businesses that didn't supply food or drinks closed for the day. A few people went to their churches and prayed.

To McCall people as to all others, the implications of the atomic bomb almost overpowered the peace it brought. As details of its awful power spread by newspapers and radio, people shivered. Might the release of such force not shake the very earth on its axis? Produce earthquakes and tidal waves? Revolutionize climate by shaking the polar ice caps loose? Even destroy its creator?

Man assumed that *up to now* he had Nature pretty well controlled. But maybe not. Maybe Nature would retaliate. Of if not Nature, God. Angry at man's impudence, or sickened by his cruelties, God might now loose his own fateful lightnings and burn everything to dust.

It would be weeks before the complete story of the bomb and its construction was released. Meanwhile there were the accounts by eye-witnesses of the unearthly spectacle, and the incredible destruction it sowed. Over the bomb itself people did no rejoicing; they shook. On Earth time had moved out of its billion-year routine into a new frightful relativity. Nothing would ever be the same again.

To Chester Stephens the freeing of American prisoners from Manila jails brought happy news. His brother Lawrence had been captured in the fall of Bataan. He was chief commissary steward on the battleship Quail, which was scuttled by her crew to keep her out of enemy hands. In prison Lawrence had lived for three years on a diet of rice.

V. J. day did not bring jubilation to everyone. As one GI after another came home—and why did it take them so long!—the rejoicing of their families somehow heightened the grief of those whose boys would never return. While the war was still in fury, the bereft had been able to push back the thought; now it must be faced. Some hadn't even the comfort of knowing that their veteran was dead. Maybe he was imprisoned somewhere under conditions too hideous to imagine, hoping, hoping in vain.

Two men who had been on Wake Island were believed dead, George Dean and Orville Kelso. Otis Morris at Warren received word that his only son Orland had been massacred with others in a Jap prison camp in the Philippines.

Bus Johnson came home. Only two months after he enlisted he had found himself on the seas. His ship, the Boise, was credited with sinking six Jap ships in the battle of Savo Island off Guadalcanal. After the Mediterranean campaign, the Boise returned to the South

Pacific and fought its way up, island by island. Bus had many medals.

Boyd Hayes, grandson of W. B. Boydstun, had been a construction worker on Wake. Now Boyd came home. In Portland he saw his son, four years old, on whom he'd never yet laid eyes. Joe Bayok, another Wake Islander, was so ill during the three years he was in a Jap prison that he was once reported dead. Kenneth Johnson had spent three years in a camp near Shanghai, one supposed to provide kindlier treatment because it was more under the eyes of the world. Its inmates got unsalted rice and soybean gruel. Later Johnson was transferred to other camps, once in a ship's hold so crowded men couldn't lie down. In one camp he encountered a Dr. Y. Shindo, a yellow man with white understanding, who used his own money to buy medicines for sick Americans.

In October Lieutenant jg Homer Davies was honorably discharged. He came home but shortly went to Seattle to report for reinduction.

Mrs. Austin Goodman was about town with a sunburn. She hadn't burned while basking on any beaches, but driving a tractor on her son's farm. On days that she didn't drive, she worked at the Red Cross.

For a while yet women would be doing men's work.

CHAPTER TWENTY-EIGHT

Even though meat was rationed during the war years, less hunting went on around McCall. Perhaps this had gradually brought about an imbalance in nature. At any rate bear had increased in numbers, or grown bolder, or both. Rosamond West, looking out a back window at her parents' home a block from school, saw a live bear. Excited, she called her sister and together they watched it climb the back steps. It meanwhile noted them, and the girls returned stare for stare. Finally it left, and the girls went out and laid a board over one of its tracks for proof. The track when measured was eight inches long.

Asa Clements living a mile east of town saw a big mean-looking bear in his yard and went for it with all he had, a shotgun blast. The bear tried to attack, took a second round of shot and withdrew.

McCall people didn't at all mind these indications that they still lived on the edge of the Primitive. They liked living *where it was different*, where life had color.

Right at the golf course near town Tech. Sgt. Carl Seiber killed a bear with a .22, though he had to re-load twice. Mrs. Charles Tinsley had seen the same bear rooting in a sack of empty tins and thought it was a horse. Her three-year-old daughter had been play-ing there a few minutes before. The bear's pelt was just under six feet long.

At B T and L everything was booming, orders hard to keep up with. Business of all kinds had waited with patience for lumber. People had waited to build houses, even to effect simple repairs. Now they were eager to catch up fast.

The road to Stibnite, where strategic ores were mined in great quantity, had been finished. Forest Supervisor Farrell believed it would open up 300 mil-lion board feet of merchantable Ponderosa pine to be cut under Forest supervision in a perpetual plan. About this road there had been heated and lengthy public discussion, whether it should go in from Cas-cade or from McCall. Some souls said that if it con-nected with McCall, Brown Tie and Lumber would profit too much.

Dr. Don Numbers, a man who had reason to be in-terested in roads, wrote this to the Payette Lakes Star: "As for Carl Brown's wanting the road mostly to get out timber, if Brown's future operations along this line are as wholly beneficial to so many others as in the past, then give us the road and the timber and a few more Carl Browns."

Dr. Numbers' errands of mercy had been done with and without roads. In December 1927 he made a trip by dogsled from McCall to the Wordenhoff mine between Warren and Edwardsburg to save the life of a 20-year-old boy, Emmett Routson, too ill with influenza and pneumonia, to be moved. Numbers and Roy Stover started out together, covered the first lap to Burgdorf in four and one half hours. The dogs they drove were picked from the teams of Stover,[54] Warren Brown and Frenchy Yriberry. Some of them were unused to the trail and before they reached Burgdorf their feet were badly cut. At this stop the men picked up two extra dogs and in Warren three. Now 60 miles from McCall they had yet to cross Elk summit, 8672 feet high; and the mine was 25 miles beyond that. They made it through, and when the doctor had done all he could for the boy and left medicines, he and Stover started back. A snowstorm raged, but in 15 hours they were in Warren. Relays of men had helped them—Brad Carey, Fred Sheifer, Bill Roden and the sick boy's father, John Routson. Across the eight-mile bare stretch of the South Fork, Dan Levan brought his mules to help.

Three years later Numbers was called at night to make another mercy run. J. D. Monroe, a 70-year-old mining man, was suffering from internal hemorrhage. The phone call said he had been carried by toboggan to Burgdorf. This time the doctor started at midnight with his own five dogs, reached Secesh in three hours, but had to stop because his dogs, not yet toughened in, were in trouble. He backtracked three miles to an old cabin, rested the dogs and left one there, going on with four. About daylight he was over the summit and down to the resort. He had come prepared to operate but decided his patient was too old.

He did what he could and remained until the man was better.

The Boise Statesman in recounting the story referred to Numbers as "famous in this section for a half dozen rescue efforts." An anonymous writer for Newspaper Enterprises wrote a piece about the doctor that probably went all over the country.

As late as 1939 Dr. Numbers was still saving the isolated sick, now by plane. To Harald Hill at the Golden Anchor mine he first flew medicine and a hypodermic so Hill could be packed over a mountain. Piloted by Chick Walker, the doctor flew to Burgdorf and brought Hill out. Number's wife Zoe, who wasn't a nurse but liked to help in the office, didn't worry even when the doctor was away over long. The U. S. Forest phone lines were a life-saver, and Grace Hoff, operator, "kept the key open" for emergencies.

While dogs were still in use, the doctor kept as many as 12 at times. They were Labradors, setters, not huskies. He drove them every morning for exercise, often as far as Sylvan beach.

A big event was due. Lyle Watts, who had been supervisor of the Idaho Forest from 1922 to 1925 and since 1943 chief of the United States Forest Service, arrived for an unofficial visit. Forest men from Boise, from Ogden, from all quarters came to honor him at a stag dinner and reception. With Forest men Carl and Warren Brown had always enjoyed highly satisfactory relations. Not only was it to a lumberman's advantage to cooperate, especially in modern timber harvesting techniques, but such was the personal quality of Foresters that to know them as friends was rewarding. Moreover McCall felt it was surely in some small way responsible for Watts' rise.

During the Chief Forester's stay Ida and Carl had him to dinner with many additional guests, a kind of entertaining they both loved. As a host Carl was his best self, and Ida knew how to make those at her table feel admired and honored.

McCall women enlistees were among the last to come home. Winona Furrey visited her parents, the Roy Mayses, then returned to her base in Shoemaker, California. Luella Meldrum, a WAVE who had enlisted in Boise and was stationed in Oklahoma, came with her parents, the Harvey Meldrums, for a visit.

Mrs. Homer Davies went to San Francisco to see her husband. Later he was discharged, and they moved back to Nampa, where he resumed managership of the Davies Hardware and began involving himself in community chores.

With building materials available now, a new Yacht club rose on the site of the burned one, this time of brick, not ties. Again the street looked whole.

And now it was Christmas time again. For the first time since the war, the Forest Service celebrated with a Yule party. It was held in the Finn Hall at Lake Fork, and though winter had set in early, people came from as far away as Weiser. How wonderful to get everybody together again, especially in the lake country, a Christmas card itself.

CHAPTER TWENTY-NINE

Spring 1946, but around the lake it was still ski season. The Payette Lakes Star noted that Stanley Harwood, eight years old, had won the championship trophy in the Bill Brown Junior ski tournament on a 1500-foot course through 27 sets of slalom gates on McCall's Number 1 hill. Just as dogsled racing had made small Warren Brown a celebrity, so now skiing would put into headlines another generation of

Browns, and start them even earlier. For the next 15 years Stan and his cousin Frank, a month his junior, would race each other almost meet for meet.

Even at eight the boys were wholly different in appearance and temperament. At any age Stan was a big boy, Frank slight. One seemed outgoing, the other reserved. There is no law that cousins shall be inseparable friends, especially cousins the same age, crazy about the same spectacular sport, cousins growing up in the same town, sometimes living next door to each other. Yet remarkably the boys were on good terms, simply looking at life from different angles.

In the Cougar derby that spring McCallites enjoyed another reminder that their environment was still untamed. For some reason a judge in a faraway state—Tennessee, no less—had offered $100 to the Idaho hunter who turned in the greatest number of cougar kills in the winter of 1945-46. The state also paid a bounty of $50 on any cougar killed at any time within its boundaries—killing one in some other state and transporting him across the line to collect in Idaho was not considered quite honest.

A Garden Valley man proved he had killed 18 cougars, and others did away with 14 and 10. Anyone with the slightest knowledge of the beast must have been pleased. This lithe, tawny six-foot cat is not charming. He is a killer, not as wanton as a bear, but still remorseless. He kills sheep, calves, pigs, fawns, even range horses, and follows school children walking home. His pelt isn't even prized much—only his demise is pleasing.

Ida Brown had never forgotten how a cougar sounded on the South Fork, especially if she and Betty were alone. Its cry always seemed to come after dark had fallen, and it was like the wailing of a woman in agony.

In May a landmark at the mill, the office building, was moved down the highway to become the Tuck Beyerle Photo and Art Shop. The Beyerles had returned to the states and settled into a home on the south shore of the lake. Starting now, Tuck advanced by degrees into the status-conscious, half-mystic field of interior decorating. At first he made trips from McCall to wherever his counsel and services were desired. Later he set up an establishment in Boise, first move in a large and engrossing adventure with the decorative arts.

To replace the outgrown office building there rose a two-story-and-basement structure with the affable look of a modern cottage. However, it housed a 14 x 16 foot fireproof concrete vault protected by walls 14 inches thick. Its crank-type phones, knotty pine interiors and its windows looking out on the lake still implied that primitive living lay not farther away than the nearest blue ridge.

A survey made at this time for The Gryphon, publication of the United Pacific Insurance company, set forth some significant facts and figures about B T and L.

For several years the mill had averaged an annual cut of 22 million board feet, yet in the region there was an estimated 10 billion feet of lumber in-the-tree. Because of the terrain where it stood, not more than a fifth could ever be logged. Or so it appeared.[57]

However, with its 22,000 acres of virgin timber west of town, B T and L was not worrying about scarcities. By this year it had supplied the Union Pacific with 2,500,000 ties, and this was only 50 percent of its production. Some of the 100 million board feet of lumber it turned out had been shipped as far as New England. An example of mill efficiency was the handling of ties. Leaving the pond in the log, within a few minutes by one continuous operation a tree became cross-ties in a railroad car. An innovation by Joe Kasper allowed the mechanized sorting of lumber direct from edger and trimmer, then stacking by dimension in racks ready to be loaded for the dry kiln.

The plant at this time consisted of six buildings: mill, planer, power plant, machine shop, kiln and truck repair shop. The repair shop was equipped to handle anything up to jammers and dual axle trucks. On the payroll were 160 people, drawing $338,000.

For two terms Carl Brown had avoided state politics, but in the June 1945 primary 94 voters wrote him in for senator from Valley county. The regularly filed Republican candidates together polled only 104 votes. However, the rising Republican tide ran strong throughout the state, and in the November election Carl defeated Republican C. L. Schoenhut of Cascade by only 18 votes—782 to 764. Just after election Carl had a serious attack of asthma, his first real illness in years; and he and Ida left for the warmer airs of Arizona. He was confident he could return in time for the opening of the legislature in January. As to the mill, he had no worries—Warren was there.

As it always did, the mighty cold came down, closing the mill but bringing ski snow. At Ski hill it lay 53.2 inches deep. During the Christmas holidays the Brown grandchildren, along with all the other McCall kids, skied every day to exhaustion. They skied, they warmed up in the ski house, they rushed out and skied while light lasted.

Now the mill would certainly close, and the fact brought back to Warren Brown once more the nagging conviction that there was some way to keep the lake from freezing around the pond logs—if one could just hit on it. Ashes on the ice hadn't helped. Now he tried blasting, with hardly more effect. When the mercury dropped to 18 degrees below there was nothing to do but let the fires die.

CHAPTER THIRTY

Spring in McCall is more brilliant than anywhere else. The vapor scarves that have been tangled in the thick firs and tamaracks begin pulling themselves free to rise slowly. As they lift, distant ridges emerge against the sky. Behind these white peaks begin to assert themselves. Then the sun bursts from its bondage and suddenly a soft warm breeze flows into town.

While the lawns are still spongy the streets and walks grow firm, and the winter-bound population comes out to hear music, the music of water trickling under snowbanks. Tomorrow green shoots will poke tentatively through the wet earth. Where snow lies so long, so long, the odors of spring are sublimely sweet.

Ida Brown had always loved flowers. Over the years she tried out many species for their resistance to cold and ability to get a quick start in a season always short. Iris, gladioli and roses were her best growers, and she gave lavish cuttings and roots of these to other gardeners. Each year the town yards were more brilliant, and Ida's friends thought of this as her warm and colorful personality extended from neighbor to neighbor.

In 1936 Chester Stephens had married a widow with two boys and a girl, a happy move for everybody. Chester and his wife both loved flowers, and once took four first prizes in the McCall flower show that the Progressive club had founded.[59]

Another flower lover was Ernie Watkins, head saw filer at B T and L. He had begun to feel the oppressive length of the winters—nothing green in the landscape but *evergreens*. Nothing blooming. So he set up a window box, a long one, in the saw loft and experimented with seeds and slips his friends gave him. In the loft the light, warmth and humidity seemed just right, and before long he had fuchsias, gardenias, poinsettias, gloxinias and even orchids blooming. Whenever his wife or daughter needed a corsage for a party, Ernie had the makings. And at all times he had this wonderment to share with visitors.

Just as the gardens were coming into bloom that spring, McCall lost one well loved. For 43 years, when there was either no doctor in town or a very busy one, Valeria McFall had served as a midwife. Two of Ida Brown's children owed their first glimpse of the world to her expert hands; to Ida she was an angel. Now at 88 she was gone. In her honor the local order of the Eastern Star, of which Ida was a charter member, renamed itself the Valeria chapter.

Newly rebuilt and ready for business, the Yacht club that spring suffered the jolt that any spot may expect if games of chance are played on a real scale. Thieves looted it and the Annex club, taking $8,500 in merchandise. This included slot machines worth $6000, bought in preparation for the opening of the house. For the Annex, which lost five machines with their cash contents, this was the second such irritation. The indignant owners of the two clubs offered $1000 reward for information leading to, etc., without results.

By mid-summer McCall was more wide awake, more lively than it had ever been. At the mill the roar of machinery was steady. In town business felt the impact of the visitor wave. Cabins and hotels were full of tourists and conventioneers. Camps and beaches swarmed with picknickers and sun bathers. Self-conscious women in incredible shorts crowded the grocery store aisles.

A single big day for nearly everybody was the Fourth of July. It was by no means the Fourth Ida and Carl saw during their first years in McCall, when it lasted three days, during which the three saloons ran practically dry. Horse racing then brought crowds

166

from Long valley and Meadows valley, and at night there was some letting off of firearms as well as fireworks. Sometimes the cowboys riding home after it was all over shot out windows along the way.

Now the celebration was mostly carnivals, boat racing, water skiing, picnics and dances. As chief of police Chester Stephens had found that some discretion was best in dealing with those breakers of the peace who during the war had been restrained overlong. People came to McCall, he thought, not really to make trouble—nine out of ten anyhow—but to relax and be happy. If you told them firmly that they'd better sober up or quiet down, they'd usually comply. You didn't have to arrest them. And by evening they'd be pretty tired anyhow, though not too tired to dance. Chester himself often sold dance tickets for some organization like the Legion. Five or six hundred tickets. People would eat, dance, eat again, drink some, go sit by the lake in the shadows, finally call it a day.

The only person Chester had trouble with this day was Ida Brown. Trouble about her driver's examination. He was with her in her car, and they were coming from Lenore street onto the highway. There stood a stop sign, perfectly visible, but Ida didn't stop. Probably Chester was telling her something interesting.

"Ida," he exclaimed, "Stop means stop!"

He made her go back around the block and approach the highway again. She would never again make that turn without thinking of Chester.

CHAPTER THIRTY-ONE

This was the year that reorganization of the school system in Idaho began to make country grade schools obsolete and also to group two or more small high schools into one. It sharpened in McCall the unwelcome fact that its high school students had to be sent to Donnelly. McCall longed to have its own school and would be wholly willing to take in other students. It felt that any consolidated high school should be set up where it would serve the area best. Obviously that place was McCall. Once it could have taken such action—with the consent of the immediate school patrons; now it would have to get the consent of a wide district. No longer was it a simple bonding question; stopping everything now was the hard roadblock of community rivalry. Donnelly would certainly prefer to have the status quo maintained.

Brad Carrey writing in the Star asked plaintively why it couldn't be arranged "to return our school back where it belongs."

Lavor Chapin, now editor of the paper, reasoned: "The bitter truth is that any other community of comparable size or larger in this section of the state has more to offer . . . New Meadows, Cascade, Donnelly and Council all have educational plants far superior to McCall's. Are we to assume that they are richer? That their people are more progressive?"

He ran both editorial and factual material about school needs, and carried a Frankly Speaking column designed to draw out public sentiment.

It is significant that though the Brown grandchildren living in McCall could have been sent off to private schools, no such move was made. Warren and Jayne, Betty and Ted would have regarded that as an

168

Ansgar Johnson Photo

Breezy Point on Payette Lake as it looks when the summer crowd comes to McCall.

**Left: Little Payette Lake on a fall day before the waterlilies have felt the cold.
Right: Warren and Jayne Jones Brown at the time of their marriage.**

**Left: The brawling south fork of the Payette, a stream that is the delight of fishermen.
Right: The skycar of the skagit, lifting timbers out of a lofty pocket.**

evasion of responsibility. The thing to do was to attack the school problem, not by-pass it. For Warren this meant serving on the school board, where he would have to keep constantly at patrons to get action, ever seek new ways of approaching the problem, and meanwhile accept criticism without sign of rancor.

The school war was not over quickly. It would be fought through one bond election after another, Donnelly determined to keep the district high school, outlying areas dividing into factions on the issue. Country storekeepers would be boycotted for their stand. It would be said aloud, angrily, "This is one thing Warren Brown is not going to get."

Meanwhile, within 13 months, three more Brown grandchildren, all girls, arrived to further solidify the clan. To Tuck and Dorothy Beyerle on May 27, 1946, was born a little maid who set a new pattern in one respect among cousins, uncles and aunts. Her eyes were not the Brown blue, which is often a highly bluish blue, but brown, like her father's. A not too scientific theory makes blue-eyed people executives, brown-eyed people dreamers and artists. As to Susan Jennifer the only certainty was her looks and bearing, both eminently satisfactory.

To Betty and Ted Harwood on October 15, 1946, was born Karen Ann, a child who would start independent action as soon as she could walk. At four she skied. At eight she walked the top bar of the back yard gym set, like the aerialists she had seen the previous afternoon at the Shrine Circus in Boise.

To Homer and Margaret Davies on June 17, 1947, was born Sharon Margaret, their fourth child, first daughter, and Homer was so overwhelmed at this signal good fortune when first shown the little girl that the nurse said to herself there must be an error in the mother's record, this *must* be a first-born.

On April 22, 1946, the ice in the lake broke up at 11:05 p.m., as indicated by an electric clocking device mounted on a float and daily inspected. In earlier times, the day, hour and minute had been determined by something more simple, a floating cask that would bob to shore when finally released by melting ice. This year over a thousand dollars in prizes had been offered to ticket buyers making guesses on the break-up time. The winner, a stranger in town, was only one minute off. Second place went to Pearl Boydstun, four minutes off; and Mrs. Boydstun did something typical of local generosity and pride: she offered her $200 toward a better school for Lardo-McCall children.

This was the summer that the ever-entertaining ladies of the Women's Progressive club found themselves in that old predicament, the embarrassing situation. That is, they had no funds. However the ladies seemed not too greatly embarrassed, and besides the Star came to their aid. The Star said citizens should turn in and help the club, because it had always had but one object, helping the town. For one thing, see what it had done about the cemetery.

A Cemetery Maintenance district had been engineered in June after long, arduous labors by Betty Harwood and her committee of Nelle Tobias, who operated summer cottages, and Mrs. William Reitmeier, wife of the Congregational minister. The Club then had the grounds cleaned; and the committee took on the job of identifying unmarked graves and bringing the record book up to date. Identification hadn't been easy. When other means failed, Betty appealed through the Star for information. Now the work could begin, placing on every grave that had neither stone nor headboard a rectangular copper marker.

One little grave stopped them. It was known to contain the body of a child that lived its brief span during the excitement of the mill fire. The father was a transient bartender, and he and his wife departed shortly leaving behind them only an unmarked mound in the cemetery.

170

CHAPTER THIRTY-TWO

In the midst of the school dilemma, a new institution was to rise in McCall and become quite celebrated, both for its outstanding appearance and urbane esprit, and as a focus for recreation and big gatherings of people. This institution was Shore Lodge.

In announced plans, Carl Brown was named president of the board of directors, men who for the most part were out-of-towners with substantial business relations. Virgil McGee of Boise was named executive manager. Presently a contract was let to C. B. Lauchs Construction company of Boise for work to start immediately at a spot on the lake shore just west of the bridge. Mr. McGee stated that an analysis of travel and vacation trends revealed that people were not seeking a night club or glamor type resort, but wholesome recreation and good service. Shore Lodge would conform to this trend, etc., etc., and accordingly *wholesome* and *service* became catchwords.

In the imagination of the directors, appeal would extend far beyond region and state. Shore Lodge would attract southern and eastern patronage. And why not. Here was the unsurpassed: view, sunshine, and a setting for summer and winter sports close to the great, mysterious Primitive area. Highways were good now, air travel possible, so why not go after the trade, the well-heeled trade.

To outsiders stock was offered discreetly, but the Brown family probably retained a good deal of it.

Victor Jones and Associates were employed as architects, and presently a newspaper picture showed Carl Brown, Mrs. Lloyd Lovegreen—her husband was one of the architects—and Mrs. McGee holding spades ready to start scooping earth at a place where, eventually, alfresco dining would be offered.

171

Surrounded by great pines, Shore Lodge rose, substantial and restrained. If the builders listened, the pines seemed to be murmuring, "Quiet! Quiet! We have already been here a long time."

From the approach side, the Lodge had an air of actual starkness, due to the cavernous entrance and the small windows cut into the timber walls. However, these windows served only hallways or offices. On the opposite side, every room looked out through unhindered glass to lake and mountains. In the diningroom, at lake level, the sweep was interrupted only by concrete columns that supported the ends of massive ceiling beams.

In lobby, lounge and diningroom, slightly exaggerated fireplaces of stone slabs again announced: "Simplicity."

Banquet and convention rooms occupied one wing, and convenient to the diningroom was a bar and clubroom. On the main floor an arcade of shops for sports wear, gifts and women's whims emulated the style and exclusiveness of similar shops in famous metropolitan hotels. There would be a drugstore, and, so the brochure implied, a resident physician and dentist.

Besides its fireplace, accessible bar, copper paneled beams and view of the lake, the diningroom had another distinction. It had been decorated by Mrs. McGee, and part of the decor was a genuine mural, painted on two walls that met at right angles. It was so real that an actual battle, as if seen through a window, seemed to be taking place.

Painted by Jack Flynn, a southern Idaho artist, the picture purported to record a fight on the narrow wooden bridge that once spanned the lake outlet. The driver of a loaded freight wagon and the driver of the New Meadows stage had raced their horses side by side for the bridge—and tied. Violently. Lard and flour spilling from the wagon churned into dough in the rough waters beneath the bridge. Lard, flour, water—dough. Lard-dough, Lardo. Thus the name for the nearby settlement.

Details of background buildings, somewhat Grandma Moses in perspective, were taken from a snapshot dated 1900 belonging to Neal Boydstun. The stage pictured belonged to Frenchy Yriberry, whose name was pronounced as if it began with W, and it was so spelled on the stage, Wyberry.

If anyone has ever said of the mural, "How artistic!" he hasn't been heard, but the furious action of Flynn's horses and the boneless grace of his humans is very diverting. Public taste in its recurring cycles will enjoy or ignore the mural. At some distant day, unless covered up meanwhile by a new decorator, it will become Idaho Americana.

The lobby was given exactly the same view as the diningroom, but here in summer sandy-footed swim-clad vacationers would startle staid Easterners, and in winter wool-swathed skiers would bolt in to leave wet spots on the floor. For quiet charm, the diningroom was the place to go.

It did more for the Lodge than any other part of it. The mural did not dominate, the general coloring was soft, and the massiveness of the building seemed to discourage noise. There was a kind of spell, felt when one made the turn on the stairway. It was nothing like the old enchantment at Payette Lakes Inn, yet it was tangible, a sophistication without indifference. Soft-footed college girls served, and the first hostess, Mrs. Ted Turner, wife of the manager, might have stepped from Vogue. To robustly hungry McCallites, it was something new to refrain from advancing to the best table in the room, to accept the modish will of the hostess as to where to sit.

The past ski season had found Browns very active. Stan Harwood and Frank Brown, still under Bill Brown, Junior, trained regularly with the Mitey Mites. At a meet at Mt. Hood, Oregon, against a field of 67 of the best skiers in the Northwest of any age,

Stan and Frank finished 16th and 17th, respectively. As different in appearance and nature as ever, the cousins forged ahead in an exacting, terribly appealing sport. Frank, a quiet boy, excelled at school, took piano lessons. Stan was goodnatured, not quiet, and always bigger this week than last.

Of local skiing Lavor Chapin wrote for the Salt Lake Deseret News: "During 1948, the Payette Lakes junior team entered six major meets and in each won not less than six of the first eight places . . . several years ago the Ski club with the unreserved support of the Chamber of Commerce and townspeople began a program of free instruction to anyone who wished to use the ski area. Special attention has been given to young skiers. Free transportation provided by a local lumber mill is made available to junior skiers wishing to use the facilities of the ski hill. Ski instruction is given by Bill Brown, Jr., a native of McCall, whose racing days ended when he was shot up while serving with the mountain troops in Italy."

Mitey Mites and Juniors wore their ski clothes to school, stacked their ski gear in the corners, and were ready to swing onto the bus when it came from B T and L after school.

Now older skiers were urged to get out and unlimber for a meet. When there wasn't a big enough turnout, Warren Brown dropped his work and with two days of practice took a second place in the competition. The next year he would be sent for again, "the old man of the mountains," this time to take first place.

In April Muddy (Murray) Numbers led the McCall team that at Sun Valley won the Western American Legion Ski meet, Muddy taking first place with 290 points.

In Boise, Tuck Beyerle, moved by the current ski enthusiasm, agreed to set up an Idaho Power company window with a display to advertise Payette Lakes winter sports. However, it seemed impossible to locate the various props he felt he must have. In mild frustration he recalled a piece of his mother-in-law's advice: When you find yourself confronted by a situation, the thing to do is sit down and rest.

He sat, he rested. Almost at once offers of mannequins, ultra sport clothes and equipment, and a colorful poster from an advertising agency flowed in. He had his window. And he was once more impressed with Ida Brown's common sense.

In June, 1948, McCall achieved its first bank. The Idaho First National bank bought the Donnelly bank and moved it with its president H. E. Armstrong to McCall. This bank and Mr. Armstrong had had a previous move indeed. In 1907 it was set up at Roseberry. In 1915 when the railroad reduced Roseberry to a memory by favoring Donnelly, the bank was moved thither. A year later Armstrong was made president and had never afterward been anything else. Now he must leave his long familiar haunts for larger ones, leave clients of more than 30 years, unless they chose to follow him. Many of these clients were Finns, and on Finns he had never lost a cent, although bank interest in early days was 10 percent and $2000 a big loan.

Armstrong had been proud of his Donnelly bank. In the late 1920's it took hard financial shaking, but it was one of three in the state that kept open through the crash of 1933. Armstrong had Finn friends who at that time offered to repay loans in advance if he were *in a bind*—they'd offer even though it meant cramping themselves. Finns who didn't know English would bring one of their children to do the talking. Then without question they'd sign where Armstrong pointed.

On July 3, 1948 Shore Lodge was formally opened. Probably it was not immediately or continuously a financial success; perhaps the directors didn't expect it to be, were thinking several years ahead. In off seasons it had to lower its rates and sometimes it would close briefly. Its payroll had to be pared, and it abridged some of its diningroom service, such as the copper-lined food carts from which guests could choose viands kept constantly at pleasing temperatures. And unfortunately it had to give up its hostess.

Unperturbed by these problems, the Lodge sat low and poised among its towering pines, bonded to the soil by dwarf juniper and hardy perennials, while managers came and went. On the lake side, pines that were unable to accept people and shuffleboards died and had to be taken down. One had been allowed to pierce the second floor balcony, but in death its wide stump was still a showpiece, a support for flowerpots.

In any case, the Lodge had come to stay. At first those who owned no stock and who had no business that was noticeably improved by its advent took dubiously its air of queenship. In the end they accepted it and its airs as the older inhabitants had accepted the first summer invaders. In time they would speak of it with pride, at least when they visited other communities.

Summer bowed to autumn. The deer and elk seasons opened. Red-hatted hunters crowded McCall, some in drugstore outfits. They didn't stay long, and they didn't usually stay at the Lodge, preferring their own camps or somebody's summer place. The Johnson Flying service flew some into remote basins. Professional packers took others. Some went entirely on their own. It proved a good elk year. Three hunters brought in bulls that dressed better than 450 pounds. Alive they'd have weighed 650 or 700 pounds.

A Brown truck rumbling down Lick Creek hill with a load of logs had to stop for a stalled car headed toward town. In the car were three hunters and their dog. The truckdriver agreed to tow them, and hooked on with his chain. However, the hunter at his own wheel either didn't understand being towed behind great logs, or he grew drowsy at they swooped down the winding grade. When the chain suddenly went slack on a curve, he ran the car over it. Before he knew what was happening a front wheel jerked off. The car began to whip. It knocked down small trees; it rolled rocks into the road; it began to fall apart. Up ahead the trucker could see and hear nothing. Besides he had enough to do himself.

One by one the hunters jumped, then the dog.

Reaching the switchbacks at the mink farm, the trucker stopped thoughtfully to see how the hunters were doing. No hunters, very little car. He drove on into town and told the Forest office, which sent out a man. He rolled over the bank all that was left of the car, found the hunters and brought them in.

Fishing too was good. In the spring spawning salmon appeared for the first time in 20 years in the waters below the lake. The river was scarlet with them. Then it was discovered that they weren't getting through the dam headgate, so McCall sportsmen and Fish and Game department people went to work. With buckets and nets they seined fish from the rapids and transported them to the lake, where the calm waters probably tranquilized them into resuming their original intention. It was thought the run came from Black Canyon reservoir near Emmett, which had previously been planted.

At Christmas time Shore Lodge opened for the holidays. How cheerful to join old friends in the lounge and diningroom and listen to Dave Steward at the organ. One evening his playing stimulated an impromptu concert. The Beyerles were there and Dorothy found herself singing request favorites. The evening was a thrill to her—she had always loved Christmas in McCall.

At Carl's and Ida's, every Brown, Brown in-law and Brown descendant sat down to Christmas dinner together. Jayne Brown's parents, Mr. and Mrs. Frank Jones of Malad, were there too.

Outside the drifts were as high as the windowsills, but inside it was warm and bright, and the youngsters sang "Let it Snow" or "Winter Wonderland," or "I'm Dreaming of a White Christmas." An older youngster dreamed of other Christmases. He was back in Whitefield, where the underwear manufacturer's canal was frozen tight. His rosy-cheeked, red-tippeted girl was on his arm, and their skates shone in the moonlight.

Just before Christmas the mill had closed, earlier than usual, with the mercury standing at 28 degrees below zero; and the 11-foot snow on Lick Creek summit had already stopped the trucks. In those drifts Bill Deinhard and Bob McBride found a mountain goat floundering. They rescued Buttons and took him to town, to Brown's lumbershed. However, the goat didn't care at all for this retreat. He worked himself loose and searching for something like an Alp he climbed lumber piles, trucks, whatever he could leap upon. So the men caught him again and took him to Boise, to join a lonely female goat in Julia Davis park.

At the permanent camp on the South Fork, regardless of snow 20 men stayed on. With the turn of the year, the Ernie Watkinses and the Brownie Hoffs[62] went on vacation trips, and Ida and Carl prepared to leave for Coolidge, Arizona. They stopped in Boise on their way and were guests of Morrison-Knudsen company, Boise-based great earth-moving constructors, at an enormous dinner party which featured famous nightclub talent. Newspapers said it was the most outstanding private party in Boise's social history, a fact of interest but no great self-satisfaction to the Browns, who enjoyed meeting people and being entertained on any scale, high or low. Now they went on to the Southwest, to return with spring.

In the legislature as throughout the state, sentiment was rising against slot machines, and slot machines were sugar on the gravy to club owners in McCall.

178

Small Idaho cities with no appeal for the leisure class, small places with no induced glamor, cried that their citizens cashed payroll checks with the one-armed bandits instead of with the grocers, that families were in desperate condition and collections terrible. One city in South Idaho threw out the slots bodily, and reported an instant improvement in economy. Tradesmen were paid; social agencies found less privation.

In McCall Mayor Glenn Howell took his duties seriously, kept the town on his conscience. He helped with everything. To him slot machines were one of the facts of life *for his town*, and so in some alarm he wrote in the Payette Lakes Star: ". . . we shall find the village shorn of about $13,500 out of the total income of around $45,000, with no way for us to get any more money . . . we are taxing so close to the limit allowed by the law that we could raise only abound $1000 more by this method . . . We'll be in a bad way if the slot machines are made illegal . . . The council wants to make it plain that they are concerned only with the revenue aspects of the question. They do not like slot machines as such."

However, the legislature failed to act, and McCall clubs, including Shore Lodge, smiled and relaxed.

In the early months of the year camera clubs convened for the first time at the lake. Probably no visitors could give finer free advertising to the place, and McCallites turned out to help them see everything. Special ski runs were arranged for them, and they were taken out on the frozen lake too. Here three earnest addicts stepped through airholes, but not fatally.

In February Jayne Brown's card club found itself invited to Shore Lodge for dessert and told to come in slacks. This the ladies found was the explanation: the windows in Jayne's and Warren's new house, erected in an addition on the south side of the lake, needed washing. And the house was about three-quarters glass.

It had been designed by Henry Allen, a millwright for B T and L, who also supervised its construction. Lumberjacks idled by the slack season at the mill did the work with the aid of two professional carpenters. The house sat modernly low—"Gosh, it looks like a shed," some viewers remarked—and it barely glanced at the highway which its front door faced. Its real concern was with the lake, through double glass. The walk and narrow gallery leading in, the neutral coloring of the outside walls, these gave little hint of the poised, thoughtful interior, where pictures, drapes and furniture spoke softly a single word. The walls, not surprisingly, reflected the tastes of several generations of wood-loving men. Each room was wood-paneled, no two precisely alike, all blending.

The house was heated by a process that would have made early McCall dwellers sniff in unbelief. A reverse-refrigeration device brought warm water from the bottom of the lake, where temperature never dropped below 38 degrees, and "exchanged" it for colder water. The exchange produced heat.

The Warren Brown house has been well used. In 1935 Jayne organized Girl Scouts in McCall, and has worked continuously with this group. She has served as president of the Gem State Girl Scout council and is a member of the regional council for Idaho, Washington, Oregon and Alaska. Recently she received her 25-year service award. Even more than in Boy Scouts, where men are already accustomed to executive work, Girl Scout leaders find themselves doing things differently, and probably better, than when they work alone. Jayne Brown liked association with these competent women—with now and then a man permitted on the finance or camp end. Much Scout activity has centered in the Warren Brown home, and it is used for other public affairs. Then too it is understood that if a McCall girl is marrying and her friends' houses are not large enough for a shower, Jayne's house is, and welcome. For instance, there was Mack Miller's wedding reception, attended by 200 people. By squeezing his mother's book-filled little house couldn't have accommodated more than 25.

Events large and small marked 1949 on the lake. Mrs. Lyle Watts visited at the home of Mrs. Joe Kasper, and at Shore Lodge Ida Brown set a luncheon for this friend of 22 years. As to the town, Mrs. Watts confessed she could hardly believe the changes.

In January Frank Brown, not yet 12, won the Mitey Mite ski meet for the second time, with Stan Harwood right behind him. Brown took first in cross country and slalom, Harwood first in jumps.

Ted Turner promised that by summer Shore Lodge would construct a water ski jump for the second annual water ski tourney, where slalom and trick riding would also be staged. Robert Taylor, movie idol, stopped over night at Shore Lodge and spent all of half an hour admiring Tuck Beyerle's giftshop there. Guests like Taylor made the management glow.

A half mile west of the Lodge the Village Store opened a new building to feature Mexican and Indian crafts, and it also had a motel. Within sight of the lake and near her cottages, Nell Tobias opened a tasteful giftshop on the bluff above the river. Churches set up camps around the lake, and eating places with quaint names sprang up. Besides lodgings the Yacht club had a diningroom extending to the water's edge; and William Deinhard's McCall hotel at the bend in the highway offered rooms. Deinhard's estimable conversation could be had too, and usually was. A tough-tender product of early times, who had knocked up against every kind of obstacle and usually come off well, stocky Deinhard knew everybody in the area and miscalculated few. His wife knew nearly as much as he, but she was too busy tending the hotel desk to tell stories.

McCall was indeed expanding, at least in summer, when population climbed to three times its winter one thousand.

Perhaps a relaxed sense of fluidity and freedom from restraint overtook the town. Whatever its name, it was interrupted by an explosion—a raid on Shore Lodge by Clyde Dominy, state law enforcement officer, C. Ben Martin, prosecuting attorney of Valley county, and the local justice of the peace, Leonard Ackaret. These officers were directed to look for anything unlawful, and their find was an elaborate private casino for big scale gambling. They did their duty, and the next morning a pile of ashes was all that remained of gambling paraphernalia.

"If you could just have saved one of those lovely tables!" Mrs. Ackaret exclaimed when her husband told her.

If in certain quarters there were hard feelings over the raid, they were not paraded. For its part the Lodge maintained the lofty air of a big hen, some of whose overbold chicks have been roughed by the cat.

As a contrast of sorts, Robert Kasper, a graduate in engineering from the University of Washington, told his parents that if they wouldn't be too disappointed in him, he'd like to enter the ministry. No, they were not disappointed, although Joe Kasper had dreamed of the day when his boy might be working in his field. Robert enrolled in the Yale University Divinity school at New Haven.

It was fall. Frost had painted the low brush red, and on the spiky green hills the tamaracks looked like big yellow candles. Suddenly to Carl Brown's ears football was calling. Any well-managed sport had always fascinated him. When Warren was at the university, Carl had enjoyed getting to Moscow for a game, dropping in at the Sigma Chi house, and perhaps showing the boys a thing or two about poker. But for a long time he hadn't had much chance to enjoy the thrill of college football, so he and Ida drove to Salt Lake to see the Utah-Idaho battle. He came home feeling better.

Halloween and the moon approaching full, temptation irresistible, but C. C. Anderson, the Bungalow store and others offered prizes and treats in exchange for good conduct pledges, and McCall youngsters fell in line. The great cold came down; snow piled on snow. The American Legion dance had to be postponed because all roads were blocked—tickets would still be good when the roads cleared.

John Maloney became new manager at Shore Lodge.

In Reno Skier Mack Miller clipped seconds from the time set by two former Olympic aces. Only 17, he won honors by finishing first in downhill and fourth in slalom. Four people, Coach Brown, Ted and Betty Harwood, and Mark Johannsen of the Forest office, drove all the way to Reno to enourage Mack.

The Winter carnival was renewed, full of life though not as swashbuckling as in the old days. There was dogracing and skijoring, i.e., skiing behind something other than a boat. It can be an airplane, a snowplane, an automobile or a horse.

Right in the midst of the cold McCall bought a new fire truck. A wise idea. In frame-house towns, fire is the villain. The only things it seems to spare are churches, blacksmith shops and outhouses.

Leonard Ackaret drove a group of men to Boise in his own car to complete the deal and bring the truck home. In Boise even when they arrived it was cold, and by time to leave, the mercury had skidded to zero. The men drew straws to see who'd have the honor of driving the new machine home, forgetting one important matter—the truck had no heater.

Ackaret won, and two others asked if they could ride with him. By the time they were wise, it was too late. At 11:30 that night when they got into McCall it was 13 degrees below, and they were as rigid-frigid as frozen trout. Their consciences had frozen solid too, and they drove up and down Main Street with the new siren open warming themselves at the alarmed faces of the half-dressed who rushed out to see what was burning.

The Progressive club now began an important project, unusual in small Idaho towns, the collection of local historical data. Mrs. Tuck Beyerle was named coordinating chairman.

People seemed unified in the conviction that Valley county history should be preserved. It was a pity the dwellers proved so disparate when it came to schools. Under the new school reorganization act, which gave Valley county two B districts and one C, Warren Brown became temporary chairman of B-district 421. He was aware of what he was accepting, and in assuming his duties he said, "Throughout our work, we want to keep everything that is done before the eyes of the people. We hope for full publication of the board's efforts so everyone in the county will know what is going on."

The immediate problem was transportation, how children were to reach consolidated schools. And the board worked with the county commissioners as to roads which would have to be repaired or rebuilt. The commissioners promised cooperation. Progress was being made, Brown reported, on a market road running east from Donnelly to Roseberry, then north to Lake Fork, then west to Elo school.

A wave of improvement now struck town, started by the Jaycee project to create a public beach east of the bridge. B T and L loaned trucks, individuals brought wreckers, loaders and jeeps. Workers removed 40 truckloads of trash, built nine picnic tables and four firepits besides constructing one log boom to keep cars out of the new beach and another boom to keep young swimmers in safe water. They provided a large rubber raft, firewood, and handy litter barrels.

184

In the Star Beth Rodenbuagh summed up this community toil: "Wonderful McCall, the town that has everything . . . we saw the Jaycees scratch out a public beach . . . the church[64] needed a new basement and Bill Reitmeier called for assistants and rolled up his sleeves and spat on his hands and was ready to pour concrete before any other place could have got past the add-and-subtract stage. We saw McCall snowed in, and they ran up a couple of square dances. We saw the smoke of forest fires boil up over the mountains, and ladies slapped together truckloads of sandwiches. Nothing small ever happens in McCall."

While the Beyerles were enlarging their house and developing a beach terrace, two local women glimpsed the serpent. One reported thus: "It looked like a big log . . . suddenly I realized it was moving too fast for a log. I saw motion at the front end. It looked 20 feet long . . . the big thing came out of the water three to three and a half feet, and showed above the surface for five or six feet." The part that showed was "dark and shiny."

At a picnic on a meadow southwest of Lardo, 500 Brown employees and their families regaled themselves on food that Ted Harwood and his committee had rounded up and the women had cooked. After food came the second thrill for the kids: contests. They raced and jumped in every imaginable style. Then the women raced each other—in sacks. Not to be outdone, the men followed them—in sacks.

In the Mamma-Baby race, Mamma tore across the field to Baby, dressed him frantically, raced back. Mamma and Baby were both men. In the tug-of-war, Les Ulmer headed the mill team, Warren Brown the loggers. Agnes Rowland captained one softball team for women, Jayne Brown another. Dazzled, seemingly, by their own performance, which went on and on, the women could hardly be induced to leave off, but the men were tired and wanted to go home.

The bright sunshine, the horseplay and relaxation, these were not all. McCallites simply enjoy homemade fun, everybody taking part. And if there were men and women present who envied or disliked the Browns—as can be alleged—today they forgot about it. They were having a day to remember, all together, one camp.

An interesting pair at the picnic was Gretchen Hoff and Diane Brown, granddaughters of Theodore Hoff and Carl Brown, nine years old, great friends. Together they were learning to water-ski; they were both keen about music. At a recent wedding shower that Mrs. Les Ulmer gave for Mrs. Jack Numbers they had sung a duet. This year Gretchen's mother, Helen Hoff, would teach in the McCall schools, so the girls would still be together.

In 1946, wide-awake Jaycees had started the McCall air breakfasts, with nine or 10 guest planes. This year there were 145 planes gliding onto the field south of town. Ted Harwood's fleet of two buses and all the available cars in town transported pilots and passengers to Shore Lodge for a space-taxing meal. The Lodge contributed 100 of the breakfasts, the Junior Chamber paid for 190 more. The descent to the field, the lovely, lively stay, then the taking off, there wasn't the smallest mishap, and the Jaycees had done something for air transportation, for nothing-small McCall, and even obliquely for themselves.

On July 30 a great if swift-passing excitement hit town. A man came in from Tamarack falls on the Payette and displayed a piece of silver-bearing ore. An instant thrill swept all males who saw or heard. The young and unskeptical, and some not so young, seized picks and headed out. When they had gone, the joker explained that though *he* had come from Tamarack

186

falls, the ore had not. It was just a souvenir picked up elsewhere.

The ash and smoke of forest fires darkened the August skies. Joe Bross, a B T and L employee, went to the Forest office for a fire permit to take on a fishing trip to Duck lake but came out with something else, an assignment to boss a fire crew. During that one week 40 fires broke out. On four that were project size, 1600 men fought the enemy. Forest rangers and area super-woodsmen, who were familiar with the lay of the country, worked side by side.

On the main Salmon north of Burgdorf, a thousand trained fighters battled along a 25-mile line. This fire had spread from a burning automobile to roar through 4000 acres of heavy timber. The Forest took out threatened mine and ranch families, though not many were actually in the fire zone.

CHAPTER THIRTY-THREE

Fall was here, crystaline, tantalizing. As Beth Rodenbaugh said in the Star, it was "that time of year when a cool breath comes out of the dark heart of the firs as you pass walking in the sun; when wood piles grow higher, layer on layer, and huckleberry bushes turn red, dyeing brush slopes into patterns like Persian rugs; when pine squirrels burrow and chipmunks scratch at their favorite nooks and crannies; and summer people all pick up and go home, thus missing out on one of the free samples of heaven in advance of the real thing."

The editor of the Star said his gesture of welcome to autumn was to order a truck-load of planer ends from B T and L, "what they call widow wood—about all it needs is a sharp look to cut it down to stove size."

It had also come time to select a fine apple for Teacher, but not especially for the school board. With reorganization, little children from closed schools would wait on the road for a bus to transport them to bigger schools. Sometimes they would be waiting before the gray wintry daylight was full, and when they reached home after school, dusk would be falling. They would wait on roads in swirls of dust, in rain, in snow, in harsh wind. But when they reached school, it would be a bigger, better building usually; and teachers, though no kindlier nor more earger to help, would generally be better trained. For instance, teaching the 7th and 8th grades this year at Donnelly would be Phyllis Ellison, with 13 years experience in Boise schools and a master's in education.

The school election in September retained all the temporary trustees in office, with Warren Brown again chairman. This seemed to indicate approval of the moves the board was making, including efforts for the best transportation possible. The board advertised for a third school bus and set up book-rental fees of $3, of which $2 would be refunded if books were neither lost nor damaged. Thus far there seemed relative peace in the district, although McCall was in a perennial burn about sending its high school students eleven miles to Donnelly, a smaller town with a bigger building.

The over-generous Payette Lakes Ski club now found that it was lamentably broke, and since Betty Harwood, like her mother, could extract money from men, she was named chairman of a committee to raise funds. The women went to people and to businesses, and came back with $700. However, Sterling Clark, president of the club, said that some of this would have to go on bills dating back two years, so the situation was still gloomy. "Desperate in fact," Clark said. He proposed that members lend their equipment and themselves to cut and stack wood for the ski hut, so as to avoid an expensive paid job. The members assented, fell to work. A woodpile grew.

Fall found Ida Brown as busy as usual. She had been reappointed chairman of the civic committee of the Progressive club (and would be over the years); and no empty honor this. Next there was PTA, though of course she had no children in school.[56] At its first fall meeting PTA got 150 parents out, a nice showing for a town of less than 1200 population. Ida also had social chores to attend to, including the entertainment of the Washwomen's club.

Nevertheless when Carl suggested that they ought to attend the Willamette-Idaho football game in Moscow, she did not demur. Although they had neither children nor yet grandchildren at the state university, they were animated by a perennial concern for all McCall youngsters bent on getting more education. So they drove to the campus, met friends in the aging, homelike Moscow hotel, and got to the game. When it was over, exhilarated that Idaho had actually won a football game, they drove nine miles to Pullman and saw the second half of another contest, the W.S.C.-Utah game.

All this carefree going and coming for a couple who had lived on a ranch on the South Fork with never a holiday, never a respite from gruelling work, not the smallest luxury, and over their heads a galling debt! Their present degree of comfort and leisure had not come by chance, however, only by unremitting effort. And it had not changed them at all. To be sure they took delight in being where important people gathered, but everyday folks were still the heart of their existence. It was everyday people, matching their own hard work and loyalty, who had made this comfort and leisure possible.

The Warren Browns also allowed themselves a small holiday. They flew to New York in less time than it once took Carl to cover twenty miles with a dogsled or packhorses. Warren's chief pleasure was the World series, and Jayne's was South Pacific, with Ezio Pinza and Mary Martin. On their way home they stopped with the friends of both Brown generations, the L. P. Drews in Omaha.

The Drews had long kept a home on the west side of the lake, where Mrs. Drew usually spent her summers, her husband coming for his annual three weeks' vacation. Drew[66] was assistant chief engineer for the Union Pacific, whose tie contract B T and L had leaned on through the years.

Not to be eclipsed in art appreciation, Betty and Dorothy took themselves and a carful of friends to Boise to enjoy the Ballet Russe. Dorothy could speak with authority about such, and found the talent superb. Later the Carl Browns, Harwoods, Beyerles and Nell Tobias made a second trip to Boise, this time to hear Patrice Munsell, who had achieved operatic distinction and, being a Spokane girl, seemed somehow to belong to everybody in the Northwest.

Carl had been inordinately proud of Dorothy's voice and thus was kindly disposed toward most singers. He admitted that the evening was nice. He hadn't had to listen to any long-haired men beating out piano pieces which had no tune and couldn't be danced to.

Every winter the heaped-up snows forced pre-school children to spend many restless hours indoors, standing at the windows, asking their mothers what they could do now. So McCall women set out to find an answer. On their own they organized a play group. Dorothy Beyerle collected "constructive type" toys, and Mrs. C. R. Johnson became teacher-supervisor. As in most such attempts, rules had to be made, tried out, adjusted to fit situations. Eventually each mother paid $4 for each child she sent to the play-school, and each month she gave one morning of her own. This chance to observe the offspring of others was no doubt illuminating. Each mother was also expected to attend

190

the monthly meeting. To get and stay abreast of the times, the group conducted a study of child problems.[67]

Mindful of other community needs, women worked on a bloodbank. Urging, heckling, pushing, they got their men to go with them and give. Mrs. Ted Koskella first lined up the workers, Betty Harwood signed donors, and Mrs. Lloyd Johnson handled canteen details. Result: 76 pints of blood. McCallites suspected it was better blood—it must hold in solution lots of summer sunshine and lots of winter muscle-work done on ski runs, hunting trips, ice skating, square dancing and logging.

Within one week, the Progressive club, as progressive as ever, conducted a Girl Scout drive that netted $465, put on a tea to publicize the needs of the village library, and firmed its plans for Christmas treats for the children.

And now women set up a new service unit for themselves, the Jay-C-Ettes. With community projects exceeding most towns its size, McCall was already organized to the neck, but what matter. True to pattern, Brown women refrained from accepting offices in the new group. Instead they showed up on the work details.

Early in November, Henry Hoff died. He had come to McCall first to work for his brother Theodore, had remained straight on through the years, and stayed with B T and L. In 1935 he left Carl to start a transfer company with Jack Hayes. In World War I, he had served with the 347th Machine Gun battalion in France, where in the fall of 1918 within two months time he fought on three bloody fronts, St. Mihiel, the Meuse-Argonne, and Ypres Lys. The American Legion conducted Henry's funeral with an opening salute of three guns. A replica of the flag used on the coffin was presented to his wife.[68]

Though the livestock-feeding months in the valley had always been long, sometimes tragically long, and the crop-growing period short and risky, cattle and sheep had always been raised. Hoff and Brown had cattle ranch assets, and later Warren Brown would put money into cattle. Now Valley youngsters were getting into the game through 4-H. Jay Garrett and Rita Barker of Donnelly took steers they had raised to a livestock show in Ogden and brought back first and second prizes.

At the University a home town boy was doing well in a different line. David Ulmer wrote his folks that he had been accepted for entrance the following September at the Washington University School of Medicine in St. Louis. And his interests weren't limited to science, either. He and a girl partner, Shirley Jacobsen of Rexburg, competing among 400 entrants from all parts of the West, pitted against teams from schools far larger than Idaho, had won four of their six debates. Previously at Whitman they had won four of five debates. Some day Ulmer's experience in analyzing a problem might come handy again—a trend toward socialized medicine, which had been tried out in England, was being felt in America.

Tuck Beyerle opened a decorating department at Carrol's, an exclusive Boise shop for women, and though continuing to advise on specific decoration problems out of the city, he would give full time to the new project. This meant that Dorothy would presently move to Boise with the two little girls. Of course they would keep their property on the lake and spend their summers there, Tuck flying up for weekends.[69]

Conscious of the responsibility that *someone* in a town even as remote and small as McCall ought to assume, Editor John Colley of the Star joined Herb Fitz, manager of Shore Lodge Pharmacy and writer of a regional newspaper column, in an attack on "funny"

192

books. Fitz classified these as (1) funny, (2) the kind that teach the finer points of cruelty and crime, and (3) books to bring romance into the lives of the wee little tots. Funny books should be censored, Fitz declared. Colley went further. He said they should be outlawed. Now the great wide world may not have noted the Fitz-Colley utterances; but McCall did. And agreed.

Christmas brought the usual dear activities that united many people, not just select groups. At the Community church, in addition to formal services well attended by Browns and Harwoods, there was a celebration in honor of the new basement. Pastor Reitmeier's speed in getting this move underway had been pointed out by Beth Rodenbaugh. This evening Reitmeier reported that 80 men had given a total of 834 hours of labor, and that practically every man present had helped in some way. A complacent evening, and rightly so.

On Christmas eve Jaycees fought through the worst blizzard of years, one that stalled 4-wheel-drive vehicles, to make Santa Claus visits to homes that the old gentleman might overlook. On the following night, with conditions a bit improved, they struggled through drifts again to any remaining homes. Bob Fontaine was Santa. If he found that children had already been put to bed, he saw no reason for not going right into their bedrooms, where round eyes peered with joy and unbelief above the pulled-up covers.

An event of the week that must have seemed significant to those who hoped for better schools and firmer cooperation among school patrons was the Christmas program arranged by Joyce Brown, music supervisor for the district. Over 400 children from seven different schools participated. There were rhythm bands, carol singing, solos, a 20-piece high school band playing a Bach chorale, and a grade school operetta, the first such unified effort the area had ever heard.

Shore Lodge, the Yacht club and the Lake View hotel were crowded with holiday skiers, and many of the lake houses were opened for the brief season. Main roads were kept plowed through the deepening snow and there were dinners, dances, parties and much singing of Auld Lang Syne. The mercury dropped to 17 below, the lake froze.

At New Years, the Harwoods gave a cocktail-charades party for 15 couples; the Beyerles were dinner hosts to guests from Australia and New York. Carl and Ida, however, decided that it was time to start to Arizona. In Boise they stopped for the huge annual dinner party given by Morrison-Knudsen.

CHAPTER THIRTY-FOUR

Warren and Jayne Brown had gone to Malad for Christmas with Jayne's family. In this orderly little town Warren observed the efficiency of the school system, and on returning home he wrote to the Star, mentioning what he had seen. He said further: "I do not have the answer to our situation but certainly feel it is high time we did something about it, even if we make mistakes . . . Was anyone happy over transporting 200 small children to Donnelly to put on a Christmas program?

"I am serving warning to those who think 'What was good enough for me is good enough for my children.' I am not asking for a fight. I am appealing for help, for it will take the cooperation of our school district to whip our unsatisfactory housing situation." This was not by any means the last appeal that Warren Brown would make.

At Shore Lodge resident manager John Maloney resigned and K. R. Putnam, owner of the Village store, succeeded him. Maloney said, perhaps wistfully, that the future of the Lodge was dependent on local, not outside support.

Looking over its own shoulder, B T and L found that in the past 12 months it had produced 16 million board feet of lumber, 10 per cent over its 1948 output. In addition it had handled 6 million feet from other mills for custom planing and drying. Most of its lumber had been shipped out of the state—East, South. Five million feet of railroad ties had gone to Union Pacific.

In January Ted and Betty Harwood went to the town of Payette for the annual Boy Scouters banquet. Ted assumed it would be just that, but at the dinner he realized suddenly that the speaker was talking about *him*. How he'd begun work as an assistant scout master at 16 under L. L. Moore in Cascade. How he'd worked on the council level and as a member of the executive board, finally president of the Ore-Ida council for a year, during which he made countless visits to troops in his district—he had a hundred to carry on his mind. How he had stayed on the board after his presidency, and of the satisfaction he found in the kind of men he worked with. How he had labored for the development of Camp Billy Rice at Warm lake, the camp given by former supervisor of Weiser and Payette Forests, William B. Rice.

Then, with Betty in a gift corsage proudly watching, to Ted Harwood was presented the Silver Beaver award, a tribute few men would receive, one he had not dreamed he'd merit.

Through January the cold continued. A storm that Bert Armstrong said was the worst in 37 years hit the area. All the snow that fell stayed. Aleen Stover said, "I get tired of shoveling the same old snow over and over."

At the ski hill it lay 51 inches deep. Winter possessed the town, the lake, the valley, a precious season if a man had a job, a warm house, and if his wife was inclined to shovel snow.

The annual Mitey Mite meet was on, and the cousins Stan and Frank see-sawed for lead, with hardly ten points finally separating them, Frank 439.6, Stan 430. Frank had now claimed top place for three consecutive years.

The Payette Lakes Open that followed was like an intercollegiate meet, five top honors being distributed among three colleges. Everybody responsible for the high development of the sport in McCall glowed with the reputation it was acquiring. And here were two boys who wanted to go to the National Jumping championship meet in Wisconsin but lacked the funds. Fifty businesses and individuals chipped in to send Teddy Nelson and Allen Smith on their way.

For kicks, Donnelly and McCall basketball teams met each other *on webs*, outdoors. Lloyd Johnson did an exhibition of skijoring behind a plane going 90 miles an hour.

Word came that Lyle Watts, supervisor of the Weiser Forest in 1921 and of the Idaho Forest (McCall) from 1922 to 1925, then in 1943 made Chief Forester of the United States, had received the Department of Agriculture's Distinguished service award for leadership in forest resources conservation nationally and internationally. Starting as a fire guard on a western forest, Watts had spent nearly 40 years in public service. His friends in McCall, who supposed his rise might have been activated *a little* by his three years in their resolute atmosphere and peerless climate, rejoiced at this honor. Who could deserve it more.

To the delight of Browns and many others, Grace McRae was nominated by Valley county as Idaho Mother for 1950. She had been a young teacher at Old Meadows in 1905 when she men Dan McRae. He ran a livery stable and owned the townsite. He also owned the Sunnyside mine in the Thunder Mountain region and was a stockholder in the Independence—that was where he and Carl Brown first met. Even then Dan was "mining glad"—his wife's word.

They were married in 1905 and her livelier life began. She lived at mines and away from them, wherever circumstances dictated, but like Ida Brown, she was forever cheerful. Once she and Ida rode along a narrow lake road so slick with ice their wagon began to slide toward the edge. Because Ida was half ill Grace was driving, and she shouted desperately to the men ahead with the horses and packstock. They rushed back and *held the wagon on the road* until danger was past. But this slowed things down and that night the party camped in the snow. Ida, it was clear, was getting worse rather than better, but she had Grace to lean on and refused to turn back.

In 1908 Bob McRae was born, and when he was three, Grace went to Thunder Mountain to live, taking two days for the ride, holding the little boy in her arms all the way. At the mine they lived in a house built by the fabled Colonel Dewey of Nampa, which enjoyed steam heat from the mine—when the mine operated. When Bob was ready for his Three R's, his mother taught him. A second child, Marjorie, was born later.[70]

In 1924-25 Grace McRae taught school in McCall, when two of her pupils were Dorothy and Margaret Brown, who loved her. During the Depression, the McRaes spent two years in Boise, then returned to Sunnyside for another ten years.

After 1945, Dan McRae was associated with the Bradley Mining company, and the family moved to Stibnite. Here Grace again taught for three years. Their son Bob, now a family man, was also employed by Bradley as chief metalurgist, and Grace had her own grandchildren in her school.

After Dan McRae's death in 1956, she moved to Mc-

Call to make her home. Strangers could hardly believe that this well-informed, carefully dressed woman had lived in isolated mine cabins, and knew the weary, sometimes dangerous trail. She was a genuine pioneer who didn't look like one.

That Mrs. McRae didn't win in the state Mother finals was a big surprise to McCall, but not a thing to grieve about. Her friends had had a chance to present her name and to dilate on her accomplishments and worth. If judges didn't realize her superiority over other candidates, that was their misfortune.

Another honor that McCall felt to be its own was Mack Miller's being asked to Rumford, Maine, for Olympic tryouts in cross country and jumping. Bill Brown and the Ski club must have felt that their years of work with young skiers was paying off.

Ted Harwood accompanied junior skiers to a meet at Snow Basin near Ogden, where the boys jumped straight into a terrific snowstorm, against a howling wind. Nobody did very well. It was still storming when they started home. They drove all night, and along those long cold miles Ted's calmness and good nature got a thorough testing. When they pulled into frigid McCall at six in the morning, the points won or lost were unimportant—they were only glad to be home, home where weather was *dependable*. That is, it stormed or it didn't.

The same blizzard had hit McCall, but nevertheless the annual Payette Lakes Open was run off under Warren Brown's direction. Though the fury of the wind increased through the day, volunteers on skis kept the new snow on slalom course and jump hill packed. The next day, Sunday, the storm still raged. On Monday schoolhouses stayed closed. On Tuesday the highway department turned back all travel between Cascade and McCall. Ted Harwood was thankful that his charges were safe at home.

Corey Engen, head ski instructor at Snow Basin, Ogden, was now engaged to manage the entire ski program for the Payette Lakes area, with instructors under him. Engen's record was impressive. In 1948 in the Olympics he had taken third in jumping in competition against top men from 39 countries. In 1951 he was U. S. national ski champion, and in the McCall meet of February 1952 he won the national title in classic combine.

Obviously the Ski club knew what kind of man they were getting. Under Engen's supervision, and using a B T and L cat, improvement began at once at the ski hill. First undertaking was to widen the space at the bottom of the jump.

McCall skiers now returned from a national jumping meet at Tahoe bringing firsts won by Frank Brown and Ralph Turner in a field of 57. At Tahoe the boys had been surprised by luxurious hotel guest beds in place of the expected sleeping bags, but had not been softened too much, it appeared.

At the permanent camp on the South Fork, a small B T and L crew was putting in the winter. Between storms they worked on next summer's roads. By radio and phone they had contact with the world, and in the kitchen they had a cook provided with groceries. Life was pretty endurable.

CHAPTER THIRTY-FIVE

In Korea the United Nations' police action had turned into an undeclared war that nobody, at least nobody in McCall, could explain, and for which Idaho boys were being drafted. This outbreak had not yet affected the lumber market, but with the government taking lumber for new camps, one could only wait and see.

Anxiety was evident all over the country, anxiety in general, then political anxiety. Carl Brown remained as loyal as ever to the principles of Thomas Jefferson, but with the coming of the primary election this year he was faced by a dilemma. As national committeeman he must either accept Glenn Taylor, campaigning for reelection to the United States senate, or he must give reasons for opposing this candidate.

He expressed his sentiments in the columns of the Star, and for one who had served as a Democrat in five legislatures and had been a delegate to two Democratic national conventions, the statement took nerve. He said that the war in Korea was "a possible prelude to a long period of undeclared or open war against communism," and that he distrusted Senator Taylor's "associations." He felt that Taylor had "betrayed and subverted" the principles of the Democratic party, and the standards of the Democrats of his, Carl's, generation. Feeling violently anti-Taylor was one thing; saying so in print was something else.

Taylor's style of campaigning may also have offended Carl. The senator would arrive in a town where he was to speak riding his horse and playing his guitar. He sang as he rode, a modern Pied Piper drawing crowds on village streets. When his concert was over, he addressed the crowd, shivering and thrilling them with his biting wit and compelling voice. However, Republicans claimed that on the far side of each town a car and horse-trailer waited to take Taylor on to his next stop, that he didn't literally "cover the state horseback to get closer to the people."

Whatever the influence of Carl Brown's words, Taylor lost the primary to D. Worth Clark, but in the fall he appeared on the Progressive ticket as running mate to Presidential candidate Henry Wallace.

In 1946 Warren Brown had become vice-president of B T and L, his voice more and more the deciding note. No one could have been more conscious that Carl Brown of the depression, sometimes the deprivation that mill employees shared each year when the icy grip of cold stopped the saws, but Warren was more aware of economic effects. To either of them the thought of hard working men and their wives suffering anxiety, if not actual cold or hunger, was painful.

The reverse-refrigeration heating in his own house had convinced Warren that there should be a way to "exchange" the lake water where the logs floated, and keep it from freezing solid. In Sweden engineers had worked out something that could be applied to running water, but he knew of nothing closer home. The ashes and blasting tried on the ice had accomplished little. He had even stirred up the water with churns and fans, to no effect.

In the winter of 1951-52 the logs not only froze but were first wind-driven across the lake as far as Shore Lodge, where they embedded for the duration.

Now Warren had a new idea to try. With the help of mill engineers he worked out a system of one-inch pipes to run compressed air along the bottom of the lake and release it at 60-foot intervals through 1/32 inch holes. The pipes were laid and connected. At five o'clock one evening, with the temperature near zero, the compressed air was turned in. By morning Warren would have an answer.

He was out at daylight. What he saw was a strip of open water 1000 feet long and a hundred feet wide. Bubbles of air were rising steadily, breaking in small ripples on the surface. From the bottom they were bringing up 38-degree water. There it was, a bubbling fluid log pond in an air temperature that through the night had dropped to 30 below.

With no excess of jubilation Warren told himself, "It seems to work."

If this much was good, more might be better. He

extended the pipe system until there was a mile and a half of it. A 200-cubic foot compressor driven by an electric motor was installed and a series of control valves.

Since frozen wood didn't saw successfully, this offered a problem of its own, so while he was about it, Warren set up a steam shed, 125 x 40, riding on floats in the open water, and into it he piped steam from the mill's power system. Left in this shed for three or four hours, a frozen log came out thawed through.

With this great change, there was nothing to prevent the mill from operating the year round. Even if heavy snow came, by nine in the morning the mill yards could be cleared and work going. If snow piled 20 feet deep at the side, the mill could still operate.

The effect on McCall was thrilling. It meant the end of anxiety about winter pay.

As always, the March of Dimes came round. Mrs. Peck collected $100 from B T and L employees in the office. Pat Hayes asked those for whom he did income tax returns to give his fee to the drive. Jay-C-Ettes put on a $100 dance, and the Masons, McCall Theatre, the Progressive club and the Lake Fork Community hall contributed.

Not to be outdone in charity, the Community church collected old clothing for foreign shipment. The previous year the women had sent 12 boxes of things to Sachsen, Germany, and received back a grateful letter.

The March was not by any means the last drive of the year, but McCall had long been drive-conditioned, for its own projects when not for national ones. Now it was Red Cross time again, and the county quota had been put $500 higher this year. Though the Brown women strove to avoid office, Mrs. Warren Brown found herself president of the Progressive club and serving as commentator[71] for a money-making style show in which her niece, four-year-old Ann Harwood, made her first appearance as a model.

Money-conscious Eastern Stars, looking ahead to a proposed Masonic temple, put on an evening of acrobatic acts and short plays. In the staging of a local version of Tobacco Road, Margaret Peck as Maw found her finest speech was being left out because another actor had jumped a half page. So Maw raised up from the floor and said in Mrs. Peck's voice, "I think we ought to go back over this—I've been cheated out of my best lines!"

So they went back; Maw delivered her star piece.

Filled with the spirit of spring Jaycees and their wives cleaned the cemetery, sawing out fallen trees, repairing fences. They also cleaned up the public beach they had created the year before, and painted its benches. In these endeavors the men had averaged four days of work apiece, besides a Sunday.

Summer picnics were still a few months away, but the Employees Benefit association at the mill felt the need of a party and held one at Short Lodge. Here an attempt was made to name the mill worker with the longest service. Ida Brown held up her hand—"Forty years working for the corporation," she insisted. When they could induce her to be quiet, Bill Harp with 33 years took the honor.

Summer brought death to a man well known to many Idahoans, and especially those with mining interests. This was Walter Hovey Hill, who came to the state in 1890. As an engineer he had laid out railroads and townsites, built roads and explored and operated mining claims for himself and for eastern capitalists. Recently he had served as consulting engineer for Rare Earths, a Long Valley project concerned with earths that were indeed rare but present in Idaho to some extent. His name was connected specifically with

Thunder Mountain, Buffalo Hump and Warren. Unlike the usual mining type, Walter Hovey Hill—and he did not like to have his middle name omitted—was small, exceedingly neat, and well groomed at all times. His white hair and goatee were trim, his dark eyes sharp and all-seeing. And if nothing else told it, his precise diction announced him as a personality and a thinker. With minds slower than his he sometimes seemed impatient.

Once on a wintry evening he rode into a B T and L camp. He knocked at the cookhouse and when a male cook came Hill asked in his usual careful speech if he could "secure overnight lodgings and food" for himself and his horse. He would also like, he said, to have his horse rubbed down.

The cook had never seen Walter Hovey Hill before. Perhaps he wasn't even sure he was seeing right. For a moment he was silent, then he went out on the porch and hollered for help. "Somebody better come. Jesus Christ is here and needs attention."

In April school board chairman Warren Brown had written in the Star that with the mud and snow that still persisted everywhere, it would be impossible for many rural electors to vote on a proposed school bond issue. For complete fairness the election should be postponed to mid-May when roads should be dry. Brown submitted drawings for a proposed grade-high school for McCall, and for the remodeling of the Donnelly high school for the grades. With such a plan in effect it would be possible to close two one-room schools in Donnelly, one at Lake Fork, one at Roseberry, one at Lardo. It would also put McCall grades back into one building—some were now going by bus to Lardo, some to the American Legion hall and elsewhere.

As Brown had pointed out before to parents, since 70 per cent of the high school students of the district lived in McCall, it was the logical place for a district high school. When he was questioned about the over-all plan at a Jaycee meeting in McCall, the plan was given unanimous approval.

In May Brown wrote a third long letter of explanation to the Star. He said in part: "It is a disgrace for people of the district to permit conditions to remain as they are now. This is not a fight between Donnelly and McCall or McCall versus Lardo. This is now a reorganized district and we are all as one."

The election was properly scheduled. The day came. In McCall transportation and baby sitters were provided, and it was soon clear that more people were registering their opinions than in any school election in history. From this Warren took some hope that people had listened to the facts he had presented to them.

But the bond issue failed of the necessary two-thirds vote. Even in McCall 52 people were against, to 524 voting Yes. In Donnelly, 235 opposed, and only 21 favored. Perhaps it was a surprise that *anybody* in Donnelly thought McCall should have its own high school. With 17 more Yes votes, the bond issue might have passed. Now there would be more delay.

On Mother's Day, Mrs. Lester Ulmer received a special gift—word from David that he was one of seven men elected to Silver Lance, upperclassmen's honorary.

Summer was bringing a new kind of visitor to Mc-Call, the travel editor. Writers converged from New York, Cleveland, Detroit and Fort Worth. They were entertained at Shore Lodge by the local Wild Life Federation and joined by other leading citizens on the patio. Guests like these and the previous camera fans were very dear to Shore Lodge management. However, there were now so many special meetings and conventions that the local paper didn't always report them in detail, not unless really famous people attended or the resolutions they passed were sensational.

Again the annual picnic of the Employees Benefit association at the mill featured races. Races for everybody. A race for "grayheaded ladies" brought a lineup of Mrs. Tony Fitzwater, Mrs. Matt Paananen, Mrs. Matt Heikkola and Mrs. Carl Brown. They raced in apparent good faith, then at the finish the coy ladies joined hands to confuse the judges. Ages of the contestants were not made public, but Ida, nothing loth, gave hers as 71.

Stan Harwood was bound for the 10-day Boy Scout Jamboree at Bad Ischl, Austria, and his parents took him to Missoula, Montana, to board the train there. His first trans-Atlantic stop would be Algiers, then Naples, then Rome. These places half way around the globe sounded dubious, maybe unsafe, even to his mother's teacher-trained ear. But if she felt tearful in bidding him goodbye at the station, she hid it. Family feeling among Browns is fiercely strong, but it is not for public display. The whistle blew, Stan's face in the window became a blur. The Harwoods returned silently to their car and started home.

In good time Stan returned. Safely. Showing slides and reviewing his trip for the pleasure of the Progressive club, he related that in overseas countries the architecture, particularly that of old churches, had impressed him most. He recounted that in Rome the Scouts had had an audition with the Pope at his summer palace.

"We sang 'God Bless America' for him, and the Scout song 'On My Honor,' and he seemed pleased," Stan reported, and the ladies applauded.

The previous year seven McCall boys, an astonishing number for so small a town, had been sent to the Scout Jamboree in Philadelphia. They were Harwood, John Kerr, Larry Gallagher, Jimmy Wilson, Dan Cook, David Calvert and Mike Hoff. When McCall boys

206

needed help in connection with worthwhile projects, the community seemed invariably to produce it.

A death in the fall brought particular regret to Carl and Ida. At 88 Clem Blackwell, their neighbor of 40 years before, passed away. His wife Fanny had worked with Ida to set up the first Sunday School, and Clem had put up the first $25 for their organ. Clem ran the original McCall hotel, a livery stable, a meat market and a saloon. He had helped lay out the McCall townsite and had handled many real estate deals for himself and others. Fanny had now been gone many years, and Clem was living with his son Herman.

Another death, untimely because the man was still young, was that of Harold Rodenbaugh, who with his wife Beth lived in McCall for a while and served as publicity manager for Shore Lodge. His photographs of wild life and his pictures of American cities for the Saturday Evening Post had made him widely known. One photograph of his would not die soon, two rearing stallions battling each other in a finish fight.

In the Boise Statesman there was running a series of pictures by a local artist that included college presidents, civic servants, and industrialists. Each with its text covered most of a page. When Carl Brown's face filled the space, McCall people proudly clipped.

A summer event that surely brought deep feeling to Carl Brown was the unveiling in the Community church of a picture, The Lord's Supper, painted by a convict at the state penitentiary and given by himself and Mayor Glenn Howell, though neither was a signed and sealed member of Pastor Reitmeier's fold. Dorothy Beyerle came from Boise to sing Gonoud's Ave Maria, Mrs. Howard Williams sang Malotte's The Lord's Prayer, and granddaughter Ann Harwood unveiled the picture.

Carl Brown rarely discussed religion, even with Ida. They preferred to live their beliefs.

CHAPTER THIRTY-SIX

Still painfully engrossed with the school riddle, for the third time within a year the board of district 421 called a bond election. The first election had failed by 17 votes, a second by a still larger margin, 35. Now Warren Brown waited grimly, saying little, as was his habit. But the defeat this time was the sharpest yet— 40 votes short of the required number. It was galling to take, but if anyone thought this meant an end to the struggle, he failed to comprehend Brown nature.

Meanwhile along the lake career-conscious women were setting up the Payette Lakes Business and Professional Women's club, a group likely to give warm support to school or other forward-looking moves. Dr. Susan Kerr, an osteopath, was elected president, and while still in its infancy, the group invited 135 other BPW's to come to McCall for a convention. At this meeting they passed resolutions demanding a constitutional amendment guaranteeing women equal rights with men.

"But don't we already have them?" an innocent female reader of the Star asked. "Don't we, in McCall?"

It was May and time for the Joe Kaspers to leave for New Haven and the Yale Divinity school for the ordination of their son Robert in the Christian ministry. Bob wrote something to the local pastor at this time that must have given people in his home town pause: ". . . the friendship and support of the church *and of McCall* in general have been a great help to me in my spiritual growth."

In June, 1952 came a triumph for which many McCall people had labored long, the dedication of the

Masonic temple, complete except for the outside finish, which was expected to be stone. A 45x80-foot building, with a lodge room that could seat 250, it had the furnishings needed for Masonry but also the facilities for a public hall. The site was a little rise, back from the highway near the state forest buildings.

Masons had contracted to cut timber on state land, timber that had to be cut. To move the logs they used equipment donated by B T and L, and they then sold the logs to the mill and applied the money on the temple. In other ways the building had been raised literally by the hands of the people. Its lovely carpeting had been provided by the Eastern Star. Into the cost had gone auctions, dinners, and tons of clean old rags collected for sale. Ted Harwood had overseen construction, rounding up workers and keeping work flowing evenly. He was associate guardian and his wife guardian of Job's Daughters; Warren Brown was on the building committee and Les Ulmer worshipful master. With frequent loads of lumber delivered unbilled or at a nominal rate by B T and L, the mill seemed pretty well tied in to the project.

Wrote the Star: "The village joins with McCall Masons in pride . . . labor cheerfully given, and time and devotion have been built into the very walls of the temple."

In June Brigadier General O. L. Fitzgerald of the British Joint Services Mission in Washington came to McCall for a liaison visit to the United States Air Force Survival school, which had been set up on Channel island at the narrows. The general brought his family along, and to insular Idaho these foreigners were very exciting. When local pride was involved, McCall could always put its best foot forward, and this it now did. First there was a large cocktail party—Washington visitors would certainly expect this—which was attended by many local people, even if they drank only tomato juice. These included city officials, legislators,

Forest personnel, and all the Browns, Harwoods and Beyerles. Then there was a motor trip about the lake, the visiting ladies were taken to the McCall shops, and there was much entertaining back and forth. By the time Virginia Zachary and Dorothy Beyerle both had teas in their homes, the visitors' allotted four days were used up.

This summer the bureau of the census released the fact that Valley county in 1950 had contained 2218 males and 2052 females, a reassuring statistical imbalance to any New England school teacher thinking of trying the county in the manner of the schoolma'am in Owen Wister's Virginian. For another fact, a well nigh unbelievable one, people over 25 years of age in the county had had an average of 11 completed school years. Furthermore, as soon as the colleges opened in the fall, not less than 14 youngsters would be setting forth for more education. Education, it could not be denied, was respected in the valley, although there was no unanimity as to what constituted a proper building in which to acquire it locally. In the next election Warren Brown was continued on the board as chairman and it was announced that more space would somehow be provided at the Donnelly high school.

CHAPTER THIRTY-SEVEN

In July in Chicago the Republican national convention nominated General Dwight Eisenhower. Carl Brown had followed the convention earnestly. Toward Democrat Harry Truman he had never warmed, although he granted that in certain emergencies, such as the decision whether to drop the atomic bomb, the

President had acted forthrightly, with courage far greater than his contact with the realities would lead one to expect.

At this time an unusual situation existed in the fact that the ten westernmost states, without exception, were headed by Republican governors. Just after the Chicago convention when Idaho's governor Len Jordan proposed at a strategy meeting in Denver that his state was the logical place for the vacationing general to launch his pre-campaign, the suggestion at first hung fire, then took hold with a boom. When Carl Brown read that General Eisenhower would be in Idaho on August 20, he made up his mind that he would see and hear this great man and shake his hand if possible.

Boise was the only place in the state big enough to handle the crowd that would certainly come. On the appointed morning, nine of the 10 governors flew in, plus Republican Hugo Aronson, who sought the seat in Montana.[72]

They were accompanied by flocks of secretaries, pressmen, and one governor's wife. Descending from his plane, the General was followed by speechwriters, secretaries, advisors, plain-clothesmen and Mrs. Catharine Howard of Boston, representing embattled Republicanism on the distaff side.

The small city had been organized to the hilt and was well aware of the honor that had come. On the way in from the airport there awaited a nearly solid line of school children with homemade signs of welcome, mothers with babes in arms, and old gentlemen on canes. On their porches sat old ladies, rocking and clapping. Of course all able-bodied males had gone to the city to join the crowd, but Eisenhower understood, and looking at the homemade signs and the healthy, friendly western faces he said thoughtfully, "These are *Americans*."

Carl Brown was standing on the street when the general's car passed, the general standing up, waving.

The visitors were whisked to the capitol and into a dinner in the office of Attorney General Robert Smylie. After that they gathered on the south steps of the building and looked down on a waiting crowd of 20,000 wedged into the grounds, the parks, the blocked off streets, the windows of office buildings.

In turn the governors were introduced. Then the general spoke, first from his prepared script, finally abandoning it and steaming ahead on his own, his warmth and sincerity evident. Cameras ground, bulbs flashed, and the crowd thundered.[73]

While the press interviewed the general in the House chamber, the governor's suite was readied for a reception. Carl Brown was there. He and Len Jordan had been legislators together, and he said to the governor, "Do you think I could meet General Eisenhower personally?"

"I'll see that you do, and that he knows who you are."

It came about, the two men talked. Afterward Carl returned thoughtfully to McCall, and the next week's Star carried a quarter-page ad that reproduced an article by Raymond Moley, eminent columnist, that could not be said to echo the thinking of Adlai Stevenson, Eisenhower's Democratic opponent. It was signed by Brown Tie and Lumber Company. The General had not only set Carl's mind at rest, he had moved him into a different political pew, one occupied already by some of his children and children-in-law.

Eight days after the Boise affair, to Carl came another big event, this one domestic in nature and Ida's as much as his—their fiftieth wedding anniversary. In the afternoon of August 28 they received guests at their home. Including employees and their families, more than a thousand well-wishers passed through the doors of the white house on Main street. That evening there was a family dinner at Shore Lodge without one chick or child missing—their own four, their four in-laws, and their 10 grandchildren.[74]

From opposite ends of the long glittering table Carl and Ida could exchange glances and look out upon the lake that had for so many years been their servant and their delight, and to the hills that had been their trial and their strength.

Small events rounded off the summer. Since around McCall age is the least of one's troubles, a 70-year-old woman went out alone for a casual walk up Brundage mountain. When she did not return, search planes flew over. Then logging crews were alerted, the Forest Service radio went to work, and people started for Brundage mountain in cars. Meanwhile the woman had caught a ride on a logging truck and rode into town unaware of the excitement. At Warren there was a shooting, the first in years, that left the victim not dramatically dead but recovering. And in typical fashion Jaycees sponsored a ticket sale for the Wallace Brothers circus in McCall to help with the medical expenses of Del Rice, who'd been injured shooting fireworks on the Fourth.

Shore Lodge often preened itself over a celebrity. En route to his home at Hayden Lake in the North, Bing Crosby and his four sons stayed over night. Film producer Hobart Brownell came to photograph Payette Lakes as part of a Standard Oil movie of Idaho. McCall youngsters Sally Thurston, Bob Hilburn and Bud Holmes water-skied for his cameras, and Carl Brown took him to White Bird to see a lumber camp. Producer Brownell seemed a bit unusual—admitted to missing his wife, who was too busy with some church work to come with him.

Late in summer McCall enjoyed a dash of glamor with the arrival of the new Miss Idaho, Barbara Norton of Burley, and her court of five. On the Shore Lodge patio, with a backdrop of sparkling lake and forested mountains, the girls entertained. If old timers, now shirted and decorous, recalled goldrush days and hoped for a variety of cancan, they were sadly let down. The Miss America contest was concerned with poise and talent, beauty and grace, and offered few honors to hillbilly music and none to black-gartered highkicks. "Measurements" were now merely a statistic. Miss Norton modeled the wardrobe she would wear at Atlantic City, played a Paderewski number, and then to her own accompaniment sang Sylvia. McCall's Alaska days were indeed past.

For healthy balance, it was probably suitable that following this feast of art and beauty, 200 delegates from 28 counties trooped into the Lodge to discuss Wildlife. And following them there the Progressive club asked Valley county senator Frank Freeman to talk to it on "Highlights in the Romance of China." Freeman and his wife Florence collected exquisite objects, and he exhibited for the ladies not only rare tableware of his own, but china, silver and crystal he had borrowed from Boise collections for the talk. McCall might not have decent school buildings, but it had Shore Lodge and it comprehended culture.

Summer did not yield to autumn without a visit from the serpent, although like Lochinvar he came late. Les Ulmer and David stood near the logboom at the mill about noon. Between two logs, where the water was perfectly calm, a large head reared, then a long gray body went undulating through the water, lifting humps eight or ten inches above the surface. The head seemed armored. For ten minutes the serpent remained visible, and the Ulmers scarcely took their eyes from him. Meanwhile near the mill office other peopled had gathered. Suddenly out on the lake a motorboat let out a muffled blast. Instantly the serpent was gone.

The Ulmers' story was verified by Blake Hancock, who added that the head armor looked like thick scales. Others who saw the serpent that day were Reed

Gillespie, Mrs. Alfred Jussila, Mrs. I. W. Rasmussen and Mrs. Hazel Griffin.

Now it was really fall, and Carl and Ida decided to take a trip east. In Cleveland they stayed with Ida's brother, then they went to Whitefield, which Ida had not seen since 1907, when she made a quick visit home, a visit and an excuse to display baby Betty. At New Hampton Institute, where he had graduated in 1899, Carl attended a reunion. They went thence to Boston, then to New York, enjoying their holiday like children. Returning, they visited the L. P. Drews in Omaha, and even went dancing. Home after six weeks, and the town, their own, had never looked better. On the hillsides the tamaracks had turned flame yellow, and in the meadows dying reeds and brown grass waited for the mantle of the first snow.

CHAPTER THIRTY-EIGHT

In March 1952 a school bond election was held and the result was a new shock. After three increasingly bad tries, success was too much to believe, yet here it was. However a group of dissatisfied voters filed a court suit to prevent construction of a high school in McCall, and it was not until December 24 that Judge Charles Winstead of the district court phoned Warren Brown from Boise that a decision had been rendered in favor of the school board, and that the board was now in position to proceed with building *if the plaintiffs did not appeal.*

From this time on contentions bitter, often dramatic, dogged the moves of the board and soured the atmosphere of the district. In battles of this kind, one side is rarely one hundred percent right and the other side one hundred percent wrong; the one certainty is

215

frustration. Following the appearance in Boise of a protest group which pointed out that with half the population and a quarter of the assessed valuation of the district, McCall had only one vote on the five-man board, the state board of education journeyed to McCall and sat for two days.

The state board now changed the boundaries within the district, but a resolution at a Donnelly meeting asking two members of the local board to vacate because they were no longer residents of their zones was defeated. Defying the directive of the state board, a substitute motion divided the district into two independent parts. Two trustees withdrew from the bristling meeting, but it went on anyhow, and board member Henry Knowles, ever sound and calm, moved that bonds not to exceed $275,000 be issued to build a grade-high school and gym at McCall on grounds previously offered the district for this purpose.

This move went on the record, but it produced no visible action. For two more years, through another court decision, through resignations, appeals, and consultations with the state board and with attorneys on each side, the problem lay unresolved. Details of the struggle must still be distinct in the minds of leaders on both sides; others seem to have forgotten.

Why the issue should have attained such proportions in an area where everybody seems to join heartily in good moves was difficult to understand. It is easy to say that youngsters should never have been sent to Donnelly in the first place, but at the time that move seemed practicable. It came during the war years when no building could be done, when the McCall school had grown to the point that the high school had to be housed in unsatisfactory basement rooms. A state educational agency refused to accredit the school longer; something had to be done.

In Donnelly there was room to spare because the closing of a MacGregor lumber camp below town had removed children attending from there. It had seemed

216

sensible to use this space for McCall students on a tuition basis.

One solution often proposed was the erection of a new all-county high school in Donnelly that would serve Cascade too and provide a really large student body. To this Warren was unalterably opposed. In his insistence on a site in McCall and nowhere else he was regarded by many as hindering rather than helping. He was called a dictator—"he wanted everything for McCall."

In November in McCall there was evidence that time had indeed progressed since 1910 when Ida Brown and friends organized the first Sunday school. This was a plan to get voices from all the churches now represented in town for one big Christmas program. And Newt McCall, manager of the McCall Mercantile company, agreed to set aside 10 percent of all drygoods sales and five percent of all food sales on a certain day for any church the purchaser named. Unanimity among the righteous is a very fine thing, and it never looks lovelier than at Christmas.

And on Christmas eve 15 Santa Clauses, all Jaycees, probably representing every church in town, carried 800 sacks of candy into McCall homes.

At Steamboat Springs, Colorado, Mack Miller, now on the freshman ski team at Western State College, Gunnison, won the crosscountry ski event. He reported that this town, Steamboat Springs, seemed to be the only one besides McCall where if children wished to learn skiing they were taught it. Here skiing was even granted physical education credit, credit from grade one to grade 12.

A very high moment of the year for the Brown family and their friends had been the naming of Ida as Valley county candidate for Idaho Mother of 1952. The letters that went to the state committee in praise of her, though loving and carefully composed, somehow rang flat against her warm, witty, springy nature. But the writers of them could hardly set down how she spoke to Carl and Warren about the company logging trucks rolling through town too fast, and how when they smilingly ignored her she went to the law and got action. The action cost B T and L around $500. The writers couldn't take space to relate how she had often left her dinner to take a telegram to somebody who had no phone, or how she always watched her two younger daughters across church to make sure they were being mindful and decorous—as Dorothy said, "I grew up with God sitting on my shoulder."

"A successful mother as evidenced by the individual character of her children," the letters declared, and that was very true, but the judges were too busy to read between the lines, and some other good mother was chosen. Actually it did not grieve Ida's friends beyond repair. As in the case of Grace McRae, they had had the loving experience of trying to put on paper her charm and accomplishments, as a woman and as a mother.

At the year's end Bert Armstrong returned to Donnelly, his home for 33 years before moving with his bank to McCall. "All through my life," he said, "I have made it a habit to leave a party while I'm still having a good time. No one in the world had enjoyed his work more than I. I've made a host of friends, and I think I've done a little good along the way." Plenty of other people thought so too.

At the bank his nephew Blair succeeded him as president.

B T and L celebrated Christmas with a solid gift to itself: a roller for logging roads. This homemade composition of ⅝ inch boilerplate was nine feet wide and six in diameter. Into the cylinder had been poured a heady mixture of 10 cubic yards of concrete and 10 tons of scrap iron. Total weight 35 tons. The roads would know when it passed over.

CHAPTER THIRTY-NINE

In January Frank Brown headed an all-star field of boys and girls in the 3rd annual Cranston Cup junior slalom combined at Bogus basin, high in the hills north of Boise. Between 40 and 50 McCallites, including naturally the Brown and Harwood families, made the trip. To local spectators who drove up from the valley floor, the view was commonly thrilling, but Lakers found the mountain road and unfenced vistas merely pleasing.

At this meet Frank won the Cranston cup for the second time, with Stan at his heels. Brown had won every meet he had entered for the season, junior jumping at Blue Mountain, PNSA junior nordic and PNSA junior alpine championship, and the American Legion junior ski meet.

The Boise Statesman's sport writer called him "the flashing 15-year-old," and another writer "the 15-year-old powerhouse of McCall."

Later Corey Engen took Brown, Jerry Jones, Bert Armstrong, and Stan Harwood to Sun Valley where teams from 11 western states and two Canadian provinces competed in a three-day meet. A group of McCall parents went along, saw the boys take second place. In these competitions hearty, bluff Stan was usually—not always—a few points behind his quiet, contained cousin. What inner drive does it take to keep a 15-year-old competing cheerfully when he has foreknowledge of second place—second place to a cousin his own age? The question is worth pausing to consider.

In McCall a new fund-raising project flared. Even for the sensation-loving village, the early effects were lurid. Dense clouds of red smoke began boiling out of the Lake club; the wail of the fire siren opened up and kept right on. Fire Chief Bus Johnson, surrounded by volunteers, rushed to the front of the club. But they paid no attention to the blaze, made no effort to man hoses. Instead they manned a loud-speaker.

The fast-gathering, excited crowd was assured that the red smoke was purely synthetic, nothing was afire, but everybody was invited to the Red Hot Firemen's carnival. This carnival cleared $300, not to pay token wages of $1.50 per fire to firemen. Oh no. It was to set up a fund to help any injured fire fighters. Besides, one-fifty didn't even pay for cleaning a man's clothes after a right good fire.

The 1953 legislature made games of chance, i.e., slot machines, pinballs, pegboards, and others, illegal in Idaho. If McCall suffered withering economic loss, as many had been sure it would, the evidence was not overwhelming. At Shore Lodge, the battery of machines disappeared from the corridor leading to the diningroom, a spot secluded enough for those who wished to pursue their hobby in relative quiet, yet an easy reminder. The other clubs in town disposed of theirs. Occasionally a sentimentalist wished he could acquire one "as a piece of furniture," handy to lay hats on, and the question then arose, wasn't it legal to possess a slot *if the handle were removed.*

Preparations were made to ship many of the machines into territory permitting their use, and this raised another question: if machines in transit were still within the state on the day they became illegal, wouldn't state police be obliged to smash them or arrest their owners. Lawyers mused on the problem; some owners had last-day headaches. However, the record doesn't seem to show any McCall owners in trouble.

220

Betty Harwood got out a letter to remind Valley county that services of the Red Cross would be lost unless the county's quota was raised—last year it fell $200 short, a nearly unthinkable lapse. Her appeal succeeded. McCall alone raised half of the $1660 asked.

Becoming literary, the Progressive club sponsored the sale of Helen Markley Miller's new *Promenade All,* with profits to help repair the city library which was housed in the town hall. Mrs. Miller's book had just been chosen by the Junior Literary Guild (as were three others subsequently), and McCall could indeed be proud that its children had studied in her high school English and history classes.

At Shore Lodge Perry Bruce, who had been associated with the management of the Hotel Boise for 20 years, succeeded Harry Grabow as manager.

In June the Payette Lakes Lumber company store, a separate corporation from B T and L situated across the roadway from the mill office, was awarded a face lifting. Originally it was a blacksmith shop, a wonderful place in the days when the mill still used horses. Then it became a truck shop, finally a store and retail lumber yard. Now an all-glass front was installed and the interior done over in style. Three hundred people crowded in for the opening. They admired the hardware stock and furnishings and drew door prizes ranging from buckets of paint to screendoors from vice-president and manager Ted Harwood and from assistant manager Wyman Zachary. During the war Ted had put in the same overtime as anyone else in the B T and L shipping department—sometimes it seemed like 24 hours a day. Now the store was his responsibility as well as the assignment as purchaser for the camps.

The new store was not the only Harwood excitement. Ted and Betty now closed the doors on their small white house near Ida's and Carl's, and moved to a rapidly built new one farther west on the lake, where a CCC camp had formerly stood. It was near

Warren's and Jayne's, and like theirs the house made every possible bid for water, sky and mountain panorama.

Betty and Ted had known for a long time that their dream house must be big enough for their children's friends as well as their own. Thus it encompassed a foyer with planters and much greenery, a large living room with one end for dining, a big kitchen also good for dining, a lengthy bedroom L, and a huge recreation room below that opened to a terrace on the lake.

This house was no ivory tower—it was meant for stout living and doing. The living room fireplace offered comfortable wide ledges for sitting, or for plants, games or TV. There were big comfortable chairs and low tables, a piano and a hi-fi. The kitchen looked as if meant for sizable people helping each other turn out a meal; and the garage had the dimensions of a small warehouse.

But all this was not space-wasting. The Harwood house, like the Warren Browns', would be open to many public affairs. There would be bride and baby showers here, church teas, community money-raising parties, and a great deal of easy, unhurried, uncalculated visiting.

A house-warming surprised the new dwellers, and a gift clock, ticking away on the kitchen wall, assured them that they were at last at home.

The Visitors' bureau, set up the previous year with Nelle Tobias and Dr. Susan Kerr among committee heads, printed now its first report, "Fishing in the McCall Area," written by Gladys Heter. "We should concentrate on our tourists," the bureau announced, "and give them the best we have to offer, aiding them to find the recreation they seek." Here again was a strictly community-manned move, all workers volunteer, nobody paid.

McCall Shriners came forth with a piece of summer thoughtfulness: they borrowed private cars and hired buses and took to the Shrine Circus in Boise more than a hundred McCall children. For many it was their first circus, and oh the excitement. The Shriners also remembered that children at home or away from home need to eat, not only a hotel lunch, but quite constantly before and after.

And now came an event that drew upon those esthetic qualities that Carl Brown's (usually) gentle nature and finely made hands implied. He had witnessed the Miss Idaho entertainment previously afforded McCall, but now he was asked *to help judge* a division of the Miss Universe beauty competition that was coming to town. Advance notice affirmed as before that there would be no measurements taken. Helen Farrer, a dramatics teacher from Boise, directed the program on the Shore Lodge patio, where before a crowd of 300 Carl eventually crowned Miss Pat Carter, 18, of Boise. And he enjoyed every minute of it.

The young women were guests of the Lodge, they were entertained at the home of Frank and Florence Freeman, and Roy May took them for a motorboat ride on the lake. Had McCall been able to think of anything else to do for them, it would have thought.

Citizens now fell to to aid a local boy, 18-year-old John E. Smith, who attended the school for the deaf at Gooding. John had been named outstanding track man for the deaf in the United States, and he longed to compete in the international games for the deaf in Brussels. This summer he was working at the mill, and Margaret Peck found out about his special longing. She and Gladys Heter solicited. The Rotary club gave them $50, the mill $100, the mill benefit association $180, and others enough to total $360. John went. He brought back a record to his friends: winner of the 200 meter race, and winner in a 400-meter double.

On Labor day, the first annual Idaho tour of horseless carriages selected McCall as its objective. With its spring mud and winter snow troubles in early days, McCall probably had worn out its own vintage cars, but what matter. The oldest car to make the climb from the south was a 1905 Reo, and a Nyssa couple won the prize for bringing their horseless the greatest distance.[75]

The serpent made a summer appearance, and Boone McCallum, editor of the Star, decided it was time the creature had a name. After all, he was neither a Johnny-come-lately nor yet a fly-by-night. McCallum said he would give $5 for the best name suggestion.

In Boise the Statesman unexpectedly assisted by offering to "add a few bucks" to the prize—hadn't a number of its readers seen the serpent? Ike Wescott, an Idaho industrialist, for instance. Once when Mr. Wescott was sipping *a lemonade* in the Shore Lodge bar, he suddenly saw the serpent in a mirror that reflected the lake. But when he ran for a closer view, he naturally ran in the wrong direction and wrenched his knee.

Now the prize money stood at $75, and letters poured in on McCallum. In these letters, descriptions of the serpent were startling in their similarity. They agreed on humpy shape, undulation, armored head and neck. They agreed on length, about 30 feet. And no one objected to being quoted. Though most of the letters came from Long Valley and the Boise area, every part of the country was represented, showing McCall's wide popularity. Suggestions ranged from names short and snappy to Latin polysyllabics. At Shore Lodge Perry Bruce threw caution aside and promised to use the chosen name on Lodge stationery.

Judges were announced. They included legislators, the governor, the McCall mayor, presidents of service clubs, and two McCall women, Mrs. Grace Hoff and Mrs. Wayne Webb.

The judges put their wits together, finally focussed on a letter from a Virginian who had formerly lived in

Twin Falls. The man wrote: "Vas you dere, Sharlie? Name him Sharlie."

The judges agreed that Sharlie was undoubtedly dere. But so far as anyone could discover, Sharlie did not come up to be christened.

CHAPTER FORTY

Frank Brown greeted the new year, 1954, by taking the Walker cup in downhill at Blue Mountain ski course near Stout Springs, Oregon, and claimed the Cranston cup for the third time at Bogus Basin, this giving him permanent possession. In February he went to Duluth for a national skiing event with 79 entries. Here he took 3rd place.

The winter storms provided McCall with three days of pseudo-pioneer life. That is, it lived without electricity. Heavy snow broke power lines and blocked roads. Families that pumped drinking water from the lake had to borrow from those with city water. The town attics were ransacked for candles and old oil lamps; stores that had either soon sold out. It was hard to find a public place to eat. Lola's served hot coffee made on a portable oil stove, and Esther's used propane gas and got by. Shore Lodge was reduced to serving cold sandwiches, then began cooking on its fireplaces, cooking for 60. Some stores managed to keep their clerks and customers half warm with oil heaters. Fortunately the mill with its auxiliary electric plant could continue running.

For three days Leonard Ackaret kept the town snowplow at work so that at least no one was marooned. And neighbors could hover around each other's fireplaces and talk about how necessary electricity was—how on earth did their parents endure life without it.

With power restored and the not irreverent feeling that God was again in his heaven, the Business and Professional women decided on a cabaret and a cake auction to raise funds for polio. The dance at the Yacht club brought in $1400, besides being very funny and thrilling. The cake affair was sponsored by Albert Fleetwood, called Curley, proprietor of the Old Oregon Trail, a lunch counter, bar, dancehall place. His parents-in-law, the Joe Morleys, contributed a cake stirred up by Mrs. Morley that contained four dozen eggs and sold for $190. Twenty other contributors' cakes brought in $327. Another $300 was collected by B T and L employees. All in all the Business ladies felt satisfied.

Through early spring the cousins Stan and Frank went to one ski tournament after another, their parents usually along. No one was more conscientious about this chore than Jayne and Warren Brown, no matter whose children were going. They were thoughtful, generous, good company—and the proprieties, everybody knew, would be observed.

At 14 Stan began working summers at Newt McCall's drygoods store. On his first morning he found himself waiting on a wealthy Boise woman and her four children, all of them needing summer shoes. Stan explained that he was right new on the job but would do his best. His boss noted what was happening but left Stan alone. However, the woman took to Stan, everybody's chillun got shoes, and left happily.

When the McCall golf tournament opened, Stan wanted time off to play, but McCall told him that he'd have to fire him if he didn't show up for work. Stan played golf, was fired. Out of a job, he went to Shore Lodge and asked if they didn't need a dishwasher. He was hired. Stan had a good time with his dishes and teasing the girls. Then the Labor Day celebration opened up. This time Stan stayed on the job.

At 15 and 16 he worked under Art Roberts on the State Forest, doing whatever was assigned him. The next summer he drove the water wagon at the mill and looked forward to being 18 when, he was promised, he could begin driving a logging truck.

Many fathers dream that their boys may follow them in the field they have already made their own. But neither the Browns nor the Harwoods considered doing more than pointing out occupations that might afford special advantages of one kind or another, or that might satisfy. At school Frank's marks were always high, his tastes on the creative side. Moreover, he knew how to concentrate. Even while he awaited a ski decision he was centering his thought on something ahead.

Stan liked the idea of business. Besides sports, he was beginning to appreciate good music—to hear it, not especially to try making it. Like his grandfather, he loved to dance, and like both Betty and Ted he was basically friendly and warm.

One more school year for the cousins, then decisions that might mean a forking of the road they had traveled together.

In June 1953 something had happened to a McCall citizen that pleased many. This citizen was Aunty Harland, saint of the Brown household in the children's early years, now living with her son-in-law and daughter, the Jack Hayeses. Before coming to live in McCall Aunty had returned once to her native Wales, sailing both ways on the Lusitania. Now her sister sent her a present, her fare home for the coronation of Elizabeth II. However, Aunty had been ill and was barely out of the hospital; and some said that Catharine Hayes would be absolutely foolish to let her mother go. On the other hand, the doctor thought it might be a good thing.

Aunty rose from her bed and went. Friends met the tired little traveler in Chicago and in New York, helped her with her connections. She sailed on the Queen Mary, and in five short days debarked not at Southampton, where dock workers were on strike, and where her sister was to meet her, but at Plymouth. Nevertheless, like a true and resourceful McCallite, Aunty, now improved by the voyage, worked out this problem with no trouble.

During her stay, besides the excitement of the coronation, she and her sister enjoyed a tremendous gathering in Wales where singing groups met in competition in a church that held thousands of people. Though home so briefly, Aunty had already recovered her Welsh speech, could understand every word she heard. Suddenly the presiding officer was calling her to come to the platform—he had heard she was a Welshwoman all the way from the States. Paralyzed by shyness, Aunty told her sister she couldn't go. Urged and urged, she weakened, although her knees were shaking more than that time when she staggered up from her toboggan spill.

She went to the platform, she made a little speech —in the Welsh tongue of course. During the waves of applause, the presiding man whispered to her that no one could have done better.

Carl Brown, who liked to tease her, should have been there. So should her grandson, Jon Hayes.

CHAPTER FORTY-ONE

In December 1953 the 1800-foot T-bar tow at McCall ski hill was completed by the Ski club at a cost of $15,000. It had eleven suspension towers spaced up the hill and could lift 600 skiers per hour. Barely two months later, right in mid-season, the ski lodge at the foot of the hill burned. Everything inside burned with it. But by the time the concrete floor had cooled, volunteers were setting up fabricated bunkhouses for temporary use. These were made by B T and L, and supplied by Warren Brown. When they could get their breath, 25 to 30 ski club members joined to donate their time to replace the old building. This didn't surprise anyone.

One hard-to-meet loss was the equipment of skiing youngsters — between 200 and 250 pairs of skis burned. The Club asked people to donate old skis so that juniors needn't be forced out of the sport. And the skis came in. They came from places as far away as Boise.

June, and the Ulmers left for St. Louis to see David graduate in medicine at Washington University. His next station would be Peter Bent Brigham hospital in Boston, for his internship.

From the age of 16 David had worked in the mill in summer. He was never careless with his money, and his father assured him that a good education for him and his sister Marilyn was his parents' dearest wish, that they would see both through college. "This is a business agreement," he explained. "You will owe only us. Then if we're ever in need, we'll let you help us."

Later when his mother became seriously ill, David wired offering to drop medical school and come home. Marilyn Sorrensen and her husband also offered their savings. Fortunately Les Ulmer could manage without accepting his children's sacrifices.

David spent two years at the hospital, two years in the army, then returned to Peter Bent Brigham, where he does research in internal medicine. He is married and has a son of his own. Marilyn has three children.[76]

A long time ago, in 1930, the McCall airport had been scraped out. In 1932 it was formally dedicated with state aeronautics director Chet Moulton and regional forester C. J. Olsen of Ogden present. Over the years it had become one of the busiest in the state. With an air strip of 5000 feet, it handled daily passengers and mail flights north and south. In addition smoke-jumpers used it to fly in and out of McCall. Sportsmen flew to meets, supplies went to remote settlements and loggers to their camps. Hunters were flown to inaccessible wilds and when they proceeded to get lost, they were rescued.

Now it was decided that the port should be rededicated and given a formal name. The governor and state officials were invited to come. The Idaho Municipal league, winding up its sessions at Shore Lodge the same day, would be on hand; and 150 attending mayors would be given a special flight over adjacent Hell's canyon of the Snake, deepest gorge in North America. Indeed a very big day it was to be.

McCall weather had not been consulted. With high winds and leaden low-hung skies, the weather said No. State officials stayed home, most of them, and the gathered mayors kept their feet on the ground, happy to remain indoors at the Lodge. Art Roberts, big sorrel-topped granitic mayor of McCall, did the dedicating briefly and specifically: To the people of McCall, the county of Valley, the state of Idaho and the United States of America. Name of the port: Municipal airport. That was it.

In March 1955 occurred the rescue from McCall of a downed pilot, and the story, written by another pilot, Jim Larkin, shows graphically some of the problems area fliers had to meet.[77]

"On Wednesday, March 9, we received word at the McCall airport that Bill Woods, veteran Boise pilot, had crashed his Travelaire on the middle fork of the Salmon river, a short distance above the Indian Creek landing field; that he was unhurt except for a cut lip and that he was making his way down stream to the field where he wished to be picked up.

"I took off immediately in our ski-equipped Travelaire. Upon reaching Indian creek and seeing no sign of Woods,

230

I began flying upstream, reaching the crash scene in approximately 10 miles. Tracks indicated that Woods had forded the waist-deep river and was headed down stream, fighting three feet of snow, on foot.

"It was evident that he would require . . . snowshoes, and possibly help, to ever reach the air strip. An extremely turbulent, gusty wind had ruled out the possibility of returning to McCall for smoke-jumpers.

"Having an extra pair of snowshoes and sufficient emergency rations to reach Woods on foot, I returned to the airstrip, made up a trail pack, and started up stream.

"Later in the afternoon a Boise-based helicopter made an unsuccessful attempt to pick up Woods. I talked to the pilot, who was able to land near me, and after being advised of the inability of the helicopter pickup, continued working my way upstream.

"Travel was difficult due to the snow condition, and I was forced to stop due to darkness about two miles above the mouth of Pistol creek. The next morning the Department of Aeronautics plane, based in Boise, was able to break through bad weather and via loud speaker notified me that Woods was a short distance above the mouth of Rapid river and on the opposite side of the Middle Fork from me.

"Soon Warren Brown began circling overhead, flying his Super Cub. Joint effort in McCall had turned up a very well planned emergency kit, including sandwiches, snow-pacs, socks, walkie-talkie, and drugs to ward off pneumonia. Warren was accompanied by Wayne Webb; and after sighting Woods, this kit was dropped to him.

"Warren had fought a series of snowstorms and almost zero visibility for almost two and a half hours, trying to reach the Middle Fork area. Warren and Wayne returned to the airstrip, and accompanied by E. G. Beckley, started up to meet Woods and myself.

"I reached Woods a few minutes after Warren and Wayne had completed their drop. He was then two miles upstream from the mouth of Rapid river. After a slow three miles we were forced to camp for the night in a pelting snowstorm.

"Friday morning after two hours we reached a packed snowshoe trail. In a short time we met Warren and Wayne who had doubled back the previous night to spend it at the guard station. On their well-beaten trail we made very good time, arriving at the Indian creek strip by mid-afternoon."

In this account are no heroics. When Larkin couldn't reach the pilot the first night he "was forced to stop due to darkness." What kind of a night did he spend? He doesn't say because he suspects the downed man probably spent a worse one.

Warren Brown, who fought a series of snowstorms and almost zero visibility for more than two hours —perhaps this wasn't foolhardy, but it sounds like crowding luck. He could not return to McCall and sit thinking about a man trapped in frozen wastes, maybe unable even to make a fire.[78]

After his family, hard work and competition, Warren Brown loved the outdoors best. That meant not only flying but skiing, riding horseback, driving. Driving pretty fast. Once on the South Fork road his pickup collided with a loaded logging truck. His head was cracked, his scalp torn. Men got him to the nearest hospital, Cascade, and there he stayed for several days until taken on to another hospital in Boise. Previous to this mishap, he was driving on the highway north of Horseshoe Bend when a truck-trailer coming at high speed jackknifed in his path, and his car crashed into the cab of the truck. With him was Bill Kirk of McCall. Both were knocked unconscious, the car was demolished. They were rushed to Boise and treated for shock, cuts, bruises. Then both men went home. Neither had time to lie abed.

Thanksgiving 1954 brought sadness to McCall. Murray Numbers, called Mud or Muddy, driving home from the University of Idaho, was killed in a car accident. He had skied among the best, first as a Mitey Mite, then as a Junior. Particularly in 1948 he had won many skiing honors. He was the younger son of Dr. and Mrs. Don Numbers, who knew well that a boy can be warm, hearty and hopeful today and tomorrow gone.

A group of Muddy's college friends, led by Mrs. Roxy Johnson of Boise, a summer resident who was like an aunt to the boy, immediately set up the Muddy Numbers Memorial cups, to be awarded in the ski season coming up, a typical McCall gesture to empha-

Shore Lodge on Payette Lake among its yellow pines. Conventions, celebrities, tourists and McCall people like to eat here.

Western white pine had gray bark broken into small squares. This tree is 6' 9" in diameter a
breast height, 207 feet tall, more than 425 years old. Idaho has the largest stand
of virgin white pine in the world.

size clean sport. The following year Dr. and Mrs. Numbers assumed responsibility for the Memorial, and the cups have been awarded each year since.[79]

After Muddy's death, the Numbers moved to Boise, and though she was happy in their new modern house, Zoe thought sometimes that she would die of loneliness for McCall days, especially for the women with whom she had played cards for 25 years. She missed the Progressive club, of which she was president for five years, and all the back fence visiting and the impromptu morning coffees.

In December Ted Harwood was presented with another recognition of his conscientious Boy Scout work, the bison award. It marked 29 years of participation, but Ted had long lost count of the trips he had made. the troops he had visited. Laid end to end, the hours he had spent at meetings, setting up camps, writing reports and letters would have bulged the time zone.

Alice and Boon McCallum had decided to retire from editing the Star. The paper had been distinguished by the work of good correspondents, it strove for complete coverage, and its proofreading, low point in most country editing, was careful. The touchy school question had been handled with tact, and in his column "As the Days Go By," the editor had spoken with a wisdom and understanding that helped unite McCall people in all their projects, their endless help-ourselves projects.

The McCallums were succeeded by Britt Nedry, a longtime newspaperman and public figure, former publisher of the Kootenai County Leader at Coeur d'Alene. He had recently completed four years as Idaho state occupational licenses director.

One of Nedry's first moves was to give the front page a livelier format, and to introduce a column called Lumberjack, which reported events important to lumber people. He "discovered" Jean Eddin, a high school girl who wrote imaginative prose and poetry on simple local themes, and often featured Jean's work.

In his masthead he spoke for development of the region—"progressive American free enterprise, competitive system in business and government." His wife Elizabeth read proof for him, and together they enjoyed the life of their adopted town.

Now and then Nedry liked to let himself go with a piece of description: "On a March day of deep, deep snow, and more coming down, the jammer heaved the last log aboard the truck, the lines were secured, and the big International was geared for the final trip to the mill. The season's timber harvest is completed until some time in June or July when the woods will again ring with logging activities."

The new editor was resolved on two particular objectives: an adequate high school for McCall and the establishment of the county fair. One of them he was to see realized.

CHAPTER FORTY-TWO

Early in 1955 Warren Brown resigned from the school board, and Henry Knowles was named chairman of the new board. Defendants in the school suit had again been upheld, and perhaps Brown felt that with the end apparently in sight he had a moral right to withdraw, a right to be let alone awhile. Amazing as it might seem, considering the continuous upheaval, the McCall-Donnelly school continued to turn out a pretty well prepared student, and if this student felt any great animosity toward fellow students whose parents and his stood at opposite poles on the issue of a new high school building, it didn't show much. The

234

youngsters seemed trying to wait with patience until their parents came to their senses.

High school graduates went on to college or they went to work, and in either case they did very well. In 1955 among the 24 who graduated were the cousins Frank and Stan. Though Frank missed no ski meets, he came up with grades that made him class valedictorian.

In the Star Bob Brandenburg presented a summary of the 1955 McCall ski season: "In addition to holding all the Pacific Northwestern championships, our junior skiers visited Intermountain at Jackson, Wyoming, February 12 and 13. Not only did they win individually in all events, all four who went . . . but they broke the existing jump hill records. (The four were Stan Harwood, David Butts, Bill Brandenburg and Frank Brown.)

"In the PNSA jumping championship, we sent three skiers and placed one, two, three.

"In the PNSA Alpine championships, our juniors won in both boys' and girls' events. In the national championships we placed four skiers in the top ten in downhill and took first in the slalom as well as placing high in jumping and cross country.

"The Western states championship is to be held at Sun Valley April 2 and 3 and we are sending the entire boys' team and half of the girls' team."

And at Sun Valley, McCall boy and girl skiers led the 11 competing teams with a total of 874 points, four ahead of second place Colorado.

At Bogus Basin Frank Brown took the Cranston cup for the fourth time. This was somewhat confusing since it had been his to keep on his third win.

These achievements of young McCall skiers were not fortuitous. They were caused. Of course there was the climate, which was cold enough and hot enough, wet enough and dry enough to encourage in kids a lusty growth and an inner something that whispered,

235

"Never stop competing." Then there were available ski slopes, and the kind of isolation that tends to keep young minds going ahead in a straight line, uninfluenced by wish-washy trends. Over and above all, there was a community that organized itself to raise funds, hire coaches, build ski facilities, rebuild burned ski facilities, help on equipment and fees for youngsters without the means, and finally to get kids out to the ski hill after school.

For a final factor, parents. Parents who must leave their businesses, their housekeeping, to accompany contestants to meets near and meets distant. Somebody must drive the cars that carried youngsters, and how often this was at night through biting cold, over strange routes. At such times no delays could occur; cars must not stall. Instead of dozing—if there came the chance—a parent must keep awake to proctor car deportment. After the meet, parents must start the children home and deliver them there in good condition.

High school for Frank and for Stan was of the past now, and neither looked ahead to anything but college. Their parents had never thought of anything else either. It would be of interest to know how many scholarships were offered the boys by athletic coaches in colleges that promoted skiing as a sport. Certainly their successes had not gone unnoticed. They wanted to go where they could ski; their parents mentioned first class academics. In the end both boys enrolled at the University of Colorado at Boulder, Frank in architectural engineering, Stan in business administration.

During his senior year Frank had married a Mc-Call girl, sparkling, dark-eyed Sherlene Lawhorn, so for them there would be an apartment which Sherlene would keep but at the same time take classes in interior decorating.

Stan joined Phi Gamma Delta fraternity, along with David Butts and Bert Armstrong, but regardless of house duties and requirements he was at the apartment a good deal. Sherlene had him over for special occasions (food) too. Either the relation between the cousins was changing, or else it had always been this way, needing only time and home-leaving to make it evident. They understood each other better; they felt closer.

Frank's ambitions would always drive him down a straight course; Stan liked to do well but didn't have to outdo everybody else. He wasn't the student Frank had always been—there were other important things. He sang in the glee club and with the house group; he with Butts and Armstrong entered a four-man bicycle relay, a 50-miler, and took first place. One summer he attended his fraternity convention at Swampscott, Massachusetts. Stan liked being and doing with others, his mother over again.

If during this first fall away the two boys and Sherelene missed McCall, they were too busy in their new world to let it weigh on them. And besides Christmas wasn't far off.

At home Jayne Brown had been elected to the board of the Gem area council of Girl Scouts and was sent to San Francisco to moderate a Scouting panel.

In January the National Geographic carried a picture of Frank Brown making the longest official ski jump at Jackson the previous season. The text said: "A bugle call shattered the chilled air. Spectators fastened their eyes on the figure poised on the top of the snow-slick runway. Taking off down hill on a low crouch, he gathered speed—and sprang upward and outward into mid air, arms spreadeagled, body thrust forward in perfect form."

In the secret hearts of dedicated young skiers stand always the Olympics, to be talked about hours on end, but always impersonally, never as if one expected to make the great teams.

At Franconia, New Hampshire, Bill Brandenburg jumped 128 feet to win the junior ski title. Carl and Ida Brown, recalling the New England snows, could picture young Brandenburg poised for take-off. Ida probably jumped with him.

In March David Butts received the Skimeister award.

Britt Nedry rounded it all up: "The repeated achievements of the McCall skiers just shows what can be done . . . on the local level, where all boys and girls start. The faith of Warren Brown, Corey Engen, Jack Setin and many others in the Payette Lakes Ski Club and their sustained efforts, year after year, this is the acorn from which the great oak has grown . . . Look Homeward, Neighbor."

In Nampa, all this time, the Homer Davies had pursued business and taken part in community labors and devoted themselves with outstanding earnestness to rearing their family of four. The sisters Betty and Margaret had remained particularly close and sympathetic, and once when the Davies family came down en mass with flu, one of the boys in the hospital, Betty dropped everything at home and went to Nampa to stay until the situation was normal.

Because she was her father's first daughter, Sharon Davies, blond and sturdy, had been Homer's great delight. Now Heaven sent him another daughter, Deborah Ida. And again the nurses were puzzled—was there an error in the chart? did a father rejoice so over a *fifth* child? But to a man who because of the war had lost out on the babyhood of his older children, the prospect of wet diapers and prattle was only joy.

McCall would always claim all Hoffs, and although Hannah Hoff had been away many years, living in Horseshoe Bend since 1914, her nomination in 1956 as Idaho Mother of the year for Boise county was regarded as a McCall honor. Then, oh excitement, she was chosen to represent all Idaho. A McCall victory.

Hannah attended all regional and state events connected with the movement, and for the final competition she went on to New York. Whenever possible and appropriate, Theodore or one of the children accompanied her, and her husband made the trip east.

Again it made no enormous difference to her friends that the national committee named someone else as all-American Mother. Their candidate was beautiful and strong in every way—anybody could see that. Her heavy braids were no longer brown, but their silver only emphasized her unusual dark eyes. Although she was seriously troubled with arthritis in her knees, she had learned to live with this and continued to keep in touch with whatever was good and essential in small Horseshoe Bend. She and her husband had no thought of ever leaving the town, where their mill provided the only payroll, and a big one.[81]

Though Theodore had bought timber "when he should have been buying bread and butter," it would seem he had made no great mistake. His closest haul for logs is now less than 10 miles, his longest about 40. The mill is strictly modern, and includes a moulding machine—their best mouldings are made of Western pine, and they ship them by the carload.

Hoff and his son Ted, who is in business with him, also buy from logging outfits. His payroll for one summer month in 1959 was $45,000, for the mill alone. This went to 69 employees. The town has grocery stores, service stations, cafes, a grade school with four teachers, and several organized churches.

CHAPTER FORTY-THREE

The school situation was back again. Warren Brown had never regretted his involvement in the struggle. However, it is not easy to take unmerited criticism and visible signs of dislike or at least distrust in others' faces. It is no less galling that one could wash his hands of the whole business at no personal loss. But the Brown way is frequently hard.

In February the board of school district 421 opened literally with prayer, and it proceeded, so the Star reported, "with decorum and serious consideration." In the interim of suits and hearings, Warren had stood on the sidelines. Now he again accepted appointment, and a new approach to the problem was suggested by William Powers, superintendent of the district.

A committee of 50 with subcommittees was appointed to present plans covering what to build and where to build it. These committees of electors returned with numerous combination plans, but the most popular—to build a high school in McCall—could not get a 70 percent vote from the overall committee, and this had been agreed as necessary.

The aid of a disinterested outside survey was decided on, but this plan was abandoned in favor of a direct referendum to the voters. Let them choose between constructing a high school or a grade school at McCall, and in either case, modernize the Donnelly building that had served so long amid such buffeting currents.

Perhaps the thorough discussion provided by the overall and subcommittees was responsible; perhaps exhaustion had set in. In any case, an astonishing spirit of cooperation and rational action now prevailed, according to the Star, and chairman Laurel Hansen urged that once more the people be asked their wishes. If they didn't approve, "let's keep on until we can find a plan they do approve."

To the amazement of many, on May 22, by an easy two-thirds, the voters of the district indicated that they wanted a high school in McCall, exact location not specified. In McCall the outcome was too momentous for noisy rejoicing. It was better just to feel thankful that what so many had sought for so long had finally come about, on paper at least, and to agree soberly with Ida Brown that "sometimes you have to try and try for a thing, even when it's right."

It would be months before building could start, and meanwhile school conditions must be improved. When the state high school supervisors reported on county schools for the year 1955-56 they had commended district 421 for the quality of its teachers and their discipline, but they had *condemned* the high school building. The referendum was the answer to that.

In September Warren Brown and Laurel Hansen were reelected to the board, and when they found that fall enrollment in the high school had increased from 132 to 145, they had not only an endorsement of the course they had worked out, but a sharp spur to accelerated action.

Brown Tie and Lumber was willing to donate land for the new building, and now it proposed to trade 22 acres in the Hoff and Brown addition for 11 acres that Boise Payette Lumber company had already offered for the same purpose. The 22-acre tract seemed a site more acceptable to out-of-town parents, and it would allow more room for expansion, for playing fields and so on. In this swap, both lumber companies became donors to the school project.

On April 12 of the following spring, with the usual bright stirring of life in the midst of melting snow, the board met again. Warren Brown moved that the members go to Boise, meet architects there, and work out a building and remodeling program. The motion carried.

CHAPTER FORTY-FOUR

With its years-long school problem now in the background, McCall began to dream of another favorite project. For at least 11 years, plans had been laid to build a hospital. It was still 30 miles to the hospital in Cascade, 40 miles to the one in Council—better roads and faster cars had shortened time but not miles. In the days before McCall had a doctor, one summoned from New Meadows might charge $25 in addition to his fee, and considering the roads he might travel and the patients at home he might have to neglect, this amount was entirely reasonable.

In 1955 the first specific proposals for a hospital were printed in the Star. In July 1956, the Progressive club, as enterprising as ever, launched a drive under president Mrs. Ralph Paris to start raising funds. With the donated help of an Emmett auctioneer, Wally Clements, the women set up a two-day rummage sale engineered by Mrs. Reed Gillespie that swept clean the town's basements, garages and attics. At jam-packed gatherings these stacks of oddments were so lustily haggled over and re-bought by citizens and summer visitors that the club wound up with $300. Moreover, everybody felt so uplifted that a Hospital Day, August 4, was set aside, the drive to continue.

By the appointed day, such fervor had developed that its myriad outpourings became difficult to keep in mind. Solicitors under Betty Harwood pledged nearly every business in town for 10 percent of the day's sales. Wage earners pledged the women a day's pay. Farmerettes and Job's Daughters sold home-made popcorn, cake and candy. Street breakfasts were served by Rotarians, and the Jaycees opened a four-day carnival while Jay-C-Ettes served lunches all week

242

for the current golf tournament. At a lovely lakeshore home the St. Andrews Guild gave a benefit tea and accepted $135 for the hospital from the earnest drinkers who flocked in.

The Stock Car racing association donated entire receipts for one day. From the Payette National Forest employees, to whom the thought of a close-by hospital was very attractive, came generous contributions; and Jane and Louise of The Cedars (not a cemetery) gave a swank style show at the Yacht club and turned over their take.

To put on the capstone, the Progressive club reported that in addition to its auction it had promoted enough other projects to raise an unbelievable total of $2400.

All in all, if any McCall citizen above the bassinet age escaped the contributor's net, if he ate no benefit food or candy, danced on no benefit tickets, watched no benefit shows; and if he didn't toil to prepare food or provide money-raising entertainment or produce rummage, then his name isn't known.

The Village board appointed a permanent hospital committee: Howard Carney, Margaret Peck, Ralph Paris, Wyman Zachary and Art Roberts. A finance committee that was already serving agreed to stay aboard. This included Dr. Eugene Pflug, Mary Thurston, and Ted Harwood.

It had been ascertained that Hill Burton, a Federal agency, would meet half the construction cost of an approved hospital. In an election, 87 percent of McCall voters favored a bond issue to cover its share of the total cost, which was $110,000. Additional funds would be required for furnishing and equipment, but, incredible or not, between bonding and independent fund raising, this local achievement, this long-dreamed hospital now started building. In November 1956 it opened its doors, and opened them *in the black*. As a non-profit institution, it would plow back its earnings into maintenance, and bank any surplus against later expansion costs. It would also have some income from the medical-dental clinic under its roof.

For the opening ceremonies McCall people crowded in to see with their own eyes what faith and toil had wrought. They saw equipment of the latest, best design. They flocked about the sterilizer, the anesthetic equipment, and fancied themselves lying on the operating table under the operating lights. They inspected the emergency ward and the X-ray and formula rooms, took special delight in the bassinet nursery and the incubator, a new sight to many. They would have tried the orthopedic beds if asked, and they wondered what it would be like recuperating in the wards or in the private rooms. Then there was the laundry, kitchen and food storage rooms, and all the other utility compartments that a building of this type required.

Most of them could think of nothing more the place would ever need, and wondered how it could require all the space it now occupied. Yet within four years a new wing would have to be added.[82]

Doctors Eugene Pflug and John W. Swartley, partners, established their medical clinic in the building and Merril G. Evans, a dentist, opened offices. (Another doctor and dentist would have offices in town.)

Mrs. Frances Vassar, a registered nurse, was made administrator. Around the corner from her desk was that of Mrs. Edith Vassar, receptionist for the two doctors. Though their names would often be confused, the Vassar women were not related, even by marriage.

A sigh of satisfaction so vigorous it might have been mistaken for some natural evocation, such as a summer whirlwind, ascended from McCall. The hospital was here, the school would come. Brown Tie and Lumber echoed this sense of uplift in its own way, with a half page ad in the Star setting forth "the principles of America," reminding citizens of the inestimable value of American freedom and the responsibility that freedom carried.

CHAPTER FORTY-FIVE

Beautiful McCall, where nothing's small, as Beth Rodenbaugh put it, now had a population of 1500 year-round dwellers, but homes available for mill workers had not multiplied. In fact, it was a good question whether they had even added. Carl and Warren Brown knew that in many instances mill workers were ready for better homes, but joint financing would bring them faster. Accordingly they developed 15 lots south of the U. S. Forest buildings and the hospital, and worked out a basic house plan that could be modified to secure variety of appearance. In this young Frank with his architectural studies took an eager hand, and the result was a compact three-bedroom house with attached garage attractively finished and set in ample grounds. The houses rose swiftly, were soon occupied. Owners were happy, and the addition greatly improved this corner of town. Carl, who worried chronically about families he thought were poorly housed, was especially pleased.

At one time he had been troubled about a mill worker who had no bathroom. The fellow was a faithful hand and certainly deserved to be comfortable. So Carl thought it over, then gathered up a plumber and carpenter and their complicated supplies and equipment, and appeared one morning at the man's house. By night, whether the man wanted it or not, the house had a gift bathroom well along.

Open shop had always been the practice at B T and L in McCall although the mill at Riggins, in which Warren held a controlling interest, was unionized. It had, however, been under several ownerships, with nothing like the continuity of owner-employee relations in the McCall set-up.

By very long odds Carl Brown preferred open shop, and his employees had always had benefits equivalent to those that unions provided. Equivalent or better.

Attempts from the outside to unionize B T and L had been made and might continue to be made, but a core of satisfaction with conditions as they were had thus far brought such attempts to nothing.

Eventually Warren Brown assembled an employee's manual that was put into the hands of each man so he could see what he was getting in benefits and what he could depend on. Employees already had their own association to which any worker could belong. It elected a committee to manage its affairs, and the committee appointed a chairman and a treasurer, the latter paid for his services.

Condensed from the manual, these are the worker's benefits in the McCall mill:

Paid vacations of a week, after one year's employment; two weeks paid annual vacation after five years employment. Group insurance, a combination of monthly paid-up contributions by employees and comparable term insurance paid for by B T and L. If employment terminates for any reason, the employee recovers all he had paid up, cash value never less than his total contribution.

Group hospital and surgical plan administered through the Employees Benefit association. Retirement plan with B T and L matching the $4 per month paid in by each employee. Retirement at 60, the worker to receive the total of his contributions plus those of the company, and *in addition*, a percentage of this sum dependent on length of service: 25 percent for between 5 and 10 years; 50 percent between 10 and 15 years; 75 percent above 15 years.

For example, a man who has worked 16 years would have contributed $768, the company would have matched this, and he would receive $1536, plus 75 percent of this sum, or $1152, making a final total of $2688. Or, for each $1 he contributed a return of $3.50. A man retiring or discharged before 60 would withdraw his contributions plus interest at 2 percent.

To the hospital plan each member contributes $3 per month, matched by the company. These benefits are outlined in detail in the booklet. They cover doctor and hospital care and death. If an employee has a fire in his home, he receives $100 assistance.

The surgical schedule, payment for operations, is stated in fine detail and includes about everything from amputation of toe to trephining of skull.

Causes and reasons for discharge are stated plainly: changes in operation that reduce the size of the crew; false statements made on application forms; incompetency, insubordination or physical disability; neglect of duty; absenteeism without bona fide excuse; dishonesty, disorderly conduct; fighting or horseplay leading to injury to fellow worker, abusive conduct or that interfering with the operation of any department; bringing intoxicants to or consuming same in place of work, or reporting intoxicated for work; smoking in prohibited areas; continued operation of or failure to report defective machinery likely to result in injury to a fellow worker or add to cost of operating.

Not covered in the pamphlet is the fact that any employee sick or needing money would be getting it in relation to his needs and honesty from the ever sympathetic Carl[83] and the more realistic Warren.

Pat Hayes, office manager for B T and L, attends meetings of the Employees Benefit association, but he goes only as an advisor.

For Carl the fall was livened by a trip with fellow Rotarians to Canadian clubs across the border. The Warren Browns laid aside work and went hunting. The Progressive club faced the town wear and tear of summer tourism and placed litter barrels about town and urged youngsters to use them as an example to their parents.

Ida Brown entertained the Washwoman's club. Winter set in.

CHAPTER FORTY-SIX

In March 1957, a reporter for the Harvester World, publication of the International Harvester company, came to McCall and was moved to near ecstasy over the way the pint-sized and the juniors of the area were encouraged in skiing. The World caught fire from its reporter and gave not only its cover picture but four pages of text and more pictures to the story.

"The town was roused in the 1940's," the reporter wrote, "to give its youngsters the same chance to shine at a strictly mountain sport as is given those interested in basketball in flatter states. Payette Lakes Ski club directs programs for juniors 13 to 18 and Mitey Mites 6 to 13. Corey Engen, 1948 Olympics team member, and U. S. National ski champion in 1951, coaches.[84]

"Warren Brown sends around a bus each evening after school and on weekends. The all-out participation idea is making youngsters crackerjack skiers. When the ski lodge burned in 1956, Warren Brown contributed the lumber to rebuild. The town furnished the labor.

"Results, 18-year-old David Butts is currently national Skimeister (best all round skier) and Bill Brandenburg last year at 18 became national jumping champion. Frank Brown skied to downhill and cross country junior championships in 1955. A year later he became national ski champion."

In the spring of 1957 at Aspen, Colorado, Frank Brown, Stan Harwood, Bert Armstrong and David Butts all from McCall skied for the University of Colorado. It was here that Frank won his Skimeister award; Harwood was first in downhill.

For the third consecutive year McCall skiers won the tournament at Jackson, Wyoming. Bill Brandenburg won first in jumping, Dee Dee McBride second in the girls' slalom race and Diane Brown third.

At Betty Harwood's house the McCall library held a silver tea and an autographing party for Helen Markeley Miller, author of two new books, *Dust in the Gold Sack*, and *Benjamin Bonneville, Explorer*. Intended for teenagers, Mrs. Miller's novels are fact-based and her research careful. Once she delayed publication in order to ascertain a certain date. In St. Louis a helpful librarian made a trip to a local cemetery to secure it for her from a tombstone.

Another party at Betty's, with Sylvia Close helping, featured local history *in person*. Many of the guests were bonafide pioneers. Blanche Darkwood had arrived in the town in 1904 to teach school while she homesteaded. Grace Bennett came in 1914. Rose Blackwell described early days in the Doumecq and White Bird country. Other guests were Marie Strode, not quite a pioneer since she was born in McCall in 1919; Hattie Sloan, who had lived in Old Meadows before coming to McCall in 1916; Alta Zimmerman who first saw Idaho in 1902; and Alta Legler who had spent her summers in McCall for nearly 55 years.

It could not be said in society page style that conversation was enjoyed. There *was* no conversation. There was only one tale topping another, billowed on women's laughter and laced with the homey clatter of teacups. As official historian for the Progressive club, Betty was doing her research in a new way.

In May Diane Brown, a high school senior, was chosen queen of Job's Daughters. While she was being elected president of the high school student body, no less, her brother in Colorado was being named to the National Collegiate ski team, four-way.

In April Carl and Ida returned from Arizona, their last winter away. With the new hospital and his favorite doctor close, Carl saw no reason for leaving the home town and all the people he loved and understood. As for Ida, she could be happy and healthy anywhere.

They came back in time to see the moving of a building that reminded them of their first days in McCall. It was the once elegant bay-windowed house that Clem Blackwell had built for his wife Fanny in 1910, next door to the Browns. He had contracted the house at a cost of $350 plus materials, the carpenters getting

$1.50 a day. After Mrs. Blackwell's death, it went through several hands, finally becoming the Silver Maple apartments. Now it was being moved onto a hill on the east side of town.

In Boulder, it had begun to seem to Stan Harwood that he was older than Frank and Sherlene; that despite their steady sticking to business and a new responsibility ahead they were still pretty young and fragile, and that he must look after them unobtrusively. (This was another bit of his mother showing up in him.) If Frank had to be away and Sherlene were alone, Stan was sure he should be available, just in case.

In addition there was the pressure of approaching finals, and the excitement of Frank's being named to the all-American ski team at the NSA meeting in Alta, Utah.

But in the end all went well, and on May 31 to Frank and Sherlene was born a little boy bonny and brown-eyed. They named him Charlie Carl.

When the news reached McCall, Jayne boarded a plane and flew to Boulder, while Ida and Carl complimented themselves on a great-grandchild. Truly they had done something pretty fine. In Boulder Stan felt as if he had become an uncle.

In the summer of 1958 the new Donnelly-McCall high school was finished in McCall. That autumn the first classes sat in the well-lighted, generous new building. Those who had gone through the struggle for better buildings and had seen families not speaking to families because they differed body and soul on the *way* to get results were willing to forget the past, and to outsiders the scars of dissent seemed practically healed.

The single-floor structure of wood and concrete contained 44,000 square feet, provided 16 classrooms, a library and a cafeteria-study hall. Across a narrow open space sat the gym, 110 feet square. In the main building was room for grades one to six, but McCall 7th and 8th graders would still go to Donnelly.[85]

A woman of unusual experience would teach here. She was Celestia Coonrod (called Lesta), and she had taught her first school in Van Wyck many years before. After this first school she was married and did not teach for 14 years. After the death of her husband Robert, a rancher and freighter, Mrs. Coonrod attended summer school in Boise, farming out her three children the while. She resumed teaching in Long Valley, continuing for the next 40 years, finally "getting to teach" in the new school at McCall. Here one of her fifth grade pupils was her own great-grandson, Randal Mundt. Previous to Randal she had taught her daughter Faye (Wallace) and her granddaughter June Wallace Mundt.

When she taught at the Center school there was no place for Teacher and her little family to live, so people made a granary into a small house for them. Faye then in the 8th grade helped her mother teach the smaller children. Her own lessons her mother heard while they washed the dishes at night. The 8th grade diplomas of Celestia Coonrod's three children all bore her signature.[86]

CHAPTER FORTY-SEVEN

In odd pockets of the land there still exist a few people, often non-taxpayers, who believe that lumbering means turning loose amid God's great trees a heartless monster; that lumbermen are responsible for all blackened stumps and all piles of wood debris; that flooding streams and diminished water supply, no matter where found, are chargeable to logging.

No lumberman with sense leaves his own lands in unsightly fire-inviting shape, and as to cutting on lands of the United States Forest, the rules there are so stringent and on the whole so tightly enforced that the forest primeval probably regards itself as improved by the passage of saw, jammer and loading truck along its aisles.

The U.S. Forest service was organized in 1905. First chief forester Gifford Pinchot, and after him Henry Graves (1910) and William B. Greeley (1920) are credited with the setting of a policy of forest preservation that was followed through by Stuart, Silcox, Clapp, Watts and McArdle. This policy, the preservation of national forests by cutting on a self-sustaining basis, was conceived by President Theodore Roosevelt.

Thirty years before Roosevelt, in 1876, the government had appointed an agent, Dr. Franklin B. Hough, to investigate and collect data on forest resources. His reports were presented over the ensuing years, and in 1881 his agency became a division of forestry in the department of agriculture. In Europe, forestry had already made advances, and in 1886 a German-trained forester, Dr. Bernhard E. Fernow, became chief of the division and gave new impetus. In 1901 forestry was made a bureau.

In Idaho a vast patchy area reaching from the north-flowing Snake to the Montana border, and from the main Salmon to the Boise Basin was organized into the Weiser and the Idaho forests. In 1944 the two forests were combined into the Payette, with headquarters in McCall.[87]

On the Payette Forest are about 75 year-round employees, an important part of the life of the village, where they and their families are valued highly. In summer the number climbs to about 400. Among men with longest service on this forest are Harold Vassar, Don Parks and Russ Brown. Frank Youngblood at Council has about the longest tenure as a ranger.

252

A forester seems rarely to know when he will be moved, those over him believing apparently in the value of experience on different forests. Sam Defler, who is a graduate in forestry at Syracuse University, worked in Colorado before coming to McCall as superviser. Here he is spoken of as "a particularly good organization man."

Bringing the forests under control had not made forestry a diminishing occupation or trained men less needed. Colleges go on teaching the subject. Private lumber firms need foresters; railroads need their help in shipping lumber products. In the South, the increasing use of pulp wood requires more forestry-trained men; and even in the Middle West there is a great deal of river-course timber to be preserved. State forests too have their considerable requirements.

Forestry was already on its feet in Idaho and Henry Bergh the supervisor at McCall when Carl and Ida Brown moved to the South Fork. When they came to McCall, Bergh had been succeeded by Julian Rothery. Grazing then was not intensive. The allotments south of Warren were filled up, but beyond that no sheep, no cattle. It was all too remote. Old timers, who hated sheep on principle, gave Rothery a little trouble, but there was no real warfare.

Timber had not suffered much from insects and was generally green and thrifty. Game was plentiful, especially on the South Fork and in Chamberlain basin. Rothery reported that the moose had vanished though a few horns could still be found, but deer and elk made a hunter's paradise, and in the breaks of the Salmon mountain sheep and goats were common.

By 1914 when Carl Brown became a lumberman, regulations on timber harvesting were beginning to be felt. The small outfits in particular found it good sense to cooperate with the Forest; the great lumber producers might be slower seeing it.

A comparison between the lumber situation that Carl first knew and that of the present day brings out interesting differences. At first Ponderosa pine, Douglas fir and larch were about all that was cut, although Hoff and Brown cut quantities of spruce. The tie production business was limited; Carl Brown secured the first Union Pacific contracts, and at times ties were B T and L's big output and nearly sole dependence.

The old high stumps—24 to 36 inches—became 14-inch stumps. Under the Forest steep narrow and dangerous roads that soon had to be closed to other travel became high standard roads on good grades, with drainage, alignment and good access. The earlier log trucks hauled loads of from three to five thousand board feet in 16-foot lengths. Now a lightweight, heavyduty truck hauls maximum loads of 23,000 board feet, and all lengths from eight to 40 feet. Dead trees that once were ignored are now utilized. Early Forest roads were built with horses and scrapers and occasional hand drilling. Now it is heavy construction equipment with rock presenting little problem. Erosion control that was seldom considered is now enforced by the Forest on road and skid trails. Once brush was left lying; now it is rated a fire hazard and must be destroyed.

Perhaps the greatest change has been the harvesting of ripe timber, the removal of useless and cull trees, and replanting to insure continuous crop.

Today between the United States Forest Service and a purchaser of Forest timber there is drawn a contract replete with fine print and many conditions. It is enforceable and enforced. Here is a summary of such a contract between Brown Tie and Lumber and the Forest:

Cutting progress must be orderly, one acre cleaned up before another is begun.

To avoid waste, stumps must be cut at an agreed height.

Unnecessary damage to stream courses and stream sides must be avoided. Logs, chunks and other debris must be cleaned from adjacent stream courses.

Erosion must be minimized by preventing gullying of roads and skid trails. In natural meadow cover, soil, and water conditions must be protected. The operator must refrain from work where ground conditions are such that excessive damage would result.

On completion of hauling, prior to a shutdown, each logging road must be outsloped or provided with ditches across or dips in the grade.

Damage resulting from slope-logging, spur roads, etc., must be grass seeded as directed by the Forest office.

Buildings constructed must meet Forest requirements.

Sawdust and mill refuse must not enter streams or lakes.

Location, width, gradient and alignment of roads must conform to Forest standards, and clearing and grubbing at sides must meet specifications as must placing of culverts. At completion of logging, operator must leave the road in satisfactory condition, roadbed smooth, with lead-in ditches clean and drainage structures working.

All ground occupied by operator must be cleared of rubbish and temporary structures, and left in neat shape.

Work roads that are to be abandoned must be treated to minimize damage from concentrated flow of water.

Maximum sustained grade of roads must not exceed 10 percent, nor pitch maximum exceed 10 percent for 1040 feet in any one mile.

Felling and skidding: trees must be felled in the direction of skidding; logs must not be "siwashed" around trees, poles or groups of reproduction. Trees and logs must be limbed before skidded; guy lines must not be attached to unmarked living trees except when authorized. Manner of turning and backing tractors is prescribed.

Fire danger is to be avoided. Smoking or building lunch fires is prohibited except under special designations. Debris is to be piled and burned as directed. No slash or camp refuse or other debris is to be burned without written consent. Spark arresters must be used on steamboiler smokestacks, and on the exhaust of internal combustion machines used in the operation.

These thorough-going measures added to the policy of cutting for sustained yield, leaving more room, more sunlight, more moisture and plant food for remaining trees, together with reseeding of logged areas and the promotion of tree farms, all this plus the developed science of preventing and controlling fires explains the great gulf separating the doomed forest empire of 1900 and the saved forest empire of 1960. Devastation has been halted, waste turned to wealth. Tree pests yield; the outbreaks of fire are less tragic.

Carl Brown will say: "If you asked them, the United States Forest supervisors in McCall would tell you that we have always cooperated in their work."

CHAPTER FORTY-EIGHT

At the University Frank Brown finished his year with a 3.7 average (out of a possible 4), and in Baker and John Day his mother as a Girl Scout official addressed Kiwanis clubs.

Diane Brown graduated from high school and asked for a job in the mill office. Here she learned things from Margaret Peck, and filled in wherever she was needed. In the fall she would enroll at Willamette University at Salem in music education. Not for her the University of Idaho where her three aunts and her father and been students. She chose to go where no one would do anything for her simply because she was a Brown from McCall.

On the morning of September 10, 1958, Carl Brown awakened to his 80th birthday. Though his body and his hair were a little thinner now than in his prime, he still stood straight and erect, fussy as to grooming, still jaunty, still emanating deference to all women and respect to all men. At his own home the Bridgettes gave him a luncheon, and reminded him of his beginnings by appearing in costumes out of the past. Special guests who were picked up in an old-time car were Grace McRae, Helen Luzadder, Betty Harland, and Jessie Moloney. About Grace McRae Carl once said, "I think she understands me better than any other woman." Better than any other woman outside his family, he may have meant.

At the office the force had been asking each other what they could buy Carl that he didn't have. Baffled, they threw the problem out the window and settled for a big birthday cake with coffee. They were in the midst of this when 50 millhands came in to wish Carl well and to present him a paper.

The paper read thus: To Our Old Friend Carl Brown, With Best Wishes and Congratulations. The Old Timers.[88]

"From the men who've known you through the
     years
To your 80th birthday, we give three cheers.
In business and health, when the going got rough
You have always proved that you were tough."
Carl was so thrilled about everything that he invited the entire office staff out to dinner.

Martin Hoff, who came to Hoff and Brown in 1918 and stayed on with Carl, died in 1958, employed to within a month of his death. In those 40 faithful years he had never worked anywhere else. As an engineer and fireman he trained many men at the mill. Martin had not married, but lived much of the time with Brownie and Lu Hoff. In whatever they did he was a part, and they made as much of his birthday as if he were head of the house. Anything done on special holidays always included Martin. The solid Norwegian family feeling had not thinned with the years.

In June 1959 Diane Brown finished her freshman year at Willamette but before returning home she wrote a letter applying for her old job in the mill office. It was not her assumption that because she was Warren's daughter a job would automatically be hers. And she didn't show up at the office until Arne Souders, mill accountant, informed her that her former position was indeed waiting.

B T and L had always given summer employment to local college students. If there was no actual vacancy, work was shifted around to create one in a place where things were't too dangerous for a beginner. This was usually in the planer, unless the young fellow asked for the woods. If he made good, he was pretty sure of a job the following summer.

About the time he finished high school, Stan Harwood began the tough and responsible job of driving a logging truck. Over mountain roads, even over those kept in the condition prescribed by the Forest, this was no picnic. He was getting day by day experience at this; he *seemed* to be doing all right.

One afternoon he was starting down a long steep hill when suddenly he realized that the 6-wheel International was going too fast. He tried to brake—no power at all. He was rolling faster and faster, with the long steep pitch ahead.

There was only one thing to do. For his own safety. For the safety of anybody he might meet at a narrow place. He'd have to bank. Bank right now.

He pulled hard and the rig struck. The shock, the rip and wrench, the shudder of resisting steel. The log weight behind him and over the cab, this weight shooting straight ahead to crush the cab and him— but it didn't. The shaking stopped and the boy sat perfectly still. He didn't think he was hurt, yet suddenly everything inside him seemed coming loose. The truck, he could see, was half over.

Slowly he turned the key, still sat. He felt like a fool or a criminal. Why did this have to happen—they'd think he couldn't be trusted.

He'd have to do something. Get to town as soon as somebody came along. If anybody did.

Finally he caught a ride. Pete Wallace, shop foreman, wasn't at the mill, so Stan went to his house. He told Pete what had happened but Pete didn't seem too disturbed. He told Stan to go back to the truck with Buck Coonrod and see what the damage was. The thing to do was pick up the logs, get the truck in and repaired. Repaired so Stan could drive it again.

"Drive it again!" Stan thought.

Wallace explained: "We'll show you how to check your equipment so you needn't get into such a jam again."

It had always been the attitude at B T and L that boys had to learn and good boys would—that was the kind the mill always needed.

The shop check showed that the brakes were actually at fault—it wasn't Stan's using a high gear and over-braking when he should have been using a low and saving brake.

The next day Stan was back at his wheel, feeling mighty fine, singing now and then.

One summer a great nephew of Ida's, Peter Wilson, came from the East. He worked at the planer and stayed at the house. Carl and Ida over the decades were slowly learning the art of being loved for a kindness but keeping the situation understood so that the incident ended with respect and/or affection on both sides. Unstinted generosity was their nature, but Ida, being practical, knew that the warm giver really ought to keep things in hand—if possible.[89]

In the summer of 1959 the foundation was laid at the lake edge south of the mill for a new office building. The red structure across from Ted Harwood's store that looked like a house but was in truth an idea and business factory had become small and crowded.

By the summer of 1960 the new office building was ready, a combination of Frank's architectural studies, his father's idea of what a mill office might be, and his mother's feeling for furnishings and decor.

On the opening day visitors approached the red-stained, rough-spruce flat-top by a walk of concrete squares that seemed to float on a rushing little stream into which small fountains cascaded. The water appeared from nowhere, then disappeared. Actually it came from under the mill, circled the office front,

259

then flowed to a landscaped area against the lake, leaving behind an effect of coolness and peace.

The visitors entered a 12-sided reception room that looked like a flight of fancy with its wide expanse of glass and huge central planter. To the south a wing led to Pat Hayes' domain,[90] to the work space, and to a concrete walk-in vault; and on the north to the split-level area of executive offices, conference room and employees' lounge. Wood and wood products of Brown Tie and Lumber set the tone of the interior. Except in the north wing ceilings were rough-beamed in red fir and larch. The offices were finished in soft-toned woods. Warren's place, up a short iron-railed stair, had an engaging wood-patterned wall and, as could be expected, a minimum of gadgetry.

McCall firms had done most of the construction, Archie Rose the building, Timm Electric the wiring, and Nelson the plumbing.

During the summer of 1959 B T and L made a gift of a summer campsite to the First Methodist Church of Boise. It comprised 40 acres a half mile west of the lake in a flat basin, part of it overlooking the water.

When the Carl Browns or the Warren Browns visited in Boise over Sunday, they sometimes attended the old turreted and domed Methodist church at Tenth and State to hear Dr. Herbert Richards. This young cleric from the East had the magnetism of a medicine show man and the godliness of a Wesley. He seemed to care about everybody and remember names. He seemed determined to remain in Idaho and become a Westerner—though he could have his choice of several big pulpits in the East.

Perhaps this Western complex appealed to the Browns. There was also the fact that the Richardses summered on the lake, and when there the pastor always attended Rotary, to which Carl was devoted. Ida's Congregational church already had a camp on the lake and didn't need another. So Carl thought of the Methodists.

The necessary clearing has been done at the site, and Boise architects have designed a structure that will give central space to counselors, girls' cabins on one side, boys' on the other. A well has been drilled. Finished, the camp will accommodate 150 sober-minded young people at a time. Through a Methodist camping commission, the grounds may be used by any of the churches in the area.

"Camping" in this sense has become a great summer outlet for city young people, but it may be that the hills behind the new camp will feel shocked for a while, no raucous voices, no shouts charged with brimstone, no noises and smells of horses. Time does not stand still, however, and today's camper may enjoy himself far more than did his forebear, to whom camping was having to be away from the log cabin fireplace and Ma's featherbed.

CHAPTER FORTY-NINE

It is late fall. In McCall a lead-gray sky sags above the housetops and in the low timber around the lake. Rain that would like to be snow slips down silently, but across the water where it is a little colder one can see small white squares among the trees, the snow-covered roofs of locked-up houses.

The lake has changed from sapphire blue to graphite gray. No pleasure boat cuts its cold surface. On the street in town ranchmen wear short wrinkled wool coats and old sombreros. Summer is dead.

In Lola's the waitress has a gold skin, gold hair, and eyes the extraordinary blue of camas flowers. Though not streamlined, she is comforting to behold. The stout-hearted Finns, of whom she may be one, do not mind days like this. From the homeland they are used to wetness, to thick-ranked evergreens, and to the deepening hush of approaching winter. Winter with snow everywhere, stock well provided for, logs blazing in the fireplace, coffee in the kitchen.

The Finns seem to understand that the seasons are not to be hurried; they will fall into place at the right time. God is a Lutheran, and he will take care.

Late fall, 1960, and a period closes. As all chronicles do, this one comes to its end. To its end, after a last look at the chief people of its pages. Betty Harwood, who shared her parents' first years in the McCall country, shall come first.

In a larger setting Betty would have found a sure niche in significant social movements, for she is happiest when giving her all to some cause, or to people who are troubled, lonely, inadequate or unjustly used. She is calm, with a great capacity for putting up with what she cannot change. To slights she is not especially sensitive and rarely flies into battle without deliberate thought. Warm but not demanding, she clings to old friendships, never rushing out to start new ones. Her friends are somebody or nobody. Unswayed by popular trends, she makes up her own mind and is long on horse sense. Through her heart runs a wide streak of family love and pride.

A fine home well kept is good, but if Betty is needed somewhere to take over as nurse, dishwasher, comforter or chauffeur, her own housekeeping can wait. Needing and appreciating others, she works better for them than for herself.

About the history of the area, especially its early days and old timers, she cares tenderly and keeps a scrapbook recording it. For three years she has worked on archive matter for the Progressive club and the town library, where is kept a tin box of data assembled by her and Ruth Speilman.

She and Ted Harwood make a good team. Possibly it wasn't easy for Ted to fit into as positive a family as the Browns, but he has done this without losing identity. To Ida and Carl he is not only dear and cherished but sometimes more thoughtful of them than their own children. He remembers the small, easily overlooked things: getting Ida's mail to her when she wants it; seeing that her front walk is clear of the night's snow; giving her car unobtrusive inspection; anticipating Carl's wants and preferences.

Ted and Betty's big Stan lost a semester at the University to the Olympic ski tryouts and didn't begrudge it.[91] He returned this fall to complete work for his degree. His fraternity means much to him, but he takes time to grade papers for an instructor and frequently works in a sporting goods store. This is both for experience and because he likes it and has always worked at something. Stan appears to have no enemies, to know no strangers. Little kids and old ladies with whom he likes to stop and visit are his friends. He is followed by dogs, he likes mill workers. He likes girls, especially if they are anything like his young sister Ann.

Ann, in an age of tall girls, is destined to be another tall Harwood. She journeys to Donnelly each day for her eighth grade work and keeps up with band and chorus. Where things are happening, there is Ann.

No Brown is a stereotype, least of all Warren, who likes to go around town looking like a lumberjack. This trait and his here-and-now manner sum up the obvious. In build he is compact like his mother's people, and his passion for the outdoors keeps him trim. Probably only his wife and the internal revenue department know how much his business interests vary. He is head of the parent company; since 1957 he has had a controlling interest in the Lake Fork Lumber company and since 1959 in the Salmon River Lumber company at Riggins. He owns a cattle ranch out from White Bird and summer grazing lands in Long Valley. He is president of Shore Lodge, Inc. Clearly he differs from his father who still believes that the whole business of a lumber company is lumber.

Money is not for show, or not very much. It is for taking calculated risks, and it is for keeping a mill equipped with the latest and best machinery. It is for some of the kindlier things, including the intangible. The market slump this year reduced lumber production and cut the payroll. It made some mill workers wonder if the wonderful new office had to be so wonderful. Regardless of the slump, the company added a skagit.

This machine, named for its manufacturer in Skagit county, Washington, is a specially built logger intended for taking timber from steep slopes or high pockets that cannot be reached easily by roads, and where ordinary logging would increase erosion and damage to ground cover and unripe trees.

The skagit is powered by a 335-horsepower diesel which lifts logs by means of a 50-foot tower and an aerial skycar traveling on a cable secured between the tower and a stump or tree across a void. The tower can swivel in a radius of 1500 feet.

When the sky-car has run out to the desired position, the loggers working below signal the operator at the tower to clamp it into position. The pickup line is attached to the logs, maybe several at a time. These are lifted and transported to trucks on the same road that brought the skagit in.

Experiment with the new logger began in August in the Zena creek area, a triangle where the Secesh drops into the South Fork of the Salmon, under the sharp eye of U. S. Forest supervisor Sam Deffler. The watersheds in the granitic soil at this point are so steep that regular logging would damage them harshly.

There are millions of steep forest acres in the West where good timber is lost each year to decay and insect damage, and the skagit may be the answer. At any rate it is intended that the Zena creek experi-

Carl and Ida Brown at their Golden Wedding dinner at Shore Lodge. Clockwise, beginning farthest left: Ted Harwood, Dick Davies, Karyl Beyerle, Frank Brown, Susan Beyerle, Margaret Davies, Warren Brown, Ida and Carl Brown, Dorothy Beyerle, Betty Harwood, Jayne Brown, Diane Brown, Stan Harwood, Phil Davies, Glendon Davies, Homer Davies, Ann Harwood, Sharon Davies. Not shown, Tuck Beyerle, who took the picture.

Ida and Carl Brown cutting their 50th wedding anniversary cake.

ment, using B T and L equipment, shall continue for six years with normal winter shut-downs.

In the modern lumber concept, the whole tree should be used. However, chips to be utilized have to be barked. A barker costs $175,000 and up. If B T and L barked its chips, freight costs to move them would still be involved. The barker hasn't been acquired.

In the generally accepted sense of the word, Warren Brown isn't downright sociable. His very blue gaze can be impenetrable; he knows and can employ the art of fending off. Some people call him ruthless. Others, noting that he gains his ends, explains that he insists on his own way of doing things because he is always sure it is best.

An idea that is either witty or weighty secures Warren's attention, but he dislikes talk that is headed nowhere, especially if the occasion is social—he'd prefer cards or dancing. He and Jayne read, listen, travel when they can. They have covered continental United States and Mexico, Hawaii and Alaska. In Alaska they made a flight over the primitive area, probably to make sure it didn't surpass primitive Middle Idaho.

Somewhere beyond his circumscribed valley and satisfying life could lie other work for Warren Brown. Improbably it would be politics, for even in a state as natural and unsophisticated as Idaho, the way to office leads through party and machine. That is, in exchange for a label, the candidate must accept identification with whoever controls the party, and this includes the thinker and the confused, the honest and the less honest. The way has to be by machine because only once in a century comes the draft that sweeps into office an able unknown, a man who has no commitments, who seeks only a chance to work his heart out. This creature has become practically extinct.

However there are jobs other than political that are worth a man's caring. Some commission, some foundation of wide repute that needs men of ideas, independence and terrible drive should tap Brown for its advisory board.

Frank Brown, still short of his architectural degree, has already piled up much useful experience. Although he skied on the 13-member Alpine team at the Squaw Valley Olympics in February, skiing from here on is diversion, not business. Last summer he began supervising the building of an A-frame house precut at the McCall mill, under the trade name Alpine Vacation homes. Demonstrated in McCall and in Boise, the houses sold. As modern as tomorrow, the Alpine is all roof and two ends, the front end glass to the peak. In 630 square feet the Swissette model actually encloses kitchen, bath and livingroom below, two bedrooms above.

A second little brown-eyed boy, Warren Leonard, came home from Boulder with Frank and Sherlene in June. Through the summer Frank flew his father's plane to Boise, returning home for weekends on the lake with Sherlene and the children. This small town boy is on his way. And no one should be deceived by his detached manner.

After two years of college, Diane Brown decided she wanted to study music abroad. Her parents did not oppose her, she was willing to go alone. But her long-time friend Gretchen Hoff, after two years at Stanford, also had European study in mind. The girls set out, although not together. Diane had a month of travel in northern countries, now studies in Vienna, where she lives with an Austrian family. Gretchen is in Paris. The girls will spend Christmas together there. It is something to note, that the granddaughters of Theodore Hoff and Carl Brown, who found it better to go separate ways, should find in each other continuing pleasure.

For the Tuck Beyerles two places are home, the handsome house in the north hills overlooking Boise, and the lake house in McCall. Dorothy is arresting when she goes on about a child's *privilege* in being able to grow up in a town where parents and children actually enjoy the same parties and sports. To her, in retrospect, McCall life was ideal, and Karyl and Susan shall have all of it that can be crowded into summer.

The tall gunmetal doors of Tuck Beyerle's maison in Boise are as inscrutable as he can be. The four white hexagon door ornaments likewise tell nothing, and the ivyboxes and coachhouse lamps at either side and the dolphin doorhandles give out little. The big adjacent window, however, does permit something of Tuck Beyerle to emerge.

An hour inside the place, amid color and texture, line and accent, is like an hour in another period of time, another atmosphere. Furniture, lamps, hangings, tapestries, these can evoke emotion when rightly chosen and rightly grouped, and Beyerle's do. Interior decorating is apparently of two kinds, that which suffices and that which produces a predetermined mood. Although he is a member of AID (American Interior Decorators) and his assignments come from many places in the Pacific Northwest and California, Beyerle's inner concern is one thing, harmony. Harmony is to confusion what goodness is to evil. Decoration is a foil for the personality of the in-dweller, whom it can interpret or betray. Beyerle has found it rewarding to put pleasure into the lives of inarticulate people by highlighting what they really are, by giving them the sense of being understood. Of course this costs them a little.

At Nampa in a two-story colonial with nine rooms, most of them big, Margaret and Homer Davies house themselves and, when all are at home, their six children. Diane, the youngest, was born October 20, 1957. They make a welded, affectionate family. Margaret's sister Betty likes to say: "Muggs is probably the best mother of us all."

Dick and Phil are at the University, a junior and a freshman, both studying business. Glendon is a high school sophomore, not an athlete like his brothers, thanks to a leg injury, but a bandman. After school he helps his father at Davies' Hardware.

In the family there is more than a little music. Dick plays the piano, with pleasure to others as well as himself, even at the end of a summer day's labor "hooking" in his grandfather's woods. That means attaching the cable to a log so the jammer can lift it onto the truck, and a boy has to be quick as a cat and strong.

Sharon Davies is in the eighth grade. She too likes her music. Her mother sings in the choir at the First Presbyterian church, where all the family attends.

Every Davies except Diane, who will soon be old enough, is a skier.

Homer has served ten years on the board, two years as president of the Nampa rodeo, one of the biggest in the United States. Former president of the Nampa chamber of commerce and on the boards of several corporations, Homer is always busy.

Like her mother, Margaret is always involved in community work. She serves on the Nampa library board. Once a week she drives to Boise Junior College for a course in stocks and bonds.

To go to State House Landing each summer[92] and have as many of the children along as possible is pure bliss to Margaret. As youngsters the Browns always began skating across the lake to this cove as soon as winter cold made the ice safe. Close to their father's docked logs they built big fires. Winter magic, this place. The property covers nearly two acres, and the Davies intend to give each of their children a piece of it for a some-day building lot.

"I have had the chance to inherit many good things," Margaret Davies will say, "but the greatest is a sound family background and a good name on both sides. I hope our children will be able to say something like that, and their children after them."

Margaret Peck, Carl's sealed box of business secrets, lost her husband, Howard, a Forest employee, in 1953.

Several years later Mrs. Leslie Ulmer passed away after long illness. Recently Mrs. Peck and Les Ulmer pleased their friends by marrying. So now Margaret, with possibly a twinge of nostalgia, has given up her job to return to housekeeping.

Helen Luzadder has had to give up the town she chose when searching for more dangerous living. On the Little Salmon in a modern home for retired people, Schoolma'am Luzadder, still sharp-witted, follows the world and its foibles.

At Horseshoe Bend the Theodore Hoffs continue active and alert. Last summer range fires swept the untimbered hills on three sides of town, darkening the skies for miles around. An inferno then, even after the fall rains the devastated earth looks like the lower regions. By sheer luck and the labor of many fire fighters, the mill and town were saved.

Last of the original Hoffs at B T and L is Brownie, who has been off and on the payroll for 45 years, sawing continuously since 1927. Last year he began to allow himself a bit of loafing. He and Lu like to visit other places, even if it is only down the Salmon in their marvelously compact mobile home.

The schools of Long Valley. Have they, despite the years of dissension, been superior to others; or are children just sharper in a do-it-ourselves atmosphere? Whatever the answer, the spirit of excelling has never let up. It is true there have been notable teachers. One of Theodore Hoff's sisters, Nora Kessler, now assistant credit manager for a huge chain store, thinks the training she got in McCall under Helen Luzadder covered "about everything she ever had to know."

Around Donnelly something extraordinary has occurred. Slender, lively Mrs. Pansy Scheline, teacher and now home extension agent, has produced some wonders, especially through 4-H. Every year since the first efforts, some boy or girl has had state or national recognition in 4-H. Mrs. Scheline's daughter Jane earned the chance to bake in the national cherry pie contest in Chicago. Two years later her second daughter Sharron baked another cherry pie in the same place, and the following year entered Make-It-Yourself-With-Wool to take second in the state among juniors. The next year Sharron was sent to the national 4-H congress, and after that not only went to Idaho Girls' State from her town but was elected to Girls' Nation.

Both the Scheline girls entered the wool contest in 1956, each winning in her district, and Sharron in the state. Further contests gave her a trip to Europe, and in the same year she won one of five $1000 college scholarships offered by the J. H. Heinz company. Sharron is now in Nepal on an International Farm Youth Exchange program. There she lives with host families, learning and teaching.

Another Valley county girl, Amelia Beth Loomis, also baked and sewed successfully. Following the Scheline pattern, she made pie in Chicago in 1958, and in the wool contest the same year did so well from the lowest to the highest division that she too was sent to Europe. Later she went to the National 4-H congress as a winner in food preparation. She is now in college.

Beverly Wallace, now at the University of Idaho, did such outstanding work that she was sent to the 4-H congress in Chicago, and also won a $300 Standard Oil scholarship.

"It isn't a big fancy school plant and ultra equipment that counts," according to Mrs. Scheline, "but good wholesome environment with emphasis on responsibility, leadership and pleasing personality."

In a different kind of competition, debate, Carol Engen of Donnelly-McCall high was three years on the school team, which for two years won district and regional meets. She and Maralee Rowland won the state class B championship in 1958. In 1959, representing the smallest school entered in the Idaho State College Invitational debate tourney, the girls were pitted against the largest school, Pocatello, in an open (all class) contest, and came off with second place. In the same tourney Carol won second place in extemporaneous speaking.

Clearly, it is not size nor geographical location that matters most. It is the mind to excel.

Grace McRae, the woman who best understood, keeps a summer home at Big Creek. The phone almost never rings, and only the trickle of a little ditch behind the house breaks the silence among the pines inside the peeled-pole fence. Along the Forest road only a few cars pass, even in summer.

In the big main room the heater backs up to an old-fashioned iron range, to share its chimney. One reads at night by coaloil or gas lamp. There are beds that look like beds and beds that look like couches; and in the loft there is enough bedding to take care of all if a big party should arrive at dusk. Grace's dishes are interesting, odds and ends that she bought from the old Thunder Mountain hotel in inundated Roosevelt.

It is a short walk from the McRae house to the ruined Edwards cabin that with its frame addition once had 13 rooms. Across the front the wide porch is intact. At the back, beyond an overgrown garden patch the hills run up toward timber. Small buildings that may have been a chickenhouse and a harness shed are falling down. At a discreet distance stands a large privy.

At Warren, which Carl first saw in 1903, there are several small eating places and a store. Many of the houses have been boarded up,[93] but in one that is woman-neat lives Otis Morris, who came to the town in 1890, when he was five, riding with his widowed mother in a buckboard. At that time the whites had dwindled to 200, but 300 Chinese reworked the tailings white miners had left. Otis' mother later married Kelly of the Kelly-Patterson store. Otis grew up to be a miner, following this until 1936, when he was named postmaster.

It was not uncommon then to send out bars of gold worth $10,000 apiece by registered mail, but there was never a mail robbery.

Otis no longer sees well. Most of his old friends are gone, and the little hamlet of empty, decaying houses and worked-over humps of mining refuse must seem peopled largely with memories. Of his only son Orland, who didn't come back from the Philippines, he can speak with a calm that is remarkable. Orland fought with the old Fourth Marines through Corregidor, survived the Bataan death march, then was a prisoner of the Japanese for three years. When the Japs heard that McArthur had landed at Leyte, they packed prisoners into a hangar, poured on gasoline and set it ablaze. Orland was among those men. Orland, "if it is really he," is buried in St. Louis.

Near Warren in 1933 died Polly Bemis, 83, who had spanned Ida's and Carl's years in the hills, a death that ended a chapter that in retrospect at least was highly sentimental. Her story has been told many times with many variations, but it seems certain that she was a Chinese slave, smuggled in by a Chinese master, when she was about 16. Her master put her up as stake in a poker game and lost her to a miner named John Bemis. Her new owner married her, and they lived together, apparently childless, until his death in 1921.

She was ever an object of great curiosity and kindly interest, is said to have been an excellent practical nurse and often sent for in emergencies. Sometimes she came out to Boise with Dr. Bess Czichek, a dentist, who kept Polly's teeth in repair. In her last years she had an arrangement with the Stonebrakes, a pair of bachelor brothers living across the river from her cabin. As long as she kept a dishtowel hanging out she was okay and they need not worry.

At Burgdorf, well known to Ida and Carl, time has slowed down. There is no pressure. The mineral pools still bubble, the Hot Hole probably as hot as ever, but even in summer few seem to need the waters. A neat log two-story hotel has succeeded the one of Fred and Jeannette Burgdorf's day. In it is the pinion pine burl furniture, more odd than beautiful, that Jeanette had someone make for her, chairs, table, stool, loveseat. The defiant burls are produced by the pine when deep cold freezes its sap.

In the main room is a stove converted from a big boiler. The square rosewood piano, a Hardeman, may also have been Jeannette's. She and Fred have been dead a long time, and Jeannette's story might as well lie with them.

Carl has not visited Burgdorf or Warren or Big Creek for years, though he must see them in his dreams. However, Ida goes. Change and decay do not dash her spirits. She is not reminded of worries or near tragedies, but of dear and nonsensical old times.

At the Doctors' clinic at the Memorial hospital Edith Vassar sits calm and sturdy behind her desk, her hair in braids around her head. Behind another desk in the fire dispatcher's cubicle in the U. S. Forest office sits lean, weather-burned Slim Vassar. After her college years, Edith did social work, then came to Mc-Call to teach—and met Slim. He was then just beginning his long Forest connection.

Whenever Edith passes the hospital's incubator she must be reminded of something that happened 30 years ago. Because the story points up the vigor, the hardiness of Middle Idaho in those early years and its still persisting why-go-soft attitude, here it is:

In October 1931 the Vassars were sent to Big Creek Forest headquarters. Later on an airstrip was developed and in flying weather planes brought as many as 15 to Edith's table. But in 1931 after snows fell and piled there was no way to get out except to walk.

The Vassars' child was due in July, so in May, two months ahead of time, Edith and Slim left Big Creek afoot. Edith's ultimate goal was Boise, where she would be under the eye of her brother-in-law, Dr. Ernest Laubaugh. Today they would walk to a mine, across seven miles of fairly bare ground, but included was a half mile of snowslide. At the mine they would meet the mail carrier and tomorrow Edith could ride the carrier's dogsled across Elk summit, nearly nine thousand feet up, and across Warren summit, only two thousand feet lower. Then they'd reach a road and travel by wagon. At Warren a plane would take Edith out.

The slide snow proved deep and exhausting to wade through, and when Edith was still a good way from the mine she began to wonder if she could make it in. And tomorrow. Could she go on, even on a sled?

At the mine they found the carrier and two old prospectors, but the foreman and his wife had gone out. The presence of another woman would have been comforting, but at least there was this, Edith and Slim could have the unoccupied bed.

A good bed, but everything else was terrifying. Through the night while young Slim walked the floor and rolled uncounted cigarettes, Edith endured and prayed—this was no place to be having a baby.

Toward morning the child was born, but for him and his mother there was nothing by way of medical aid, and all the baby's things had been sent ahead. Slim wrapped the infant in whatever he could find and put him in a cardboard box by the stove. The miners, waiting up anxiously, had contrived one real production, a bedpan made from a cut-off, hammered-down gallon syrup can.

When the mail carrier left at daylight, he took the news with him, and before the first day's end, someone came riding through the snow to the mine. It wasn't one of the Wise men or a King of the Orient, but an angel. The angel was Mrs. Ann Spillman of Warren, and she brought baby bottles, tinned milk, little blankets and diapers, also clean pieces of her husband's old wool underwear, from which she was soon fashioning little shirts. She even finished them at neck and wrists with crochet.

After only three weeks, the Vassars resumed their journey. Regardless of his inconvenient timing, young Robert throve in his new world. Eventually he grew to be over six feet tall. About that time the Coast Guard took him. He was sent to Ketchikan for three years, and is still there, statistics supervisor in a big pulp mill.

Robert Halferty, who in 1925 ran against Carl Brown for the state senate "because Carl had beaten him on other things," still lives near his original 900-acre ranch at Donnelly. He not only defeated Carl but held the seat four terms. His nature is still a fine mixture of kindness and pepper, his wit impertinent, his health good, although he has had to slow down since he lost a leg. He drives an adapted car and gets around neatly. He and his wife observed this year their 60th wedding anniversary. Besides their own two daughters, they always made a home for any of the five Butalla children who needed one.

Looking back, Halferty feels his greatest contribution was his part in getting the highway through the valley. It took 12 years. As chairman of the legislature's committee on highways and bridges, he was responsible for buying up nearly every necessary right-of-way between McCall and the mouth of Payette canyon. A county commissioner and a schoolboard chairman (for 18 or 20 years, he's not just sure), he didn't intend to be a banker. However he served as president of the Roseberry bank and stayed as a director when it moved to Donnelly. In the legislature he sponsored the Payette Lakes bill which prevented the lake being made into a reservoir with widely changing water levels.

As a family name, McCall slowly fades out. In January of this year Benjamin Blackburn McCall, a son of the Thomas McCall who settled on the lake in 1888, passed away at the age of 90. Thomas McCall had bought a squatters right from Sam Dever, said to be part Indian, and moved his family into Dever's log house. The only other cabin on the lake at the time was that of Jack Wyatt, better known as Jews Harp Jack.

Ben McCall built the town's first hotel, the Lakeview, which stood until 1957, when it burned. From the late '80's until after 1900, Ben carried mail in winter from Council to Meadows and McCall, using snowshoe or skis, sometimes with a 75-pound load on his back in addition to his rifle. Often his route lay over trails 14 feet deep in snow. Later he worked for Theodore Hoff at the mill and for Hoff and Brown.

In the cemetery, where each year a few of Ida's and Carl's friends come to rest under the pines on the south-sloping hill, small bushes have their way and rocks crop up when they like. Graves are not sowed with lawn grass. Instead the original native grass riffles in the breeze. Some graves do have iris, or the energetic succulents like hen-and-chickens that like to cover peaceful earth. After Decoration Day there are artificial flowers and a sociable assortment of coffee cans and pickle jar vases, but even these come to seem indigenous.

The graves are rather widely separated, as if even in death McCallites enjoy elbow room and their own thoughts. Most of the upright stones make no effort to impress, and if there are fences around the plots, no two are alike. Some are wrought iron, some chains, some low white pickets, hand-hewn. These are not at all pathetic, just individual. Many of the plaques placed by the Progressive club are for infants. Baby Hernden and Baby Horton lie side by side on a fine sunny slope. Baby Lytle lies at the foot of a yellow pine four feet in diameter, its singing top brushing the sky. Many markers indicate military service, and an unusual number are for men who died in early manhood. Perhaps this suggests the dangers of trapping, mining, and the treachery of the long, long winter trail.

One stone is for "Our Pal."

Near the entrance to the cemetery stands a big pine blasted half way up by lightning and divided into a candelabrum. Still living, it could be thought of as a symbol.

The town that the Browns have helped to make will probably continue to grow as a resort, as a haven from heat and dust, as a summer and winter sports place. If it can hold tight to its spirit of uniting and doing, avoid the garish and cheap, it will remain a delight. If it can escape waves of wealthy visitors demanding service, it has a chance. And it should be thankful meanwhile that it sits on no transcontinental railroad and that its sky is not darkened with commercial flight.

Idaho, the state, grows slowly. Its wide open spaces are still pretty wide, and the Federal government owns more than two-thirds of its exciting body. Industry comes gradually, but the population doesn't seem avid for an overwhelming rush of it, just as the early McCallites were dubious about summer residents. Its industries are commonly based on the development of some natural resource, or on the production of something needed in that development.

Lumber, second to agriculture in the state, will probably be produced here forever—unless science finds a way to do without wood and wood products. And whether direct descendants of Carl and Ida Brown will be operating at McCall by the beginning of the 21st century depends on how much sawdust and sap have invaded the Brown blood. It would seem disappointing if four generations of successful lumbermen were not followed by a fifth, a sixth, perhaps more. Some McCallites look to Stan Harwood as the next logical head of B T and L. His grandmother could get money out of millmen, his mother could get cooperation, and Stan, whom the men like, could get work.

And what of Carl and Ida themselves. Carl in the last few years has had to concede that modern drugs, hospitals and air-conditioning do ease one's day. Nevertheless he stands straight and alert, insists on good lines and unusual textures in his clothing. He hears well enough, especially with his hearing-aid glasses, and when he wants to. Surgery for cataract a year ago was successful, and he reads, and enjoys seeing his friends. Sometimes in good weather he goes to the permanent camp on the South Fork, and he rarely misses a Rotary luncheon.

When a worried friend asked Bill Deinhard if he thought Carl could again see pretty well, Bill said: "I couldn't say. But the other day we were sittin in Shore Lodge waitin for Rotary and along come a dame. She had on one of these here tight swimmin suits with stripes. She walked right in front of us. *Maybe* Carl never saw her at all, but he sure give me an awful dig in the ribs."

Carl has never ceased to believe that an employee should be treated like anyone else, with respect as long as he deserved it. With no lack of warmth for long-time employees, he thinks that over the years mill workers have improved, not in faithfulness, but in capacity. Today many of his men who had no chance to go to college are seeing that their children go there, and this gives them more to live up to.

Carl insists that he is no longer interested in the stock market, merely "in how it's going." He disclaims following the business affairs of the firm but likes "to know how much comes in and goes out."

For the record, B T and L's gross payroll for the year 1959 was $1,218,628. For 1960 it may not be as large. That mills like his are going to stay in business Carl is, however, convinced.

Lands now owned by B T and L in addition to the 22,265 acres on the ridge between Meadows and Mc-Call include:

> 160 acres on Nelson creek above Sylvan beach.
> 160 acres at the head of Nelson creek.
> 160 acres on Boulder creek, on the east side of the valley.
> 970 acres on Hayward creek, in separate pieces.
> The Reed ranch (Dead Shot Reed) which has a landing strip.
> The Parks place, 60 acres, on the Secesh river.

Eighty percent of the timber B T and L cuts is cut on U. S. Forest lands.

The hardships of Carl's early Idaho years forbade time for appreciating the arts. For outlet he substituted devotion to his family and concern for those he carried—miners, trappers, hermits, whose life could depend on his bringing their necessities; and employees whose pay must be found somewhere.

He could hardly bear to look on suffering. Once on a trip into Mexico he was so upset by the plight of beggars that he could never go back. He didn't mind giving; he just couldn't stand the sight of misery. Once in Phoenix he read in the paper of a Negro girl of six who risked her life to save two younger children from a fire that destroyed their house and everything in it. Carl couldn't get the child out of his mind. So he arranged with a Negro policeman to bring her and her mother to a store where he bought the child two complete outfits of clothing, one for school, one for Sunday.

Recently he learned of an elderly New Englander known to him only as the brother of a woman who for years had been a warm friend of the Brown family. On the man's house an $800 mortgage was about to be foreclosed. This was very bad. It shouldn't happen. Not to an old man, probably deserving since he was a New Englander, and practically a friend of the family, since his sister was. Carl saw to it that the note was quietly paid.

He has lost most of his onetime bitterness about the waste of time and physical strength of his early Idaho years. Fanatically hard work, he called it. Fanatical, perhaps, but not futile. The constitution he developed under tough going he passed down to children and grandchildren, along with the fanatical belief that one must be outdone in nothing, in fact achieve the impossible.

His highest recommendation for any man is that he is a hard worker, and honesty is still the first test. However, if a man *appears* honest but is an unfaithful husband, he is a poor risk. A liar he can forgive but never trust again.

Among the small things that please him are the bright flowers that McCall grows, and good food. Properly, all food should be prepared the way Ida does it. Her apple pie and the way she used to roast lamb at the Shiefer ranch are still perfect.[94]

Although it is a long time since he has marked a tree for cutting, trees are the same miracle they were when he was eight years old in Whitefield. Their ordered contours. The faint, secret rustling of their needles, even when no breeze stirs. He would veer any road to save a good tree.

His speech, unlike Ida's, has remained strongly New England. He deals in hosses, idears, and Pocatellers. Whether it is a Yankeeism or a Brownism, when he is quite amused or pleased he slaps his knee and breaking the word in the middle exclaims, "Prittee good!"

He used to take an occasional drink, but felt no disapproval of those who went further than occasional, provided that on Monday they were at work shipshape and on time.

Ida Brown has altered little in spirit. A love of nature that made life bearable when the going was hard stays with her. At 80 she drives her own car,[95] the present one a big white dream with red leather upholstery. She misses no bridge parties nor church affairs, knows what's on the radio nationally and in the news journals. And she travels at the word.

She relishes nothing more than a trip of several days over any sort of road into the old mining country. She can sleep in any kind of bed, eat whatever is available, and return home the freshest of the party.

Her humor is still sparkling and a trifle wry. Praise or compliment she is likely to take with a backhand crack, but this is modesty. She loves her grandchildren whole-heartedly, but can admit their shortcomings, at least their amusing ones, if she has to. Inside, she is sure she has her own shortcomings.

She steps out briskly, keeps her health, never fails to recognize a male acquaintance at home or in Boise no matter what his age. Though her brown hair is threaded with gray, it is set modishly, and dress and appearance are to her an important matter. Her eyes, with the same gold-flecked glint, miss nothing.

She hasn't abandoned diplomacy. When she wanted a small window in the kitchen replaced with a big one of plate glass, Carl was against the idea. Not because of the cost but because of the muss. But Ida wanted a better view of the lake than the small window allowed.

The next time Carl was to be away she hurried in a carpenter. It was all done, the woodwork painted, no muss around when Carl came home. It is probable that he slapped his knee and said "Prit-tee good!"

—

The afternoon wanes and the blue cold creeps. Below, the stream is frozen. Overhead the sky is paling, but where the evergreens brush against it, the color is almost indigo. The sun is gone, yet one high peak in a distant ridge flashes a spill of gold light. Here in the timber it is shadowy. Carl Brown halts his horses to listen, to feel the silence.

What he is thinking will be put into words some day by another New Hampshire man:

"The woods are lovely dark and deep.

But I have promises to keep,

And miles to go before I sleep,

And miles to go before I sleep."*

Finis

---

* From: THE POETRY OF ROBERT FROST, edited by Edward Connery Lathem, Copyright 1951 by Robert Frost, Copyright 1923, © by Henry Holt and Company, Inc. Reprinted by permission of Henry Holt and Company, Inc.

FOOTNOTES

[1] New Hampshire had prohibition, but Massachusetts next door did not. In Whitefield there were "blind pigs," but the French Canadian loggers probably bootlegged their own liquor.

[2] Westerners should not disparage the Presidential range. It has 10 peaks exceeding 5000 feet, and except for Mt. Mitchell in North Carolina and Clingman's Dome in Tennessee, Mt. Washington would dominate the skyline in the eastern half of the United States.

[3] In early operations the Browns were always losing mills by fire. A pulp mill costing $75,000 was barely operating when it burned. Six months later a moulding and box mill burned at similar loss, with insurance on neither. To stop this, the company acquired 2500 feet of leather hose—this was before the day of fabric-covered rubber hose—and a powerful steam pump to bring water from a distant reservoir.

The company owned 40,000 acres of pine and spruce, whose value steadily increased. Its annual sales of lumber sometimes reached $500,000. It rented houses to 75 mill families, operated a store with a yearly volume of $125,000, and maintained a 14-mile railroad, the Old South Branch, between Whitefield and Jefferson. In the woods it had camps under a supervisor.

[4] The twins, Lucie and Laura, now nearing 90 years, are with Ida the only surviving children of the Harringtons.

[5] "Profile Sam" Willson had prospected near the gap in 1902. Today an inscription on polished granite set in cement at the top of the ridge tells the traveler that Sam's latchstring was always out to Sourdoughs passing through. The memorial is supported by boulders veined in orange and brown, some of them lichen covered.

[6] John Napier also invented numerating rods, commonly called Napier's Bones, for performing complicated multiplication and division. He seems to have been the first to use the decimal point.

[7] Accompanying Ida and Betty part of the way to Big Creek was Grace McRae, wife of a mining man who had been in the mountains for several years. Mrs. McRae had taught school at Meadows before her marriage to Dan and was herself pregnant with her first child. To protect herself from bumping into the saddlehorn, she kept a strong pie tin in the right place. The two women were to meet often in the future and to become such dear friends that when in town they sometimes wore each other's best dresses.

283

⁸William Allen White, famous Kansas editor and author, made a trip to the Thunder Mountain area around 1900, and probably stopped at the Shiefer ranch. His party traveled from Council to Meadows by stage, spent the night and mounted cayuses, "which is the mountain name for ponies," according to White's later account in the Saturday Evening Post. He spoke of the stations along the trail "which are called hotels, uniform price is four bits (50 cents) for meals and four bits for lodging." The buildings, he wrote, were invariably of rough-sewn pine logs, unplastered, furniture all home-made, cutlery and tableware scanty. In only two or three of the stations were there sheets on the beds, "but a tenderfoot weary with travel can find unexpected comfort between folds of warm blankets, especially when the weather is freezing cold."

The road to Meadows, White said unsympathetically, would be called impassable in Kansas, and a ranch might consist of 10 acres or even a hundred, it didn't matter, the name was still the same.

⁹When Mrs. McCormick returned to Chicago she sent Ida a gold horseshoe pin set with pearls that Ida still cherishes and sometimes wears.

¹⁰Husk's Dressing can still be bought in a drugstore in McCall.

¹¹A palouser (pa-loo-ser), probably from the Palouse country of southeastern Washington, sometimes means a resident of this area; sometimes one who carries his lunch in a newspaper; sometimes, as here, a lantern made from a lardpail. The pail is turned on its side, and the bail is rehooked to carry it in this position. A candle is thrust up through a hole in the new bottom. The flame is protected from the wind by the sides of the bucket and the bright interior makes a reflector.

¹²Once Ida invited a gentle girl from a mining-ranching family living on a little-traveled trail to visit her. Though 16, the Willey girl had never seen a wagon or a telephone. When invited to try the phone, she was too timid until Ida offered to do the ringing. "Then you just talk like you would to a person in the room," Ida explained.

Carl Brown liked afterwards to say to his children when displeased with their school marks: "You don't know as much as the Willey kids, and they learned to read out of the Sears-Roebuck catalog." Since they had to be home-taught, perhaps this was true. The uncle of the gentle 16-year-old, Norman B. Willey, had been governor of Idaho territory from 1890 to 1893.

¹³Until dogsled racing became a popular sport in Idaho, dogs bred to the sled were practically unknown. An intelligent mongrel with wide shoulders, well-sprung ribs and a thick coat had only to be started young and used with some love.

284

¹⁴Carl was years getting over the effects of his illness, and sometimes had warning twinges. Ida thought the red medicine he brought home looked like capsicum (cayenne pepper). Once she went to a McCall druggist, Harvey Parks, and had him fill some capsules with capsicum. He did, Carl took them, seemed to profit. Joe Bross, a McCall man, even tried some of Ida's capsules.

¹⁵The house at the Shiefer ranch has been gone a long while. In its place on the bench overlooking the river stands a neat Forest building. A few fruit trees remain, but it is doubtful that they were there in 1910. Time has disposed also of the alfalfa fields and the garden.

¹⁶Following World War II the island was used by the United States defense department for survival training. In 1960 Dr. Russell Brooks of Meridian built a two-story house there and moved in with his family. Thirty-six tons of material required for construction, including gravel for cement, had to be transported by barge.

¹⁷Still living in McCall, Stover runs a popular club called these many years The Dog House. He has also put in a good deal of time as Democratic county chairman.

¹⁸Stover later bought this ranch and ran cattle on it. During World War I he served in France with the 40th Division, but his company was broken up and used for replacements, so that he came home with the 81st. As to his overseas service, Stover will only admit that "probably he took a little shrapnel." In his three or four years with Carl Brown he hauled hay and grain, drove dogs and horses on the mail route, working wherever he was needed—he even milked cows. He didn't mind—Carl wouldn't ask anybody to do anything he wouldn't do himself.

¹⁹Three supervisors who served in McCall went to the top in Forestry. Besides Rothery, there is Lyle F. Watts, supervisor first on the Weiser Forest, then on the Idaho Forest, who in 1943 became Chief Forester of the United States; and James W. Farrell, now in charge of Planting and Timber Stand Improvement with headquarters in Washington. Farrell grew up in Meadows.

²⁰Permission to quote the letter has been granted by Julian Rothery's widow, Jean, who lives in Cotuit, Massachusetts.

²¹The first school that Florida attended had a dirt floor and long benches. The desks were long boards fastened to the benches ahead. When the little girl was 11, she made a trip with her father to Boise and for the first time saw fruit growing on trees. When winters were especially severe in the valley, schools had to discontinue. However, summer schools were often opened. Florida never had a full nine months of lessons until she was in the 8th grade.

285

²²Mrs. Luzadder often asserted that in schools and colleges far more attention should be paid to political history. A Democrat, like her friend Carl Brown, she would exclaim: "When I look at our Idaho legislature I think, God Save the King."

She helped in the struggle to build the Community church and always supported it. But being a Presbyterian she didn't join—that is, not for 40 years. Then at about 87 she thought she might feel "more respectable" in the fold and gave in. However, she noted no great change in her condition.

²³Two of his best dogs were Jack and Colonel. Colonel died from a rattlesnake bite. Jack was unusually smart, and learned when at home to go down to the confectionery and make a big racket until he was admitted. Then he accepted a dish of ice cream.

²⁴The Harringtons had moved in 1907 to Littleton, and there John's health began to fail. At his funeral in 1910, fourteen ministers were present, one being his brother. Besides the presiding Baptist minister four other divines spoke of the character of the deceased, and there were also numerous prayers, special music and "selections." Said the Farmington, N. H., weekly paper: "The ministers . . . stood around the casket, each placing a pink flower upon the breast of the departed, singing 'Blest Be the Tie That Binds.' " All business places were closed during the service.

²⁵Living the life of a miner, freighter and logger, Chester Stephens had never married, and when World War I came, nothing looked more important than enlisting. He snowshoed out from Warren and signed up. With the 27th Engineers he went to Scotland, then to Havre and Dijon. When men over draft age who knew explosives were sought, Chester went somewhere on that detail. Discharged at the end of the war, he hurried back to Warren. For a while he jippooed on Dead Horse creek on the biggest contract the McCall mill had ever let. But exposure and hard work over the years now demanded pay, and he found himself in the Veterans Hospital in Boise for a long stay.

²⁶Boston Brown was doubtless born in Boston. He stated that he had "surveyed the Fifth Standard Meridian in Africa." At one time he had been married, then lost wife and child. He talked little about himself, and after he came to Warren he never lived anywhere else. Sometimes he had stayed a week at the South Fork ranch with the Browns, enjoying Ida's cooking and the New England she made him think of.

²⁷One man who remembers this incident thinks the horse crossed the river *twice*, but Carl says No. The story is good enough either way.

²⁸Funeral services were almost as elaborate for Warren Brown as they had been for John Harrington. Prayer began in the big house on the hill. Then the coffin was taken to the Baptist church

where two pastors officiated. Town businesses closed, and the Masons attended in a body. Said the Plymouth Record: ". . . he possessed original ideas, honesty of purpose, strict integrity and blunt frankness . . . firm adherence to his word . . . democratic plainness in all things, a broad liberality combined with natural caution."

[29]Other Hoff employees at this time were Johnny McMurren, Bill Harp, Bill Land, Bill Mink, Charley Arnold, Charlie Cruse and Theodore's brothers, Henry and Peter.

[30]Ties could be used for other purposes. The walls of the McCall hotel and the first Yacht Club were made of stuccoed ties.

[31]The first summer home on the lake was built in 1906. Sam H. Hays of Boise sent his uncle Amenzo J. Hubbard and his son James B. Hays to McCall to select a location on land already owned by Hays and build a house. It was one story, covered with pine slabs from a sawmill at Van Wyck, down the valley. Framing came from Green's mill, located in a draw south of town, which could not supply slabs. Site chosen for the house was the spot where the Bowlings later built their main house. The Hays house stood for about 30 years, then burned.

In 1907 Sam Hays, aged 13, accompanied his brother James to the house, just before the Fourth of July, to get things ready for the family. They put in a fireplace and fixed a large water tank in the kitchen into which a hand pump raised water from the lake.

[32]Carl Brown never used mules. He wanted only horses, whose nature he understood. Mules were to horses as cats were to dogs as women were to men—sharper of intuition, more subtle, less predictable.

[33]At five Brownie got from his older brothers the name that stuck with him forthwith. Wearing his Buster Brown cap he was running on his stout little legs trying to overtake the others and yelling for them to wait. They cried back, "Brownie, go home! Brownie, you're too little!" Most people do not know that he has any other name.

[34]At Boydstun's store at Lardo one could buy hardware, mining equipment, groceries, coaloil, gasoline in tins, clothing, and probably much else. In one corner was the postoffice, and in the center the usual pot-bellied stove, around which clustered the usual community gossips (male), cracker-barrel philosophers, and weather prophets.

Boydstun's son Neal, who followed him in business, built a number of the pleasant summer homes around the lake and did much of the construction at Sylvan Beach below the Inn.

[35]Mrs. Harland lives next door to the Browns, in the home of her daughter Catharine, now Mrs. Jack Hayes.

³⁶Warren and friends once collected a bucket of green slime scraped from old logs lying in the mill pond. They fastened it above a doorway at the mill, so that the first person going through would get it. This turned out to be Millwright Joe Kasper.

³⁷John Moore, one of Carl's employees, was in no doubt about the legislative thing, probably assuming as many did that being a legislator meant *moving* to Boise. "Carl," he said, "you haven't got no business in the legislature, and I'm not goin' to vote for you!"

³⁸Irwin later became secretary to Senator Henry Magnusson of Washington, "the only Hoff," his mother comments, "on the wrong side of the political fence." Harvey has his own lumber and home furnishing business in Caldwell.

³⁹Bill's wife Nell, who died early this year, had been something of a logger herself. One winter when Bill's leg was broken in three places, she took over for him, driving a team and doing all that a man ordinarily did. Another winter, she and her daughter (now Bonnie Comstock) cut and skidded all the black pine necessary to heat their house through the winter.

Mrs. Harp's father and brother Vernon were among seven men who died of poison believed hid in a sack of flour at a mine camp. Someone, it was alleged, had been out to get the manager.

Sometimes the Harps kept as many as eight horses at a time. But in 1924 they gave in and bought a Model T Ford.

⁴⁰Ulmer married Nellie McGinley, a school teacher, and they had a son and a daughter who went through the McCall schools.

⁴¹One of the committee's early projects was to place stout wood benches at places in the village where visitors could rest and enjoy the scenery. The bench in front of the library disappeared, but was discovered at the golf course. Ida sent the sheriff after it. The golf club, she said, could provide its own benches.

⁴²The "nice comfortable" churches in Roseberry are long gone, but a prim white Finnish Lutheran church still stands on a hill east of Lake Fork. Its cemetery contains the names of many well known Finn families who settled near Roseberry in the 1880's.

⁴³Theodore Hoff was available because his cattle ranching had not prospered and he was quitting it. And the year before his box factory at Horseshoe Bend had burned, with a loss of $40,000 and only $10,000 insurance. It was a time of troubles.

⁴⁴Warren and his CCC charges were called out one night to fight fire. Untrained in such work and excited by the heat and roar, one city boy trying to chop off a limb chopped his foreman instead. Warren bled profusely but it seemed later that this blood-letting had actually improved his general health, perhaps as a change of oil does an engine.

[45]Four years later they purchased the pleasant house surrounded by flower gardens and white fences that sits in a shady meadow outside the southern limits of town. Three of their former employees, J. L. Thornton, William Baker and John Bridwell, were still at work and these men are still with them. So is Jimmy Draper, who has worked "since he was big enough."

[46]Arlen Beyerle has been called Tuck so long he thinks of it as his name. His business enterprises have been registered under the name Tuck Beyerle.

[47]Honorably discharged in 1945, Beyerle stayed on for a few months at Prince Rupert Port of Embarkation in civilian status. During the Beyerle's stay, Carl and Ida made a trip to Prince Rupert. Carl had first seen the place with his father in 1903.

[48]Later 40 acres of this land would be given to the First Methodist church of Boise for a summer camp.

[49]Each year about 80 smoke-jumpers are trained in McCall, then a detail of around 20 is sent to Idaho City. The Payette Forest ends with between 55 and 60 for its own. They are men of varied background—teachers, preachers, etc.—but the one thing they must have is coordination. Says Sam Defler, present supervisor in McCall: "We have to check them to see if they are 'free thinking' when they jump. They may freeze or confuse right with left. Some are found unsuited." Some jumpers are repeaters from other summers, keeping it up for six or eight years. Forty is the age limit. The chutes are steerable and a man is never *pushed* from the plane. He either jumps of his own free will or he "breaches"—he can't go. If a man breaches more than once, he is usually given up. A new loft building was completed last year in McCall for drying, inspecting and repairing chutes. Silk is no longer used, but the nylon has to be shaken out each time.

On June 25, 1958, a ceremony of awards was made for smoke-jumpers by Supervisor Defler and Boyd Rassmussen of the regional office in Ogden. It was noted that Wayne Webb of McCall had made 155 jumps, Del Catlin 140. Other men were honored, some for a single season, some for as many as five.

[50]For some time Ted Harwood had been working with B T and L in the shipping department where he was not replaceable. The defense department also asked that Warren Brown stay where he was, turning out lumber.

[51]It is true that very large sturgeon have been taken from the Snake. The author saw one caught near Cache creek. It was being moved by two men with a pole on their shoulders. The pole had been thrust through behind the disproportionately large head; the tail dragged on the ground. The fish furnished the main dish for three meals for three days for a shearing outfit of about 30.

289

Older Snake river ranchers report sturgeon long enough "to fill a wagon box."

[52]In Idaho county, next door to Valley, one woman teacher had to take on high school athletics. Her basketball team played through the conference—at every game she was with the boys from start to finish.

[53]Newspaper correspondents described the way the pillar climbed, until it was level with the plane, changing color from purple to brown to white. Then it shot from its top a mushroom that rose to 45,000 feet, seething in foam. The mushroom detached itself and continued higher, perhaps 60,000 feet. Then as if the pillar had decided to grow a new head, a small mushroom burst from the top. As the first boiling mushroom floated off, it changed into something like a dreadful flower with a great downward petal of white lined with rosecolor.

[54]Stover continued to raise and race dogs. His teams went to meets in Ogden and Truckee as well as to Ashton, where he took a first in 1931. For a team of seven he usually took along nine dogs, ones he had raised himself, crosses between a setter and a foxhound. He found dogracing a wonderful hobby—and an expensive one.

[55]Valley county men who gave their lives in World War II, that is men killed in action, dying of wounds or as prisoners of war, are these: John Allen, Donald Buman, Herbert Collins, Morris Crawford, Willard Gribble, Charles Hall, Warren Hall, Paul Kerby, Eugene Maki, Clarence McPherson, Phillip Johnson, Leo Morris, Orland Morris, John Patterson, Walter Ruuska, Robert Rietze, Louie Southerland, Jay Summers, Fred Wood. There may be others.

[56]Snap Palmer, a cougar hunter at Shoup, Idaho, is credited with killing 1526 in his years of hunting, five of them in one day.

[57]Recent experiments in lifting logs by cable from lofty pockets that roads cannot reach may affect this one-fifth figure radically.

[58]Horses were last used in logging operations in 1945.

[59]Mrs. Stephens died in 1952 after six years of paralysis. During those years Chester cared for her tenderly, and some people thought he had never seemed happier than while doing for her. His wife's children often visit him at the Soldiers' Home in Boise, taking their children along, and he is sure he wouldn't be fonder of them if they were truly his own.

[60]This explanation of the name Lardo is not accepted by all old timers.

[61]Armstrong has never married. However he has made other people's children his. He has helped crippled youngsters get into the Crippled Children's hospital in Portland—maybe 15 or 16 of

290

them—and he has aided students in securing college loans. A Mason for more than 50 years, he has always been "mixed up" in community affairs.

[62]Brownie had married Lu Muth, a widow with a pretty teen-age daughter, Barbara.

[63]Miller is the only son of Helen Markley Miller, McCall author of numerous teenage books. Once when Mrs. Miller was worrying over how Mack might do in a meet, Ida Brown told her firmly: "Don't saddle your children with your fears, Mrs. Miller."

[64]The building was erected in 1916 by the Congregational church. Until this time services were held in the school house. Other denominations in McCall are Latter Day Saints, Catholic, Episcopal, Nazarene, Full Gospel Mission and Seventh Day Adventist.

[65]Edith Kasper, another PTA veteran, keeps on paying dues and attending although she now has great grandchildren.

[66]Paul Drew has since retired, and he and Alma live in a handsome white house by the highway on the lake shore. They relish the McCall spirit and climate. Their idea of fun is walking in the wooded hills.

[67]Whether or not the explanation bears scrutiny, McCall has seemed quite free of child delinquency, disturbed minds, and that grown-up female idleness that can produce community havoc. Doing things with and for one's children, without asking for state or government help, is possibly the answer. At ceremonies held in the basement of the Community church this pre-school group last year "graduated" 34 youngsters.

[68]In 1920 Henry married Grace Exum of Emmett, and from that time on they made their home in McCall. Mrs. Hoff runs a gift shop but puts most of her time into teaching figurine painting and ceramics, which she has studied in Seattle.

[69]Sometimes Dorothy stayed for a couple of autumn months, so that the girls could start school in McCall. She appreciated having them begin under teachers like "the Maki girls," now Mrs. Glenn Burnside and Mrs. Fritz Prinz.

[70]When old enough to handle horses Marjorie went out one morning at the Sunset to catch her mount, but he kicked her arm and broke it. She and her mother were cooking for 20 men, but Grace dropped everything to take Marjorie out horseback. First she called Carl Brown to meet them at Yellow Pine. Carl brought them to McCall where Dr. Ross of Nampa, who was vacationing, took Marjorie on to a hospital, another four or five hours ride.

[71]In her first years in McCall Jayne Brown wrote news for the Boise Statesman. While *Northwest Passage* was being filmed she sent down daily reports. She has written special articles for the

Statesman, and each year does one for the Idaho Hunting and Fishing Guide.

[72]Aronson won it.

[73]National magazines and news services sent to this compaign opener reporters and photographers who barely knew that Idaho was one of the states. An editor of the Saturday Evening Post, possibly thinking that bandits still carried on, air-mailed a query to a local newsman: "In the enclosed picture of the General on the capitol steps, who is the man who appears to be picking his pocket?" The answer went back that the man was Governor Jordan, pointing, not picking.

[74]Two more grandchildren would presently bring the number to 12.

[75]The tour continues each year, with more and more cars, though some barely arrive before the celebration ends.

[76]In 1959, after long illness, their mother passed away.

[77]Larkin has flown for Johnson Flying service out of both Missoula and McCall, has had his own flying service, done crop and tree dusting, and not long ago flew a plane into Soldier's Bar in the primitive country to bring out some horses—the horses had to have tranquilizers before they would board the plane. Larkin was recently the subject of an article in the New York Times about dusting for spruce bugworm on Long Island. He presently works summers for the Boise National Forest, flying out of Idaho City.

[78]Warren had learned to fly from Bob Fogg in McCall in 1942. First he bought a Piper Cub, then the Super Cub which he still owns and flies, on business or for an occasional fishing trip. He has never—so far as his wife knows—had a close call.

[79]There are three cups for boys and three for girls in each of four divisions—expert, intermediate, novice and Mitey Mite, an annual total of 24 plus the traveling first prize, which is more nearly a bowl than a cup, and is kept a year by the winner, his name engraved on it. Cups and bowl are all silver.

[80]His father said to Frank: "I can teach you lumbering, so major in the next thing you might prefer, something solid, so that if you find lumber isn't to be your career, you'll be prepared for something else."

[81]In 1955 the Hoffs celebrated their 50th wedding anniversary, and for this all six children came: Irwin from Washington, Harvey from Caldwell, Priscilla Hayes from Homedale, Erma Kling from Spokane; Ted and Helen Hoff Frye live in Horseshoe Bend, where Helen teaches. The Boise Statesman carried a picture of the anniversary group, a handsome set of people.

The Hoffs have 13 grandchildren and two great-grandchildren.

292

[82]The new wing cost $37,000, half of which was again provided by Hill-Burton. It allowed for a new solarium, two ward rooms and additional storage space.

[83]Jack, an old-time employee who looked after the horses at the logging camps, liked to take small Stan and Frank out to the woods with him, especially after snow fell. He told the children that Santa Claus was quite likely to show up out there, and they believed him. Years passed, Jack's health failed. He had to go to a sanitarium in Gooding. Carl made a trip down to make sure that he had all he needed. Care was good, Jack was happy, but he didn't have any bathrobe. Carl went to the hotel and brought back his own, an elegant red rayon the family had given him, and plenty big for Jack because Carl's shoulders were broad. Jack put it on and strutted around exclaiming, "Nobody else here has a silk overcoat!" Carl didn't explain that he'd never cared for the robe.

Once in McCall Jack had bummed Carl on the street for some money. Knowing Jack's habits, Carl handed over but said nothing. Instead of getting himself a drink, however, Jack bought a T-bone steak for Buck, Brown's dog.

"You thought I was going to do something else, didn't you?" he chortled.

Carl laughed. Only Buck would suffer—from disillusionment the next time he was fed table scraps.

[84]Engen was recently named 1960 winner of the National Ski association's Russell Wilder Memorial. The committee annually names one person who had done the most for junior skiing.

[85]For the year 1960-61, 157 high school students were enrolled, of whom 20 came from Donnelly. Nine teachers taught them. Until now an athletic field away from the building has been used. Next spring work will begin on a field and a playground on the property.

Vern Hoss is chairman of the school board, Warren Brown still a member, along with William Willard, William Eld and Herbert Krause. District clerk is William Kirk, and high school principal is Allen Blair. At Donnelly Kenneth McIntosh is principal of the junior high school and John L. Beitia is serving his first year as superintendent. Mr. Betia came "from away" (North Dakota State Teachers College) but has a masters degree from Idaho State.

[86]The ingenious Coonrods learned to make their own skis. The shaped wood is boiled—it would take a pretty big boiler—then placed to dry between two logs, with the ski tips exposed and bent over. Then they are boiled again, dried, finally waxed. The Coonrods also made their own cheese and soap, and jerked their venison and carded wool for their comforters. The Finns by whom

they were surrounded set them an example in expert spinning and weaving of wool, using it in everything from socks to rugs. They also preserved wild huckleberries, and if they had no jars, they poured the hot fruit into beer bottles which they sealed with a clean cloth covered with hot pitch.

[87]Weiser Forest supervisors from 1906 on were: J. B. Lafferty, L. F. Watts, Ben Rice, John Raphael and J. G. Kooch. In the Idaho Forest were Henry Bergh, beginning in 1908, Julian Rothery, Herbert Graff, Herbert C. Williams, Walter Mann, John Raphael, L. F. Watts, C. S. Scribner, Henry Shenk and James M. Farrell.

Farrell became head of the new Payette Forest in 1944 and was succeeded by Tom Mathews, J. G. Kooch and Sam Defler, present supervisor.

Charley Connaton, another Payette Forest employee, is now with the Pacific Forestry and Range experiment station at Berkeley.

Of the supervisors above, the following have died: Rice, Raphael, Bergh, Rothery, Graff, Scribner.

[88]Signing were the following: Henry Allen, Fred Adkins, Eino Arold, Robert Bruce, Harvey Bloom, Glenn Burnside, Fred Brown, Bob Brandenburg, Lee Bruno, Bob Coonrod, Theodore F. Drewniak, Ronald Dunlap, W. J. Dooley, Lawrence Dutton, William Coburn, Cash Crawford, Tex Chitwood, Edwin Fors, Red Gantz, Matt Heikkola, John Hillberg, Martin Hoff, Milt Hansen, Hud Henderson, Bill Harp, David H. Jordan, Alfred Jussila, C. R. M. Johnson, Harry Krahn, Dick Krahn, Ben Lawrence, Bud Mason, Howard Meador, J. D. Moore, Mat Paananen, Dutch Rutherford, George Strode, Walter J. Smith, Don Sanford, John Takkinen, John Takala, Les Ulmer, E. A. Watkins, Ray Watkins, Frank C. Woods, Warner Willey, Keith Webb, Glenn Wright, Don Willis and Ernie Ward.

[89]Once a mill employee's wife with a new baby seemed to need a place to stay where both could be looked after better. Ida insisted on taking them in. When they went home the baby was three months old. If Ida's cleaning help complained of not feeling tops, Ida was likely to put the woman to bed and keep her overnight.

[90]Pat Hayes, Scottish born, came to Boise when he was 14. When grown he worked for Boise Payette Lumber company, and in 1936 came to B T and L. He married into a sturdy Finn family, the Paananens. John Paananen, his father-in-law, who homesteaded in the valley, brought himself thither on a bicycle. Sylvia and Pat Hayes have one daughter, LaVonne.

[91]Although at Squaw Valley in February of last year Stan missed making the Olympic ski team, his regret was not for himself but for his parents who might be overwhelmingly disap-

pointed. He had known for a long time that his size was not especially in his favor for skiing, and he was philosophical about it. However, at the Sun Valley Open, on a tricky fast course he had won the downhill race against two Norwegians slated to go to Squaw Valley.

[92]Over a recent Fourth of July there arrived 25 extra guests, either high school or college friends of the children. Sometimes guests appear unannounced in the night. In that case Margaret merely gets up and "puts them to bed."

[93]One place still open has the cheerful sign Cest la Vie.

[94]Ida's apple pie: Use good tart cooking apples. If quite juicy, add some flour to the sugar. Put chunks of butter around over the sliced apples and cinnamon. After the top crust is rolled, spread it with soft lard, then flour. Do this by hand. When the crust is in place, sprinkle generously with milk or water. Bake hot for ten minutes then lower heat until it is done.

Leg of lamb: The night before if possible, and at least an hour before roasting, rub the meat with vinegar to give it tang and to tenderize. Take off the top skin and most of the fat. With a sharp knife make small cuts in the meat and push in pieces of garlic, then sprinkle salt and pepper. Start the oven hot, then roast slowly.

[95]Helen Miller says Ida handles a car at all times like a woman driving a horse and buggy on a mountain road.